TRANSACTIONS

OF THE

AMERICAN PHILOSOPHICAL SOCIETY

HELD AT PHILADELPHIA
FOR PROMOTING USEFUL KNOWLEDGE

NEW SERIES—VOLUME 44, PART 3
1954

AN ANNOTATED COLLECTION OF MONGOLIAN RIDDLES

ARCHER TAYLOR

Professor of German Literature, University of California

THE AMERICAN PHILOSOPHICAL SOCIETY
INDEPENDENCE SQUARE
PHILADELPHIA 6

AUGUST, 1954

Copyright 1954 by The American Philosophical Society

Library of Congress Card
Catalog No. 54-7499

PREFACE

Few collections give an adequate idea of the rich enigmatic lore of Asia and these few are not easily available to most of us. There are, for example, good Yakut collections in Polish and Russian and excellent untranslated Turkish collections. The only easily found Asiatic collection is an anthology of riddles from Middle India made a few years ago by Verrier Elwin and W. G. Archer. These collections contain few comparative notes. In making this collection I have sought to offer a survey of Asiatic riddling as far as it could be based on the riddles current in a single language. The numerous Mongolian collections provide a good foundation for such a survey. I have used all the printed Mongolian collections that have come to my knowledge but have not sought for riddles in oral circulation.

With some minor modifications I have arranged the riddles according to a system devised by Robert Lehmann-Nitsche and used in his *Adivinanzas rioplatenses* (Buenos Aires, Imprenta de Coni Hermanos, 1911). This system is based on the way in which the solution is described and not on the solution itself. Riddles are comparisons of an object to an animal, a man, a plant, or a thing, or describe an object in terms of several comparisons (which do not add up to suggesting a false solution) or in terms of number, form, color, or acts. The other varieties of word puzzles that are loosely called riddles are here put into the chapter entitled Shrewd Questions.

The collection contains all the published Mongolian riddles that I know. The original texts, which were printed in various places and especially in rare Russian journals, were printed in Mongolian script or various kinds of transcriptions and were occasionally accompanied by translations into a European language. In all instances the original Mongolian text has been used as a basis for the translation offered here. Square brackets are used around added material; parentheses enclose words already in the Mongolian text. The collector's name and the number of the riddle in his collection are cited. The riddles cited in the notes are arranged in an order proceeding roughly from east to west, that is, from the tribes nearest to the Mongols to the peoples of Western Europe. The references in the notes are to collections of riddles, which are cited according to the collector's name and the numbers of the individual riddles. When the riddles are not numbered, they are cited according to the pages on which they appear. The books and collections cited are listed in the "Collections of Riddles Cited" in my *English Riddles from Oral Tradition* (Berkeley, 1951), pp. 871–897. Some additional books and collections that were not available to me in 1951 are cited in "References," pp. 411–412 below.

I am indebted to Professor F. D. Lessing for the translation of more than eight hundred riddles and a reading of the manuscript. Professor N. N. Poppe generously gave me translations of both his own collections and a very rare lithographed collection made by Zhamtsaranov and Rudnyev. Professor Wolfram Eberhard lent me an indispensable book for a long term of years and translated a large number of Turkish riddles. I express to them once more my gratitude for help that has made this collection possible.

A. T.

AN ANNOTATED COLLECTION OF MONGOLIAN RIDDLES

Archer Taylor

CONTENTS

	PAGE
I. Comparisons to a Creature Not Identified as an Animal or a Man, Nos. 1-38	321
II. Comparisons to an Animal, Nos. 39-339	322
III. Comparisons to a Man, Goblin, or Devil, Nos. 340-543	335
IV. Comparisons to Several Persons, Nos. 544-636	343
V. Comparisons to Plants Nos. 637-680	348
VI. Comparisons to a Thing, Nos. 681-908	349
VII. Enumerations of Comparisons, Nos. 909-919	358
VIII. Enumerations in Terms of Number, Form, or Color, Nos. 920-950	359
IX. Enumerations in Terms of Acts, Nos. 951-971	360
X. Shrewd Questions, Nos. 972-1027	361
Comparative Notes	367
References	411
Index of Solutions	414
Index of Conventional Elements and Formulas	425

I. COMPARISONS TO A CREATURE NOT IDENTIFIABLE AS AN ANIMAL OR A MAN, NOS. 1-38

In order to keep together the riddles based on a comparison to a creature having a small body and a loud voice (Nos. 31-36), a few texts that rather clearly suggest a man are included among them.

1-4. FORM

1, 2. A MEMBER LACKS SOMETHING ESSENTIAL

1. Though it has a gaping mouth, it has no throat for swallowing.—Scissors.

Gomboyev, 38.

2. There is a gaping mouth, there is no food to be swallowed.—Scissors.

Klukine, 37.

3, 4. THE BODY AND ITS MEMBERS

3. Ninety-nine eyes in a very small thing.—Thimble.

Kotvich, 204.

4. It has many thousand eyes.—Thimble.

Poppe, *Ekhirit*, 6.

5-17. FUNCTION

5-16. MOTION

5. It comes from Mongolia climbing on *moilokhon* trees.—Spider climbing in its web.

Bazarov, 128.

6. It leaps *bung bung* and jumps awry.—Hare.

Gomboyev, 24.

7. It runs through ravines, it runs with bare feet, it finds its prey on the road.—Wolf.

Rudnyev, 33.

8. Going eastwards and once chased away, going eastwards and once more chased away, it went and crossed over the Barguzin pass.—Chewing and swallowing of food.

Bazarov, 88.

9. I do not walk on the ground, I do not fly in the air, I make no noise, and I give birth to children.—Fish.

Kotvich, 263.

10-16. SPECIAL VARIETIES OF MOTION

10. It enters here and protrudes (*bultai*) there.—Defecation of cattle.

Mostaert, 135.

11. When he spreads his legs, something having the shape of a ball appears.—Button passing through the buttonhole.

Mostaert, 71.

12. When one sprawled out one's legs, a bulb came in.—Button and buttonhole.

Poppe, *Aga Buriat*, 16.

13. Coming nearer and nearer, it disappears.—Firebrand.

Gomboyev, 35.

14. It moved, it moved, and it disappeared from sight.—Log in the fire.

Bazarov, 108.

15a. It goes and goes; there is no trace. It cuts and cuts; there is no blood—Boat.

Kotvich, 162.

15b. It goes, no trace is left; it stabs, but there is no blood.—Boat.

Kotvich, 161.

15c. On looking for it, there is no trace; on pricking, there is no blood.—Boat.

Gomboyev, 48.

16a. It goes and goes, there is no trace. One cuts and cuts; there is no blood.—Shadow.

Kotvich, 162.

16b. It goes, no trace is left; one stabs, but there is no blood.—Shadow.

Kotvich, 161.

17. EATING

17. It can eat but not eliminate.—Bag or satchel.
Mostaert, 159.

18–38. FORM AND FUNCTION
18–24. FUNCTION WITH THE APPROPRIATE MEMBER LACKING

18. It has no back (*sēr*) and bends its head backwards (or: it sticks out its head) ;/ it has no thin skin (*semeji*) covering the intestines and moves on wriggling.—Snake.
Mostaert, 174.

19a. It walks without legs; it flies without wings.—Cloud.
Kotvich, 186.

19b. It has no legs but it ran; it has no wings but it flew.—Cloud.
Sanzheev, p. 168.

20. Though he has no feet, he runs; though he has no wings, he flies.—Cloud.
Poppe, *Aga Buriat*, 21.

21. Though without feet, it walks;/ Though without a neck, it carries.—Boat.
Zhamtsaranov, 20.

22. Although it does not walk, it has feet./ Although it does not fly, it has wings.—Vertebra.
Gomboyev, 13.

23. Although he has no feet and hands, he opened the door.—Wind.
Poppe, *Aga Buriat*, 22.

24a. It has a voice but no mouth; it has a name but no glory.—Echo.
Gomboyev, 4.

24b. It has no mouth but a voice; it has no fame (*aldar*) but a name.—Echo.
Klukine, 2.

25–30. MOTION

25. It runs by leaps/ In shagreen boots.—Magpie.
Mostaert, 149.

26. It runs by leaps/ In shagreen boots.—Antelope.
Mostaert, 149 var.

27. It runs with a hop, is higher than a camel and lower than a dog.—Bird.
Kotvich, 135.

28. A little bladder, *yā yā*;/ A little boneless bladder;/ A little bladder than runs;/ A little bladder without a paunch.—Tick.
Mostaert, 29.

29. His eyes are of fire and glass; there is a side where he runs alone.—Wolf.
Kotvich, 256.

30. It jumps *böng böng*/ And has neither kidneys nor heart.—Saltwort (*khamkhak*).
Mostaert, 182.

31–36. SMALL BODY, LOUD VOICE

31. The height of a finger, but as vociferous as a man.—Bullet.
Sanzheev, p. 168.

32. A body as big as the index finger, but a manly loud voice.—Cicada (pheasant?).
Bazarov, 178.

33. It has a body as big as the forefinger,/ And a man's sonorous voice.—The green grasshopper.
Rudnyev, 22.

34. Although he has a body the size of a thumb, he has a masculine and lovely voice.—The voice of a wasp.
Poppe, *Aga Buriat*, 58.

35. A body as big as [the bead of a] rosary, the voice is as sonorous as that of a man.—Bee (Bumblebee).
Klukine, 36.

36. It has a span-high body, a steep bench. When you seize its beard, it counts its years.—Steelyard.
Rudnyev, 16.

37, 38. OTHER FUNCTIONS

37. A round body, a round mouth, it eats flesh all the time; its belly is filled with water. It has no stand, no feet.—Chamberpot for men.
Mostaert, 122.

38. I flung something noticeable at the mouth of the river Tar. When I returned to see what happened to it, I found that it pricked up its ears, goggled its eyes.—Grain not yet harvested.
Kotvich, 147.

II. COMPARISONS TO AN ANIMAL, NOS. 39–339
39–51. AN UNIDENTIFIED ANIMAL
39–45. FORM

39. A blunt snouted one glitters like silver.—The scales of a fish.
Bazarov, 158.

40. A *dendžin* one spotted in alternating lines, a spotted one with four feet that point outwards, in another people's country a wrinkled spotted one, in our country a very spotted one.—Frog.
Mostaert, 52.

41. A spotted one that hops. It has little round spots that are clearly seen, spots as big as a camel.—Frog.

Mostaert, 51.

42. A spotted one with spots in groups,/ A spotted one with four feet that point outwards,/ With flat mouth and tongue.—Frog.

Mostaert, 50.

43. A green and mottled disheleved one,/ A green and mottled shaggy one,/ It spread its [painting] brush.—Hoopoe.

Bazarov, 165.

44. It has a body spotted with green and three wooden claws.—Hobble.

Rudnyev, 59.

45. *Mogdoe*, somewhat short, potbellied, with wooden horns.—Abomasum of a ram filled with blood.

Bazarov, 94.

46-48. FORM AND FUNCTION

46. It runs trotting along, with dun-colored boots and two ears perked up.—Wolf.

Mostaert, 43.

47. Running [and] flattening itself out, with a garment as yellow as a [dry] leaf.—Fox.

Mostaert, 42.

48. He has a long tail; he has a face like a calf. When he trots, he is playful; when he gallops, he is violent.—Jerboa.

Kotvich, 131.

49-51. FUNCTION

49a. It eats goat's meat and mutton and finds shelter in a hollow tree.—Knife.

Bazarov, 99.

49b. It has a hollow as a night-shelter and mutton for food.—Knife.

Klukine, 11.

50. When seizing it from behind, it is peaceful. When seizing it from the front, it is ferocious.—A log of wood burning at one end.

Bazarov, 76.

51. After sucking its teat,/ One cauterizes its navel.—Pipe.

Zhamtsaranov and Rudnyev, 27.

52-55. INSECTS

52. A body the size of a flea, with six sides each of which has its own importance.—Anklebone (dice) used in gambling.

Mostaert, 21.

53. On the hill/ There are seven flies./ One single fly/ Looks downwards.—Offering cups on the altar.

Zhamtsaranov and Rudnyev, 26.

54. In the center of a shelf/ There are five flies.—Buttons on a pillow.

Poppe, *Aga Buriat*, 31.

55. On a peg/ There is a hungry louse.—A scraper or trowel.

Zhamtsaranov and Rudnyev, 70.

56. FROG

56a. The frog Mak (variant: Yak) with eight [jugular] sinews.—Saddle and accessories.

Rudnyev, 65.

56b. A swamp frog with nine sinews.—Saddle [with its accessories].

Gomboyev, 43.

57-66. WORMS, SNAKES

57. A big-bellied snake on top of the yurt.—Rope.

Kotvich, 66.

58. The house is full of skin worms.—The thongs holding the wall together.

Zhamtsaranov and Rudnyev, 86.

59. An iron snake has a wooden foot.—Gun (rifle).

Poppe, *Aga Buriat*, 71.

60. In a box a multicolored worm.—Eye.

Mostaert, 144.

61. In a deep well/ There is a wattled snake.—Long rope for the smoke opening.

Zhamtsaranov and Rudnyev, 23.

62a. The water from a deep well is good. The tongue of a snake (or: lizard) is good.—Ink, goose quill.

Bazarov, 96.

62b. The water of the deep well is black. The nose of the wattled snake is black.—Ink well and ink (probably the pen is meant).

Poppe, *Aga Buriat*, 89.

63. From a flying black thing a crawling white thing is born.—Fly, larva.

Klukine, 35.

64. A long yellow worm consumes itself completely.—Incense.

Mostaert, 39.

65. A fallow snake makes a coil.—Enclosure made of willows.

Mostaert, 187.

66. Beyond the vapor that is rising to the sun, small gray snakes are coiling.—Waves.

Kotvich, 187.

67–99. BIRDS

67–72. UNIDENTIFIED OR MYTHOLOGICAL BIRDS

67. A nestling is in the fire.—Flat cakes baked in ashes.
Kotvich, 43.

68. On an undefiled dune an innocent white bird.—Sheep lizard.
Mostaert, 119.

69a. In a deep well a red bird makes the sound *gynger*.—Heart.
Mostaert, 10.

69b. In a deep well a many-colored bird makes the sound *gynger*.—Heart.
Mostaert, 10 var.

70. It makes the sound *shir shir*,/ It is a little bird of Genghis Khan,/ It has twelve tongues,/ Plump round sides,/ A golden ring.—Watch.
Poppe, *Barguzin*, 2.

71. The land that men cannot reach was reached by the bird Kurulda.—Key to the trunk.
Kotvich, 71.

72. The place that a human being could not reach was reached by the bird Kurulda. The person who wanted to get this bird got a bird of an entirely different name.—Taking out redhot iron with tongs.
Kotvich, 89.

73–84. DOMESTIC BIRDS

73–76. *Chickens*

73. A black hen with a red bill.—Lamp.
Mostaert, 127.

74. A red hen with a green tail.—A red onion.
Mostaert, 151.

75. A white hen with a green tail.—A white onion.
Mostaert, 152.

76. There is a rooster on a shelf./ His voice reaches to heaven./ His shadow reaches the earth.—Church bell.
Zhamtsaranov, 23.

77, 78. *Ducks*

77. Fifteen ducks flew away from a lake the size of a cup. A fast black duck started after them.—Bullet.
Kotvich, 273.

78. Ten black ducks on an island the size of a cup. One fast black duck is trying to overtake them.—Reading what is written.
Kotvich, 196.

79–84. *Geese*

79. Four geese on an anvil.—Four teats of a cow.
Kotvich, 105.

80. Five geese on a rack.—Five fingers.
Kotvich, 25.

81. A goose tracked over the earth.—Plowing.
Zhamtsaranov, 2.

82. A voiceless goose in a thick forest.—Louse.
Kotvich, 146.

83. Four geese came honking. Something with a black handle on it caught them.—Milking a cow.
Rudnyev, 71.

84. Four geese came flying [and] making a noise. Something black was put underneath noisily.—Milking cows.
Bazarov, 147.

85–99. WILD BIRDS

85, 86. *Crows*

85. A lame crow licks the burial mound.—Cutting hair.
Kotvich, 238.

86. A lame crow walks around a hillock.—Shaving the head.
Rudnyev, 28.

87. *Dungping*

87. The small bird called *dungping*, bowing, bowing its head,/ Drinks from the middle of the river/ And walks in the pasture, making patterns, patterns.—Writing with a brush.
Mostaert, 183.

88. *Falcon*

88. The falcon penetrated into the lower part of the yurt.—The sun penetrates into the yurt.
Kotvich, 175.

89–92. *Magpie*

89. The magpie chisels and pushes it on;/ The mouse mixes and throws it into the well.—Eating.
Zhamtsaranov, 15.

90. On the top of the Alkanai there is a particolored magpie.—Button indicating the rank of an official.
Bazarov, 12.

91. A limping magpie went around a hill.—Spinning wool.
Poppe, *Barguzin*, 11.

92. A limping magpie makes a turn around a hill.—Drawing water from a well.
Zhamtsaranov and Rudnyev, 5.

93. *Parrot*

93. The parrot drank from the dripping water./ Afterwards on the white snow mountain/ A trail is visible.—A book is being written.
Zhamtsaranov and Rudnyev, 108.

94, 95. *Shakchaga*

According to Bazarov, note to No. 151, the shakchaga is a gray steppe bird akin to the lark. This identification is uncertain, for some translate shakchaga as magpie.

94. Seventy shakchagas dug the ground.—Wall of the felt tent, the lower end of its lattice wall is sunk into the soil.

Rudnyev, 73; Bazarov, 151.

95. Seventy shakchagas dug the earth.—Matches.

Poppe, *Aga Buriat*, 74.

96, 97. *Swallow*

96. On the top of a black hillock sits a bird called a swallow.—Plug of a kettle.

Kotvich, 85.

97. A swallow laid her eggs at the source of the black river; that which no one among the living knows, the lop-eared butterfly found out.—Alcohol and a little brush inserted through an opening in the cover to test the alcohol.

Kotvich, 248.

98. *Swan*

98. From the south came a swan; it quenched its thirst from a canal (a channel of silver) and went to graze on the eternal mountain.—Writing a letter.

Bazarov, 173.

99. *Yavalak (a screechowl with a clumsy gait)*

99. The yavalak has laid eggs on the rock where it is impossible to walk, they say. While I ask how I shall catch it, an old Ölöt who has driven it out comes unexpectedly, they say.—Lock and key.

Mostaert, 155.

100–339. MAMMALS

100. JERBOA

100. A jerboa without bones is crossing the sea.—Butterfly.

Kotvich, 134.

101. MARMOT

101. A bottomless burrow, a bellied marmot.—Man in a felt tent.

Bazarov, 111.

102–104. HARE, RABBIT

102. I dig; a small hare lies [there].—Taking care of a fire. At night a small channel is dug in the glowing embers and a piece of cow-dung is placed in it. The whole is covered with ashes.

Mostaert, 94.

103. The rabbit screamed. His ears are twisted.—Balalaika.

Kotvich, 217.

104. A jumping hare comes hopping; I take it by the rump, I shake it and make it fall [to the ground].—Wiping one's nose.

Mostaert, 36.

105–108. PIG

105, 106. *Form*

105. A pig in the woods.—Louse in the hair.

Zhamtsaranov, 16.

106. The iron pig has a tail made of string.—Needle.

Kotvich, 253.

107, 108. *Function*

107. You cannot block the head of a pig.—Watermelon.

Kotvich, 159.

108. A pig runs around inside on the ground.—Alcohol running through a curved pipe during distillation.

Kotvich, 47.

109–142. SHEEP

109–112. *Form*

109. A sheep has a hundred coats in a severe winter.—Onion.

Kotvich, 260.

110. The ram's neck is curved.—The trimming (*enger*) of the upper part of the kaftan.

Bazarov, 34.

111. A year-old, six-legged sheep.—Crab.

Kotvich, 264.

112. Behind the mountains there rises a bald uncastrated ram.—Moon.

Bazarov, 46.

113–116. *Color*

113. The black sheep lacks the lower part of the jaw.—Wooden jug, mitten for a kettle.

Kotvich, 92.

114. A black sheep (cow?) without a front leg.—Woman's upper garment (*oji*) without sleeves.

Bazarov, 69.

115. A gray sheep with a hole in its navel.—Lock.

Bazarov, 78.

116. The belly of the gray ram is torn.—An oblong bag serving as pillow (*dyre*).

Bazarov, 187.

117–129. SEVERAL SHEEP

117–121. Form

117. Sheep with bad intellects are put together in the morning and separated in the evening.—Button and button-loop.
Zhamtsaranov and Rudnyev, 92.

118. A crowd of rams in an iron fold.—Grains of rye in a sacrificial vessel.
Bazarov, 127.

119. The rams outside; the sheepfold (courtyard) inside.—Woman's garment or ornament.
Bazarov, 101.

120. Among a thousand sheep a massive round ram.—Stars and moon.
Mostaert, 77.

121. Ten thousand sheep/ Are beaten with an iron lasso and brought together.—Cutting hair.
Zhamtsaranov and Rudnyev, 66.

122–129. Color

122. A stable full of sheep, among the sheep a golden ram.—Stars and sun.
Klukine, 8.

123. After ten thousand sheep have gone to pasture, a stout white ram awakening from sleep rises and goes to join them.—Morning star.
Mostaert, 103.

124. The white lambs of the southern mountains cannot serve us as cattle; they cannot serve as food for Manjushrī.—Cotton padding.
Mostaert, 108.

125. A courtyard (sheepfold) with a hollow in it, the rams are black.—Mortar with tea in it.
Bazarov, 186.

126a. The enclosure is white; the sheep are black.—Paper and writing.
Kotvich, 199; Klukine, 23.

126b. A white courtyard (sheepfold); black rams.—Paper, writing.
Bazarov, 55.

127. Black sheep; a white sheepfold.—Writing and paper.
Mostaert, 46.

128. The sheep is black, the pen is white, the shepherd devours it.—Reading a book.
Poppe, *Dagurskoe*, 1.

129. The corral is white,/ The sheep are black.—A letter.
Zhamtsaranov and Rudnyev, 87.

130–142. Function

130. A gray sheep conceived while spinning.—Spindle.
Gomboyev, 47.

131. A gray sheep grew fat [while] lying down.—Ashes.
Gomboyev, 36; Bazarov, 59 (ram).

132. A grayish sheep grows fat while lying down.—Heap of ashes.
Mostaert, 188.

133. A gray sheep gains so much weight that it is unable to get up.—Spindle.
Kotvich, 97.

134. I dropped an unborn sheep at the source of that river; when I looked [to see] whether she was born, I noticed that she goggled her eyes and pricked up her ears.—Grain sowed in the field.
Kotvich, 258.

135. An earless sheep loves its lamb.—Lock and key.
Bazarov, 61.

136a. The courtyard is narrow, the ram likes to butt.—Mortar and pestle.
Bazarov, 102.

136b. In a narrow sheep pen [there is] a butting ram.—Mortar and pestle.
Klukine, 9.

137. The sheepfold is narrow;/ The sheep are many;/ The ram butts continually.—The mortar for hulling millet; the millet to be hulled; the pestle.
Mostaert, 6; Poppe, *Barguzin*, 6 (the ram is accustomed to strike with its horns).

138. The black ram makes a rustling sound *khart*;/ Ten thousand sheep make a crackling sound *birt*.—Toasting millet.
Mostaert, 45.

139. Ten thousand sheep leap;/ A buxom woman jerks.—Toasting millet.
Mostaert, 44.

140. A sheep fell on a rock; the sheep is not uncomfortable, but the rock is.—A piece of meat between the teeth.
Kotvich, 14.

141. In the morning the sheep grazes at the back (lit.: west);/ In the evening the sheep grazes in the front (lit.: east).—The flap (*örkhe*) of a smokehole of a yurt. It is opened in the morning and closed, falling toward the door at night.
Mostaert, 26.

142. They could not kill the black sheep.—Shadow.
Kotvich, 166.

143–167. CAMEL

143–164. *Form*

143. It has a body on which one sees undulations as in a camel; it has eyes [sparkling] like the planet Venus, like a divinity (*tenger*).—Wolf.

Mostaert, 196.

144. The leading camel has a large star (blaze) on its forehead. The female camel is wrinkled. There are numberless little camels with a halter of red silk.—Sun, moon, stars, the Milky Way (called Heaven's Seam).

Bazarov, 159.

145. A thin female camel, a clumsy male camel, no end of little camels; reins made of silk shreds.—The sacred book.

Kotvich, 198.

146. Eighty thousand ear-marks (brands) on a perfectly black camel.—Circular roofpiece on the top of the yurt.

Kotvich, 59.

147a. The gelded camel is bushy; the camel is curly.—Pine and larch.

Poppe, *Aga Buriat*, 87.

147b. A castrated camel with curls; an uncastrated camel with kinks.—Answer lacking.

Bazarov, 10.

148. A camel without a neck is able to carry a load.—Shelf.

Mostaert, 81.

149a. A camel without a neck went over the top of a ridge.—Road.

Bazarov, 48.

149b. A camel without a neck has climbed over a pass.—Road.

Poppe, *Aga Buriat*, 79.

150. The camel without a neck crossed the Kuma.—Road.

Kotvich, 231.

151. No one can catch up with a camel without a neck.—Road.

Kotvich, 183.

152. A camel without a chin reaches Peking.—Road.

Zhamtsaranov and Rudnyev, 48.

153. No one can catch up with a camel without a neck.—Wind.

Kotvich, 183.

154. No one can catch up with a camel without a neck.—Smoke.

Kotvich, 183.

155. A five-year old camel stamped and arrived at the Tungut country [Tibet]. The water of a fountain flowed. [The camel] drew [lines] with a short tusk.—Writing.

Rudnyev, 27.

156. A three-year old male camel comes prancing along,/ The grass of the plain is falling.—Cutting hair.

Mostaert, 31.

157. A camel fell into the sea. The camel feels no discomfort, but the sea does.—Speck of dust in the eye.

Kotvich, 12.

158a. A castrated camel yawned; it lightened beyond there.—Bow, arrow.

Rudnyev, 26.

158b. A gelded camel opens its mouth; a remote country glitters.—Bow and arrows.

Zhamtsaranov and Rudnyev, 2.

159. A gelded camel suddenly opens its mouth. At a distance there is a flash of light.—Archery.

Mostaert, 27.

160a. The castrated camel yawned; the end of the rope flashed.—Lightning.

Kotvich, 212.

160b. A golden camel opens its mouth/ And suddenly a tether flashes.—Lightning.

Mostaert, 89.

161. A castrated camel has yawned; the end of a lasso has glittered.—Thunder and lightning.

Kotvich, 271; Bazarov, 2; Poppe, *Aga Buriat*, 15 (thunderstorm).

162. The castrated camel yawned; the end of the rope flashed.—Snake.

Kotvich, 212.

163. The gelded camel took a step;/ The end of the lasso glittered.—Flint (for striking fire).

Poppe, *Aga Buriat*, 85.

164. On a hill a baby camel was strangled to death.—Buttons of a coat are buttoned.

Poppe, *Aga Buriat*, 48.

165. At the foot of the mountain a young camel is wrapped up.—Button in buttonhole.

Bazarov, 18.

166. Among many camels/ There is a black, open, male camel.—Smokehole (the circular roofpiece and the radiating sticks).

Zhamtsaranov and Rudnyev, 60.

167. Among a hundred camels/ There is a biting black male camel.—[The rafters and] the circular roofpiece of the yurt.

Mostaert, 54.

168, 169. *Making a Noise*

168. Over there a camel throws down [its rider]. At the spot [thus marked] dust has risen.—Gunshot.
Bazarov, 126.

169. A camel makes a noise on the other side of the Don; dust rises at a given point.—Gunshot.
Kotvich, 222.

170, 171. *Eating*

170. A male camel grinds its teeth; the grass of the slope falls down.—Cutting hair.
Mostaert, 15.

171. A camel without jaws finishes the hay.—Scythe.
Bazarov, 174.

172. *Making Tracks*

172a. The traces of a three-year old female camel/ Are not effaced [even] in three years.—Ruins of a yurt.
Mostaert, 181; Kotvich, 50 (three-year old camel).

172b. The traces of a castrated camel will not be erased for ten years.—Place where the yurt was.
Kotvich, 51.

173–217. OX, COW, CATTLE

173–177. *Form*

173. Thirty oxen in a ditch.—Teeth.
Kotvich, 16.

174. A four-year old cow has four legs.—Table.
Kotvich, 79.

175. A three-year old cow has three legs.—Tripod.
Kotvich, 80.

176. Pregnant in coming, a non-pregnant cow in going.—Water pail.
Klukine, 21.

177. All the king's cows are with a halter.—The longitudinal poles supporting the roof of a felt tent.
Bazarov, 57.

178–183. *Color*

178. At the edge of the felt tent there is a black cow.—A cast-iron kettle of Chinese make.
Bazarov, 168.

179. A fallow cow has a black calf.—Steelyard (the beam and counterweight).
Mostaert, 195.

180. On the river bank there is a brindled cow.—Woman's garment or ornament.
Bazarov, 105.

181. Under a hollow there lies a grayish bull.—Ashes in a stove.
Mostaert, 145.

182. A blue ox is rolling over on ashes.—Tongs.
Zhamtsaranov and Rudnyev, 72.

183a. The king's cows all went to the pasture. Only two stayed: a black one and a mottled one.—After the birds have flown away, only the crow and the magpie remained.
Bazarov, 56; Sanzheev, p. 169 (The prince's cattle have all gone away).

183b. All the king's cattle have come back, a black cow and a motley cow have remained.—Crow and magpie.
Poppe, *Aga Buriat*, 72.

184–193. *Color and Form*

184. A red one-year old calf with a stomach of stone.—Jujube.
Rudnyev, 39.

185. A black calf with a stone stomach.—Bird-cherry.
Bazarov, 95.

186. A yellowish cow with black stripes has a shovel for a tail.—Piece of felt that closes the door.
Mostaert, 41.

187. A multicolored cow has tasty milk, but pointed (sharp) horns.—Bee.
Bazarov, 13.

188. A hornless black calf/ With a callosity on its withers.—The plug (lit.: navel) of a kettle.
Rudnyev, 61.

189. A bluish ox without ribs.—Cloud.
Bazarov, 45.

190. A bluish bull with a wooden nosepeg.—Ax.
Rudnyev, 36; Zhamtsaranov and Rudnyev, 80.

191. The side of the black cow is swollen.—Covering up the fire for the night.
Rudnyev, 35.

192. The horns of the red cow look in different directions.—The grate of the yurt.
Kotvich, 207.

193. A black ox/ Cannot be chopped [to pieces].—Shadow.
Zhamtsaranov and Rudnyev, 90.

194–217. *Function*

194. The nose of the black bull is strong.—Lock.
Poppe, *Dagurskoe*, 4.

195. The black cow walks around the yurt.—The shadow moves around the yurt.
Kotvich, 244.

196. The gray ox stays motionless; the brindled ox spreads its legs; the dock-tailed ox ran out.—Gunshot (gunbarrel, trigger, bullet).

Kotvich, 223.

197. A little bluish bull drags its little halter.—Needle with thread.

Zhamtsaranov, 26.

198. A multicolored ox is unable to pull a crumb of manure.—Eye.

Bazarov, 15.

199–209. *Lying Down, Tied, Kept in an Enclosure*

199a. The red calf is tied up inside a fence of bone.— Tongue.

Kotvich, 236.

199b. A red calf within a bone fence.—Tongue.

Zhamtsaranov and Rudnyev, 3.

200a. A particolored two-year old calf behind a fence of bristles.—Eye.

Klukine, 15.

200b. A motley calf within a fence of the hair of a horse's tail (and mane).—Eye.

Zhamtsaranov and Rudnyev, 1.

201. A red calf is tied up on the mountain.—Tassel on a cap.

Kotvich, 34.

202. On a slope a grayish bull is lying, they say./ When, saying "Tchoo!," one wants to push him in front of one's self (i.e., to lead him away), he did not rise. If pricked [with a stick], he rises.—Lock.

Mostaert, 16.

203. On the slope a grayish bull is lying./ If you beat him, he won't rise./ If you prick him, he rises.—Lock.

Mostaert, 16 var.

204a. At the side there lay a black cow./ No living being was able to lift her up./ A boy as big as a small finger was able to do it.—Opening a lock with a key.

Rudnyev, 32.

204b. On the side a black ox is lying. No one can lift it, a boy the size of the little finger lifts it, when he prods it.—Lock.

Zhamtsaranov and Rudnyev, 8.

205a. A bluish ox was lifted by a lever.—Unlocking a lock.

Bazarov, 47.

205b. After striking the black ox, one makes it get up.—Lock.

Zhamtsaranov and Rudnyev, 7.

206. Where shall I tie the black cow? I shall tie her to an empty rock. Where shall I tie the calf? I shall tie it to her tail.—Trunk and lock.

Kotvich, 70.

207. On the ground on which a three-year old cow has lain there grows no grass for three years.—Hearth.

Bazarov, 84.

208. In the place where a big ox lay grass did not grow for ninety years.—The place where dry dung lies.

Poppe, *Ekhirit*, 2.

209. They were unable to keep the black cow within the fence;/They were unable to wrap anything around the gray one.—Water.

Bazarov, 65.

210–217. *Various Activities*

210. A brindled cow produced a foolish calf./ Whoever caught it, became foolish himself.—Milk brandy, often made of cow's milk.

Zhamtsaranov, 28.

211. The black cow looks upwards; all the living look down on her.—Kettle with food.

Kotvich, 83.

212. In the north a cow lowed; in the south a stirrup got loose.—Archery.

Bazarov, 64.

213. A red cow licks a black cow.—Fire and kettle.

Mostaert, 131.

214. A red cow licks a black cow and makes her weep.—Fire and kettle.

Mostaert, 131 var.

215. In the morning a gray bull defecates (or: belches).—In the morning tea is pounded.

Poppe, *Aga Buriat*, 39.

216. The Barguzin oxen went pasturing to the north. —Stars.

Poppe, *Ekhirit*, 9.

217. A dark cow makes the sound *khud khud*,/A dark calf makes the sound *up up*.—A cow is milked.

Zhamtsaranov and Rudnyev, 54.

218–267. HORSE, DONKEY

218–222. *Form*

218. The long thin horse has eighty thousand brands. —File.

Kotvich, 251.

219. A horse under the daughter-in-law, a pacer with its front legs (lit.: up to its loins or abdomen).—Ant.

Kotvich, 142.

220. Twelve horses, all with foal. If one looks carefully, one finds that even the stallion is with foal.— The bones of the four legs and the skull. The bones of the legs contain marrow; the skull contains the brain.

Bazarov, 98.

221. A fallow stallion *yil*/ With ninety-nine mares;/ The mares are still without young this year;/ The stallion is with young.—The head: bones and brain.
Mostaert, 137.

222a. A numerous herd of horses has its pasture ground in the northwest.—Rising stars.
Bazarov, 33.

222b. Behind the Altai and Khangai mountains/ There is a herd of a hundred thousand horses, they say./ Those who count them are only seven;/ Those who rule them are three;/ Two are separated by a distance as long as a pair of scissors.—Stars; the Seven Buddhas (Ursa Major); three stars forming the shoulder belt of Orion; two stars (perhaps Castor and Pollux) standing together that one calls the eyes of the wolf.
Mostaert, 3 var.

222c. Behind the Altai and Khangai mountains/ There is a herd of a hundred thousand, they say./ Those who count it are seven, they say./ Crowded together, six are there, they say./ Those who separate the black from the white are two, they say./ One is abandoned, they say.—Stars: the Seven Buddhas; the Pleiades; the sun and moon; the morning star.
Mostaert, 3.

223–228. *Horse and Accouterments*

223. A big stallion carries seventy [poles with] loops (used for catching horses).—The circular roofpiece that permits light to enter and smoke to escape. The poles fixed to it support the felt roof.
Bazarov, 97.

224. A mettlesome horse in the courtyard,/ The end of a lasso in the felt tent.—Sun and sunbeam.
Zhamtsaranov, 9.

225a. A black horse has a green bridle.—Boot.
Zhamtsaranov and Rudnyev, 10.

225b. A black horse with a green halter.—Boot.
Klukine, 7.

226a. A big white horse with seventy blankets.—Birchtree and bark.
Bazarov, 153.

226b. On an old white stallion there are seventy-seven pieces of saddlecloth.—Birchtree and bark.
Zhamtsaranov, 2.

226c. A flat white horse with seventy-five pieces of saddlecloth.—Birchtree.
Bazarov, 39.

227. A flat white horse with seventy pieces of folded saddlecloth.—Lily.
Rudnyev, 50.

228. The black bay horse is rather strong, the strong hobble is safe.—Lock.
Bazarov, 73.

229–238. *Color*

229. No matter who owns the bay horse, it suits everybody.—Fur of an otter.
Kotvich, 39.

230. A bay pacer with his children on his back—Ant.
Kotvich, 141.

231. The thin light bay horse has eighty thousand brands.—Thimble.
Kotvich, 252.

232. Outside of the listener/ A yellow foal is hitched.—Ear.
Zhamtsaranov and Rudnyev, 67.

233. A bay, two-year old colt is outside the listener.—Earring.
Kotvich, 41.

234. At the door of the listener a bay two-year old colt is tied to the stake.—Round earrings.
Mostaert, 85.

235a. A sorrel horse behind a fence of birch trees.—Tongue.
Bazarov, 52.

235b. A roan horse within a birch fence.—Tongue behind the teeth.
Klukine, 14.

235c. In a fence of birches a brown mare.—Tongue.
Poppe, *Aga Buriat*, 53.

236. Behind the rocks there is a trained sorrel horse.—Tongue.
Gomboyev, 11.

237. A bluish horse with perspiring sides.—Whetstone.
Bazarov, 77.

238. It makes the sound *shur shur*,/ It has a short blue horse.—Sewing (with sewing machine).
Poppe, *Aga Buriat*, 92.

239–267. *Function*
239–252. *Motion*

239. It trotted upstream Selenga,/ It trotted, losing eight bright buttons.—Camel.
Poppe, *Aga Buriat*, 77.

240. Nicely mottled, ambling like a donkey.—Windhorse.
Bazarov, 190.

241. A black colt is pacing on saltmarsh mud.—Grinding a knife.

Kotvich, 77.

242. A black colt paces the salt marsh.—Shaving the head.

Kotvich, 20.

243. A gray horse jumped up;/ The skies thundered.—Firing a gun.

Rudnyev, 29.

244. The pacer of the drove of horses goes to the watering place three times a month.—Old woman who fasts [three times a month].

Kotvich, 229.

245. A moving, moving enclosure,/ A fallow ambling horse.—Mirage.

Mostaert, 158.

246. Surrounded by fences and fences,/ A dark brown stallion ambled.—Teeth and tongue.

Poppe, Barguzin, 3.

247. Leaving the black felt tent, a sorrel horse gallops, perking up its ears.—Steppe fire.

Bazarov, 87.

248. The gray horse swings to the left and the right.—Door.

Kotvich, 243.

249. In a hollow without grass a donkey wags its tail.—Washing a kettle with a brush.

Mostaert, 96.

250. On the corner the drove of horses was rounded up with the aid of the bay Bultchik.—Taking apart the yurt.

Kotvich, 52.

251. He gathered the scattered herd of steppe horses with a swift grayish [mare].—Mowing grass.

Bazarov, 44.

252. He collected a herd of gray steppe horses with bluish gray steel.—Cutting hair.

Bazarov, 19.

253–259. *Making a Noise*

253. In the steppe a bay horse with black tail and mane grinds its teeth;/ From time to time dust rises:/ It seizes [in the manner of the] *joodak khorkhoi* (an insect)./ Make ready your thing that ought to strike blows.—Bellows, smoke, tongs, hammer.

Mostaert, 74.

254. When the roan prairie stallion neighed, the mares, about one billion head, at once appeared with their udders and began to foal.—Thunder, rain; grass and grain grow.

Kotvich, 270.

254b. A brown stallion that groans, sixty mares yelling simultaneously with a shrill voice. They, having developed large udders, foal at the same time.—Thunderstorm.

Mostaert, 142.

254c. The dark gray foal began neighing; ninty-nine mares of the world began to foal.—Thunder and rain.

Kotvich, 182.

255. When a blue stallion neighed, all the grayish-white mares became pregnant.—Cuckoo.

Poppe, *Aga Buriat*, 28.

256. Noise is approaching; the sorrel's reins are down.—Rain, wind, thunder.

Kotvich, 184.

257. A cropeared bay colt with the voices of a swan and a tsepa (a bird).—Balalaika.

Kotvich, 219.

258. The cropeared stallion has the voice of a one-year or two-year old colt.—Balalaika.

Kotvich, 220.

259. From behind a rock [comes] a red horse that has made a noise,/ A red horse that has caused all the people to make a noise.—Fire, i.e. a forest fire or fire in the steppe.

Poppe, *Aga Buriat*, 2.

260–261. *Eating*

260a. A gray two-year old colt gets fat when fed.—Spindle and thread.

Kotvich, 98.

260b. A gray two-year old colt is spinning around and around and jumping until it gets fat.—Spindle.

Mostaert, 111.

261. Another two-year old gets fat when fed.—Ashes.

Kotvich, 99.

262–267. *Various Activities*

262. The white horse kicks it with its front legs;/ It pushes it back and forth./ The fallow horse mixes it;/ It pushes it into the well.—Eating: the teeth and the tongue.

Mostaert, 115.

263. Two mares are tied together: Isabella, the colored colt, is tied up.—Kidneys and heart.

Kotvich, 119.

264. They skinned the two-year old gray colt while it was standing.—Taking apart the yurt.

Kotvich, 206.

265. A two-year old colt fell into the sea; the colt feels no discomfort but the sea does.—Speck of dust in the eye.

Kotvich, 13.

266. A motley horse cannot stand the dust of dried dung.—Eye.

Zhamtsaranov and Rudnyev, 9.

267a. A fallow horse is straddled morning and evening (i.e., all the day through).—Threshold.

Mostaert, 191.

267b. A gray colt in its second year is straddled time and again (i.e., at every turn).—Threshold.

Mostaert, 191 var.

268–285. GOAT, ANTELOPE, CHAMOIS, GAZELLE, DEER

268–277. *Form*

268. Twenty goats in a hole.—Teeth.

Gomboyev, 10.

269. On the southern slope of a height/There are eight yellow goats.—Sacrifices to a Buddhist statue.

Poppe, *Aga Buriat,* 65.

270. A burned he-goat/ Has been brought from Kudara.—Iron kettle.

Zhamtsaranov, 27.

271. A three-year old goat had six horns. When a bad year came, there remained two horns.—Unmarried women wear six plaits. When they marry, they combine them into two.

Bazarov, 107.

272. The horns of a kid are in this and that direction.—Top of the walls.

Zhamtsaranov and Rudnyev, 22.

273. A goat that is good for nothing is hobbled with dried skins.—Basket (*dosser*) for gathering dry cow-dung.

Mostaert, 60.

274. A one-horned Chinese goat.—Handmill.

Mostaert, 55.

275. A chamois with a bone stomach.—Jujube.

Mostaert, 92.

276. A white goat/ Has holes in its groin.—A white trumpet.

Zhamtsaranov and Rudnyev, 76.

277. The gray-blue little buck has little feet.—Steppe onion.

Bazarov, 200.

278–285. *Function*

278. A gray she-goat ran, dragging behind herself a rope.—Needle (sewing awl).

Gomboyev, 39.

279. A black goat runs,/ A cloud moves over the kettle,/ A white goat runs.—The black goat is the soot over which, in the winter when the kettle is cold, the fire (the white goat) used to run.

Gomboyev, 34.

280. A running, running female gazelle,/ A female gazelle with which no one can catch up,/ A lingering, lingering female gazelle,/ A female gazelle that no one can seize.—Mirage.

Mostaert, 157.

281. On the other side of the mountain a male and a female antelope butt each other.—Saddle girth and loop (*zirum*) through which it passes.

Rudnyev, 30.

282. A hundred black she-goats and one biting he-goat.—Circular roofpiece over the smokehole and the poles in the roof of the yurt.

Kotvich, 58.

283. A hundred red goats bitten by a black uncastrated ram.—Coals, tongs.

Bazarov, 92.

284. A Chinese goat yelled once and died.—Smashing of porcelain.

Mostaert, 56.

285. Every morning a deer called.—Tea is pounded.

Poppe, *Aga Buriat,* 24.

286. ELEPHANT

286. The elephant yawned, all the worms of the world began to stir.—Morning dawn.

Bazarov, 91; Poppe, *Aga Buriat,* 38 (*waved* for *yawned*).

287, 288. MOUSE

287. After having harnessed a mouse, he sowed two *d'est'in* (a measure of length) of sowing.—Sewing, i.e., drawing a leather thong through a hide).

Poppe, *Aga Buriat,* 17.

288. They put a collar (*khomut*) on a mouse.—Putting a ring on the finger.

Poppe, *Aga Buriat,* 54.

289–303. DOG

289. *Form*

289. In every house there is the thigh of a dog.—Short-handled broom (*s'ooji,* a Chinese word).

Mostaert, 134.

290–303. *Function*

290–293. *Motion*

290. A dog when he became thirsty went into Lake Djolton (Lake Elton).—Spring floods.

Kotvich, 163.

291. A black dog runs on the white snow.—Writing.
Kotvich, 274.

292. An emaciated white dog waddled over thirty mountain passes.—Spinal cord.
Kotvich, 28.

293. The fawning dog passed over sixty rivers.—Spinal cord.
Kotvich, 239.

294–299. Barking

294. The dog of one hamlet (*khoton*) barks at one side.—Reed, smoke.
Kotvich, 150.

295. A short dog barks in the woods. It throws out everything that it finds and that is lying there.—Felling trees, when the chips fly about.
Bazarov, 161.

296. In the woods there barks a lonely dog.—Sound of felling trees.
Klukine, 30.

297. In the woods a furious dog barked.—A large ax.
Poppe, *Ekhirit*, 4.

298. The uncle's dog started to bark; the wood of Bargusi started to creak.—A baby's crying; the sound of rocking the cradle.
Bazarov, 35.

299a. A voiceless dog among the reeds that have no joints.—Louse.
Kotvich, 145.

299b. On a black tree without limbs there are black dogs without voices.—Lice in the queue.
Mostaert, 172.

300–303. Various Activities

300. A Tangut dog/ Is vomiting its brains.—Plane.
Zhamtsarano and Rudnyev, 78.

301. The yellow dog is getting fat shaking its tail.—Spindle.
Kotvich, 205.

302. A thin red dog (or mushroom) came for sale.—(untranslatable) coral.
Bazarov, 183.

303. A little black dog curled up and lets no one in or out.—Lock.
Kotvich, 72.

304, 305. FOX

304. The fox offered a sacrifice with its tail.—Head of a reed.
Kotvich, 152.

305. A fox is squeezed between rocks. The fox feels no discomfort, but the rocks do.—Meat between the teeth.
Kotvich, 15.

306–309. WOLF

306a. A bluish wolf is running through a ravine.—Mucus, snivel.
Rudnyev, 76.

306b. A gray wolf ran through a valley.—Mucus.
Bazarov, 51.

307. A gray wolf runs, dragging a blanket.—Needle and thread.
Kotvich, 96.

308a. Under a hollow there runs a bluish (or: gray) wolf.—Smoke following the hollow of the chimney.
Mostaert, 146.

308b. A gray wolf runs up the hollow tree.—Smoke.
Kotvich, 170.

308c. A gray wolf comes out from the hollow tree.—Smoke.
Kotvich, 169.

309. Other Activities

309a. In a hollow there lies a bluish (or: gray) wolf.—Knife in its sheath.
Mostaert, 63.

309b. In the hollow tree a bluish wolf.—Knife in its sheath.
Mostaert, 63 var.

309c. A blue wolf in a cave.—Knife in sheath.
Poppe, *Barguzin*, 9.

310–312. POLECAT, CAT, TIGER

310a. After eating meat, it is proper to get into a hole like a polecat.—Knife.
Kotvich, 76.

310b. Like a human being, it eats meat; like a polecat, it goes back into its hole.—Knife.
Bazarov, 71.

311. In front of the trunk [in the yurt] is a cat.—Lock.
Kotvich, 73.

312. A tail attached to the tiger's head.—The circular roofpiece (*tōno*) and the rafters attached to it.
Mostaert, 133.

313–320. TWO OR MORE ANIMALS OF DIFFERENT KINDS

313. All the animals overate on a piece of fat the size of a knucklebone.—Sun.
Kotvich, 174.

314a. Twenty sheep coupled together,/ A red cow with an arched back is tied.—Teeth and tongue.

Mostaert, 13.

314b. Twenty sheep are coupled together, a bluish horse with an arched back is tied up.—Teeth [and tongue].

Rudnyev, 1.

314c. Two sheep are coupled together,/ A short red horse is hitched.—Teeth, tongue.

Zhamtsaranov and Rudnyev, 107.

315. Looking [at it] from a distance: a chamois; getting alongside it: a goat; catching and looking at it: a sable; and looking at it: a horse.—Hare.

Kotvich, 128.

316. He took a camel in his mouth, concealed a horse under his bosom, and led a goat behind him.—Hare.

Kotvich, 127.

317. That which is perfectly round ambles like a calf;/ That which is round and has a horn ambles like a donkey.—Handmill.

Mostaert, 87.

318. A goat and an ox wrestle on the steppe.—Button and buttonhole.

Kotvich, 32.

319. Only a black dog with a white stripe (or: spot) on its forehead can catch the dark-spotted snake on a noisy river.—Tongs.

Bazarov, 100.

320. From the back of the house Gendel (the dog) and Shankhor (the falcon) come forward singing.—Fly and mosquito.

Kotvich, 216.

321–334. ANIMAL(S) AND (MEN)

321. Younger brothers, younger brothers are four together,/ Four geese are coming close,/ A pretty girl is going [away] after squandering her property.—Milking a cow.

Zhamtsaranov and Rudnyev, 55.

322. Younger brothers, younger brothers are four,/ Four geese are gaggling,/ A smart uncle is tittering,/ A leather bag is sucking,/ A red calf is crying.—Milking a cow.

Zhamtsaranov and Rudnyev, 105.

323. A cow with brown hair marked with black stripes arches its back;/ Bending its neck, it gathers itself up;/ The son of its father opens his legs with straddling steps;/ Something glitters between his thighs.—Plowing a field.

Mostaert, 68.

324. A hornless cow likes to butt; two maidens who were just here [are] like remnants of curd.—Snuffing tobacco.

Gomboyev, 50.

325. A man strikes a sheep; the sheep strikes a cow; the cow strikes the earth.—Walking: the foot, the sock made of felt, the leather boot.

Mostaert, 194.

326. A piebald horse, a carpenter penetrating everywhere.—Woodpecker.

Bazarov, 143.

327. A roan horse throws off Bujantui (Meritorious, a name) and Sanbo (Good, a name) is looking on.—Incense stick in front of an image.

Bazarov, 28.

328. People stand around,/ A dark stallion ambles.—Teeth and tongue.

Poppe, *Aga Buriat*, 91.

329. People, people stand around,/ A dark stallion is ambling,/ A plump thing makes sounds,/ Five fingers are snapping.—Spinning thread.

Zhamtsaranov and Rudnyev, 62.

330. He has a herd of dark mottled horses./ Who is that rich man in a fur made from the skin of a wild goat?—The little roots serving the field mouse for food.

Bazarov, 104.

331. Gloves were pasturing,/ An owl was jumping,/ An elephant waved,/ An idle being made the sound *khurī*.—When sheep pasture, a wolf eats them.

Poppe, *Aga Buriat*, 37.

332. A white person cut,/ A mouse stirred [it],/ They pushed [it] into the well.—Eating

Poppe, *Aga Buriat*, 55.

333. On a white dune resembling a cup/ The white bird Dungkhulä;/ Looks into the distance to see the southern (or: right hand) hills./ The giver is a wise man;/ The receiver is a rich man.—Weighing and handling over silver.

Mostaert, 184.

334. *Ebēdei, khebēdai,*/ A flying bird, a sitting Buddha,/ An attacking wise man.—Saddle, bridle, horse, man, whip.

Zhamtsaranov and Rudnyev, 84.

335–339. AN ANIMAL AND A THING

335a. From a white cow a white caparison.—Cream.

Whymant, p. 39, No. 5.

335b. The white cow has a paper blanket.—Cream.

Kotvich, 44.

336a. The dun-gray horse could not be trained; the silver whip could not be held back.—Wolf and snake.

Bazarov, 62.

336b. You cannot mount a bluish-gray horse; you cannot get hold of a braid with a handle [taken] from a thornbush.—Wolf, snake.

Kotvich, 213.

336c. You cannot take a braid with a handle from a bush; you cannot bring to reason a free (muscular?) . . .—Snake, wolf.

Kotvich, 214.

337a. The city of Dendžin having come from above;/ the city of Peking on earth;/ A mule with a white muzzle that enters through the gate;/ White meal that drips from a sleeve.—Distillation of brandy.

Mostaert, 162.

337b. Through a door a white-muzzled mule breaks its way;/ From the sleeve there comes a white flat cake.—Distillation of brandy.

Mostaert, 161.

338a. Behind thinly scattered trees a Russian rides a piebald horse.—Eye.

Bazarov, 6.

338b. Behind numberless birches is a Russian with a motley horse.—Eye.

Poppe, *Aga Buriat*, 60.

339. A stand of a hundred horses is good; a seam on the counter of the shoe is good.—Features of the head.

Kotvich, 29.

III. COMPARISONS TO A MAN, GOBLIN, OR DEVIL, Nos. 340–543

Note also the comparisons to a small creature with a loud voice (Nos. 31–36), in which a comparison to a man is sometimes intended, and the comparisons to an animal and a man (Nos. 541–543).

340–385. STATUS INDICATED BY FORM, COMPANIONS, OR ACTS

340–370. RELIGIOUS STATUS

340–361. *Form, Color, or Companions*

340. Between two mountains/ An ingot of camel excrements./ The lamas of former generations/ Are letting fly their robes.—Bell, drum.

Zhamtsaranov and Rudnyev, 15.

341a. A black lama on a trunk,/ The thoughts of all are on him.—Food in a kettle on a fire.

Rudnyev, 54.

341b. She puts the big black one in place; the thoughts of all are on him.—Cooking millet or rice.

Mostaert, 88.

342. In a well an amber lama.—Eye.

Poppe, *Aga Buriat*, 19.

343. Has he a vessel? Has he holy water? Has he read [the scriptures]?—Nectar, bee.

Bazarov, 37.

344. Before the presiding lama/ There are a shoulder blade and bones (*chomoge*).—A small drum (*damaru*) made of the upper parts of two human skulls and a handbell.

Mostaert, 79.

345. A lama sitting in the back part of the house/ Has a bell and a drum.—The Four Teachers.

Zhamtsaranov and Rudnyev, 75.

346. He has a little ball in his mouth, a drum in his belly, and holy water on his back.—Male camel in heat.

Bazarov, 170.

347. On the summit of the southern mountain/ There is somebody with a jacket striped like a tiger's skin,/ With the hat of a priest from Kwantung [Manchuria],/ With a trumpet of sandalwood [the color of] copper./ He celebrates a church rite that lasts three seasons.—Peewit or lapwing.

Mostaert, 1.

348. The same as No. 347 with the addition: With a tapering hat like a vessel for holy water.—Peewit or lapwing.

Mostaert, 1 var.

349. He has a tapering lama's hat./ He has a gold-colored coat;/ He has a trumpet of sandalwood the color of copper./ He celebrates a rite that lasts three seasons.—Rooster.

Mostaert, 153.

350. He came from the west, is subject to the Bandida Lama, wears a striped kaftan and a cap called *panchen shva ser*.—Woodpecker.

Bazarov, 38.

351. The abbot has come from the north, his two ears are sticking out, he has eyes of lead and a peacock's tail.—Hand drum.

Rudnyev, 5.

352. Ten accompanied the significant master.—Putting on a hat.

Kotvich, 202.

353. The lama Dondok has seven disciples.—Seven offering bowls.

Bazarov, 43.

354. Something is seen from afar with sixty white buttons, with two nails that resemble a rod (*ochire*) used in ritual and only one hammer.—Pegs and hammer.

Kotvich, 211.

355. With a handsome body as if it had been modeled by an artist,/ With six beautiful hands,/ Smelling of *agur* (?) sandalwood./ From what country does the noble lama hail?—Stinkbug.

Mostaert, 22.

356. He has a cushion of sandalwood, he has a seat of quince wood, he has six beautiful hands, he feasts on a whole sheep.—Tick.

Mostaert, 30.

357. A ribbonlike black body/ With six nice tufts (*manchuk*) of red silk or hair,/ Smelling like resin and sandalwood./ From what country is the noble lama?—An insect called *joodak khorkhoi* or *khorkoin chono* (the wolf of insects).

Mostaert, 72.

358. The novice (*bandi*) who has come from the west is bald-headed.—A kindled incense stick.

Bazarov, 31.

359. A buxom red nun in front of the Buddha.—Lamp.

Rudnyev, 60.

360. In front of the Buddha statue/ There is a plump red nun.—Sacred bowl (*bumba*) used on a home altar.

Zhamtsaranov and Rudnyev, 63.

361. Over a Buddha there is a fat Red.—Candle in front of a Buddha.

Zhamtsaranov and Rudnyev, 88.

362–370. *Acts*

362. A wag of a novice (*bandi*) has lost his vessel.—Hare forsaking its lair.

Mostaert, 83.

363. In a well an earless lama performed a [religious] service.—Churning kumiss (*airak*) with a churnstaff.

Rudnyev, 77.

364. In the ravine twenty shamans shamanized.—Something bubbling like a fountain.

Bazarov, 74.

365. In a hole twenty shamans shamanized.—In a saucepan rye is boiling.

Poppe, *Aga Buriat*, 51.

366. With a body as large as a forefinger,/ Bearing the epithet "Precious Thunderbolt,"/ Carrying blessings wherever it goes,/ Beneficent to a great number of people.—Medicine.

Rudnyev, 14.

367. Although he did not travel to Tibet, he has a woolen jacket;/ Although he did not go to office, he has a leather belt;/ Although he did not hold any jobs, he has the legal hat button;/ Although he was not attacked by a disease, he has a water bottle.—Bowl (*sabari*) for holy water.

Poppe, *Aga Buriat*, 40.

368. From the west he came,/ Having a Baljing Shaser cap,/ Having a jacket of tiger fur,/ Bearing the name Badan Sadan.—Hoopoe (*Upupa epops*).

Poppe, *Aga Buriat*, 62.

369. As if he had come from the west,/ He has a motley tiger jacket./ Although he is not a novice, he reads.—Hoopoe.

Poppe, *Aga Buriat*, 73.

370. Somebody that has come from afar has a throat,/ A double button placed on it,/ A nice round mouth,/ And eight lotuses placed on it.—Musical instrument resembling a flageolet (*bushkyā*. Tibetan *gling bu*) used in temples.

Mostaert, 70.

371–385. SECULAR STATUS

371. He has a coral button and a juicy (*shȳsy*) rump.—Lamp.

Mostaert, 126.

372. He is a son-in-law of a prince coming from afar,/ A son-in-law of a prince with two hanging ears,/ A son-in-law of a prince pursued by the dogs of two yurt-groups.—Jerboa.

Zhamtsaranov and Rudnyev, 109.

373. A jumpy prince who has come from the north,/ A prince both of whose legs pace,/ A prince with a banner-like tail,/ A prince with a calf's snout.—Jerboa.

Poppe, *Aga Buriat*, 83.

374. The wife of Abai beile has a suite of twelve and one silver spoon.—Breastbone with the ribs.

Rudnyev, 3.

375. Three government officials, three round administrative officers (*zassak*) with two corporals as retinue.—Kettle, tripod, and tongs.

Rudnyev, 67.

376. A mist rising to the sky,/ A golden gate leaning upwards,/ Four officials in a circle,/ Three ministers of the time,/ Twelve chiefs in the intervals,/ Two servants executing orders.—Fire: smoke, flame, tripod, belts [on tripod], nails, tongs.

Zhamtsaranov and Rudnyev, 111.

377. When the Amban Tse proceeded from the "inner country," five aides went out to meet (lit.: seize) him.—Mucus and the five fingers of the hand.

Rudnyev, 19.

378. A great governor comes/ And five pages meet him.—Blowing one's nose.

Zhamtsaranov and Rudnyev, 33.

379a. He walks with a proud step and has a retinue of ten thousand.—Horse and its tail.

Bazarov, 157.

379b. He has a rhythmic walk./ He has a thousand white followers./ He has a rhythmic walk./ He has ten thousand white followers.—Horse.

Poppe, *Aga Buriat,* 81.

379c. He has a rhythmic walk./ He has a thousand, ten thousand followers.—Horse, horse's tail.

Zhamtsaranov and Rudnyev, 98.

380a. He has a rhythmic walk,/ He has ten thousand white followers.—Horse's tail.

Poppe, *Aga Buriat,* 30.

380b. Thousands and thousands,/ A thousand white followers.—Horse's tail.

Poppe, *Aga Buriat,* 52.

381. The beloved queen fell ill, five ministers set forth [and] having called in Dr. Toothpick, the latter removed some harmful stuff as big as a lizard.—Picking one's teeth.

Mostaert, 73.

382. The little professor fell ill, five ministers galloped off to call in Dr. Incense-stick. He removed some nuisance as big as a lizard.—Picking one's teeth.

Mostaert, 73 var.

383. A master passed the night with his servant.—Dog.

Gomboyev, 22.

384. With a younger brother good at serving, with an older brother good at commanding, with a herd of bluish-gray horses, with [two] dogs called Khassar and Bassar.—Gun, bullet, report of a gun, powder.

Rudnyev, 18.

385. The representative of the law is in front of the official.—Lamp [in front of the divine statue].

Kotvich, 250.

386–394. MAN (DEVIL) AND HOUSE, HEAP, PIT, CUP, OR WELL

386. He has a grayish hut, he has grayish food. What a beautiful child!—The mouse, its hole, and its food [little roots of plants].

Bazarov, 20.

387. He has a grayish hut and grayish food.—Pit (*otari*) for smoking sheepskins to give them a yellow color.

Bazarov, 21.

388. The Mongol's son has a palace of wood.—Eggs.

Kotvich, 138.

389. The Yankhal's son has a palace of bone.—Tortoise.

Kotvich, 139.

390a. In a big house there is a small house. In the small house there is a fat little boy.—Boot, sock, leg (foot).

Mostaert, 193; Zhamtsaranov and Rudnyev, 34.

390b. Inside a big house there is a red house, inside the red house there is a fat yellow girl.—Boot, stocking, and leg.

Kotvich, 35.

391. It is impossible to find out whether grandmother in the trunk is in a heap or a pit.—You cannot tell whether there is a boy or a girl in the mother's womb.

Kotvich, 3.

392. In a cup there is a devil.—Eye.

Poppe, *Aga Buriat,* 61.

393. A beautiful maiden in a well.—Churnstaff, used in making kumiss.

Rudnyev, 46.

394. There is a hornless devil in the well.—Bullet of a gun.

Rudnyev, 45.

395–440. FORM

395. There is a dried-up devil on the road, a devil standing guard against everybody.—A hidden bow (*sali*) like a spring-gun set for killing game.

Bazarov, 72.

396. A strong man with two pillows.—Bow.

Gomboyev, 46.

397. A small boy is a match for ten men.—Bow.

Gomboyev, 46a.

398. A tall person has stirrups of thread.—Logs for fastening the lattice to the grate.

Kotvich, 60.

399a. A long (or: tall) man did not reach the mane of the colt.—Road.

Gomboyev, 58.

399b. A long (or: tall) man did not reach the sole [of the boot].—Road.

Bazarov, 167.

400. A small girl full of sores and wounds.—Thimble.

Zhamtsaranov, 29.

401–415. SEVERAL DESCRIPTIVE DETAILS

401. With an *arshin*-long body, with a handful of wool, with hollow testicles, with a blue penis.—Arrow.

Poppe, *Aga Buriat,* 10.

402. With a grown, grown body,/ With three times seven joints,/ With a body as white as a rabbit,/ With a face as red as a date (or jujube).—Sarana bulb (*Lilium sarana*).

Zhamtsaranov and Rudnyev, 20.

403. Its name is Gün Gürwe,/ It has a body the size of a stomach,/ It gets its booty in a place where [anything] can be found,/ It brings luck to many tens of thousands.—Medicine bag.

Zhamtsaranov and Rudnyev, 57.

404. It has a posterior of flour,/ A body of grassy pearls,/ A fiery head,/ A deep well.—Ashes, fire, smoke, kettle.

Zhamtsaranov and Rudnyev, 83.

405. It is a plump miracle,/ A miracle with five belts,/ A miracle with a hole on its top,/ A miracle with no chin.—Teapot.

Zhamtsaranov and Rudnyev, 59.

406. With a body as big as a hat, he has the voice of Mahākāla.—Cymbals used in religious services.

Bazarov, 129.

407. His abdomen is bone,/ His spine is wood,/ His back is flesh.—Arch [of a saddle].

Poppe, *Aga Buriat,* 95.

408. It has a disheveled head, sits like a Buddha, has the color of a camel, and eyes like the morning star.—Eagle owl.

Bazarov, 109.

409. It is camel-brown in color,/ It has eyes like Venus,/ It has a head like a hillock,/ It keeps the teachings of Buddha, the teacher.—Horned owl.

Poppe, *Aga Buriat,* 80.

410. With four plaits, with forty black eyes, dear to the king, respected by the people.—Steelyard.

Bazarov, 150; Poppe, *Aga Buriat,* 32 (friendly to its khan, faithful to all the people).

411. With forty black eyes,/ With a pigtail of four strands.—Steelyard.

Poppe, *Aga Buriat,* 13.

412. Your ears are turned back, your eyes are red.—Tune of a balalaika.

Kotvich, 218.

413. The nape of the neck is glossy, the abdomen protruded.—Thumb or end of the finger.

Kotvich, 26.

414. On the saddle-like pass there is a leather-covered shooter,/ A spread-legged shooter, who has spread out his legs.—Rifle.

Zhamtsaranov and Rudnyev, 6.

415. With twisted feet and a clapper with a swollen head.—Steelyard.

Bazarov, 131.

416–429. HEAD AND PARTS OF THE HEAD

416a. An unlucky rich person,/ A wise person without a tongue.—Abacus.

Poppe, *Aga Buriat,* 68.

416b. A rich man without measure,/ A wise man without a tongue.—Abacus.

Poppe, *Ekhirit,* 7.

416c. Tongueless wise, incomeless rich.—Abacus.

Klukine, 29.

417. A Russian whose top has a hole.—Gun (rifle).

Poppe, *Aga Buriat,* 56; Bazarov, 163 (Russian official); Poppe, *Ekhirit,* 5 (Russian master).

418a. A black old woman with a hole in her cheek.—Lock.

Bazarov, 49.

418b. A parsimonious old woman has a hole in her cheek.—Lock.

Poppe, *Aga Buriat,* 14.

419. From our courtyard there proceeded smoke,/ On the goblin's head there was fire.—Tobacco pipe.

Gomboyev, 49.

420. Outside our house fog has come down./ On the Russian's head fire has been lit.—Smoking tobacco.

Poppe, *Aga Buriat,* 36.

421. The lanky Russian burns from the top.—Candle.

Zhamtsaranov, 12.

422. A long man come to his end from the top.—Candle.

Poppe, *Ekhirit,* 17.

423. A beautiful red-haired maiden with unkempt hair.—Fox.

Klukine, 16.

424. A high (or: tall) man has only one eye.—Needle.

Zhamtsaranov and Rudnyev, 81.

425. A cross-eyed girl peered through the sky.—Fish.

Gomboyev, 28.

426. A skew-eyed [person] coming from Kiakhta,/ A climber up a hair.—Spider draws in its cobweb and climbs.

Poppe, *Aga Buriat,* 59.

427. A one-eared soldier.—Cock of a rifle.

Klukine, 28.

428. A covetous woman has no smell in her nose.—Lock.

Gomboyev, 31.

429a. There came a toothless guest,/ They cooked boneless meat for him.—Baby, breast.

Zhamtsaranov, 18.

429b. The newly arrived guest has no teeth,/ The sheep killed for him has no bones.—Newborn baby, breast.

Gomboyev, 6.

429c. A sheep was killed and served to a toothless old woman.—Nursing a baby.

Kotvich, 5.

430–440. A MEMBER OTHER THAN THE HEAD

430. One has a lot of trouble with her, her bone is brittle.—Incense-stick.

Bazarov, 86.

431. Its privileged position is great, its bones are fragile.—Porcelain cup.

Zhamtsaranov and Rudnyev, 29.

432. The hand of Arji Borji [is] full of knots.—Pine.

Bazarov, 14.

433. One fist in the house (lit.: tent), one fist outside.—Thong in lattice wall.

Mostaert, 66; Kotvich, 56.

434. A square boy with a hole in the middle.—Plane.

Bazarov, 152.

435. While all beings in the world have their bellies in front, Janggar Jana [has] his belly behind.—Calf of leg.

Rudnyev, 4.

436. The woman as big as a fathom has a button behind.—Door and latch.

Mostaert, 148.

437. An official arrives from the north. He has a tusk behind.—The female of a wingless grasshopper.

Bazarov, 188.

438. An official has come from the north. He wags his rump and paces with two legs—an ambling official.—Jerboa.

Bazarov, 189.

439. He has a posterior the size of a bucket.—Bell.

Poppe, *Aga Buriat*, 29.

440. The noyon Denzen, who came from above, has four crooked legs and they are colored gray.—Frog.

Kotvich, 257.

441–448. COLOR

For riddles describing the color of a garment see the following section, Nos. 453–457.

441. Hard and black [one], Tungus white [one], friendly red [one].—Boot, sock, leg.

Rudnyev, 12.

442. A reddish little boy rode in a stagecoach. Since then, "Forgive!"—Spark.

Bazarov, 172.

443. I will give you whatever you want, but catch me the black madcap.—Shadow.

Kotvich, 165.

444. At the foot of wormwood there is a yellow-red grandmother.—Fox.

Kotvich, 108.

445. A tall white hellion sways morning and night.—Grass.

Kotvich, 155.

446. A long yellow boy eats his [own] body.—Incense.

Mostaert, 39 var.

447. A tailless, multicolored carpenter who penetrates everywhere.—Woodpecker.

Bazarov, 156.

448. The master of the riddle is completely black./ When one comes after solving it, it is blind black.—Human thought.

Poppe, *Ekhirit*, 1.

449–462. DRESS, PERSONAL BELONGINGS

449a. The son of the empress has seventy suits.—Young shoot of a reed.

Kotvich, 153.

449b. With thirty suits of clothes, with a cap of fox fur.—Reed.

Kotvich, 149.

450. A ball-like, red novice/ Has seventy-two pelerines.—Onion.

Zhamtsaranov and Rudnyev, 47.

451a. He has a lithe body and a fox's tail for a hat.—Reed.

Mostaert, 86.

451b. He has a flexible body,/ He has a cap made from the breast of a fox.—*Lasiagrosis splendens*, a kind of grass.

Zhamtsaranov and Rudnyev, 95.

452. A child who came from a market (or: factory) adorns everybody.—Needle.

Bazarov, 41.

453–457. COLOR OF DRESS

453. A red flower with petals that form a ball are fixed on the top of his head;/ He is dressed in all there is of beautiful clothes./ When he sounds his loud voice,/ A thousand single gates and ten thousand double gates are thrown open at the same time.—Rooster.

Mostaert, 154.

454. Wearing a little red tassel, I was not aware that I was adorned. Wearing a little red plate (?), I was not aware that I was a master.—Woodpecker.

Bazarov, 199.

455a. Having a noiseless step, with a lama's yellow fur.—Fox.

Klukine, 17.

455b. He has a tittuping walk,/ He has a yellow lama's coat.—Fox.
Zhamtsaranov and Rudnyev, 97.

456a. It steps *tek tek*/ In shagreen boots;/ It wears a multicolored fur/ And drags a golden rope (a loop attached to a pole and used for catching horses) behind itself.—Magpie.
Gomboyev, 27.

456b. It has a jumpy walk,/ It has goatskin shoes,/ A motley coat,/ and it drags a golden lasso.—Magpie.
Zhamtsaranov and Rudnyev, 16.

457. A round girl dressed in silver.—Kidneys.
Gomboyev, 16.

458–462. SPECIAL ARTICLES OF DRESS

458. Byrgyt has lost his belt.—Traces of a yurt.
Gomboyev, 56.

459. A Tangut boy with five belts.—Teakettle.
Klukine, 20.

460. A good man has three girdles.—Trivet.
Zhamtsaranov and Rudnyev, 35.

461. A man in the steppe without flint stone.—Wolf.
Bazarov, 54.

462. An elegantly dressed gentleman/ Without tinderbox and tobacco pouch.—Statue of the Buddha.
Mostaert, 164.

463–499. FUNCTION
463–465. TEMPERMENT

463. In a flimsy house a timid old woman.—A hare lying down in its lair.
Mostaert, 176.

464. In a house made of a fatty skin a timid old woman.—Stomach of ruminants.
Mostaert, 160.

465. Subject to the king,/ Trusted by all.—Steelyard.
Zhamtsaranov, 4.

466–469. MANNER OF LIFE

466. Our folks sleep,/ A boy covered with scratches watches the house.—House lock.
Zhamtsaranov and Rudnyev, 85.

467. Do not touch me, for I will fall apart.—Dew on the grass.
Kotvich, 168.

468. "Round little boy, where do you come from?" "From the country of fat and grease." "Why are you not soiled with fat and grease?" "It is our custom [not to be soiled]."—Excrements of sheep, goats, and camels.
Bazarov, 135.

469. An early riser at dawn,/ A collector of meat refuse,/ A runner behind the house,/ A collector of women's excrements.—Magpie.
Poppe, *Aga Buriat*, 76.

470–490. MOTION

470. The naked devil crept into his hole.—Putting on a shoe.
Kotvich, 235.

471. The nimble old woman jumps on the grate of the yurt.—Leather dipper for kumiss.
Kotvich, 93.

472. He runs with a skip; he has a face like a calf.—Jerboa.
Kotvich, 130.

473. Upwards it goes goes, the leaping motley one;/ Downwards it descends, the . . . motley one.—Sleet.
Poppe, *Dagurskoe*, 5.

474. The protruding one could not turn his posterior.—Pestle.
Poppe, *Barguzin*, 5.

475. He walks here and there,/ He has a medicine-like cool body.—Frog.
Poppe, *Barguzin*, 9.

476–486. *Motion and an Accompanying Act*

476. The khan left the room, raising his dagger.—The dog went out, raising his tail.
Kotvich, 113.

477. He screamed "Oh!" and ran out.—Steam escaping from a kettle containing alcohol.
Kotvich, 88.

478. He screamed "Oh!" and, lifting his ax, left.—The dog went out, raising his tail.
Kotvich, 112.

479a. He springs from the earth, becomes frantic from above, dies in the well, perishes in the steppe.—Saltwort.
Gomboyev, 54.

479b. He springs from the earth, rises from above, perishes in the steppe.—Saltwort.
Gomboyev, 54 var.

480. From the emperor's country an envoy dressed in a black jacket/ Comes singing; he sits down and strokes his beard.—Fly.
Mostaert, 91.

481. He threw off the cover, [and] moved his feet.—Pulling the main artery of a sheep.
Kotvich, 116.

482. He jumped and jumped and lost a silk belt.—Horse's excrement.
Kotvich, 124.

483. He jumped and jumped, but did not reach his mother-in-law.—Lung does not go down in the kettle; person does not move over the pommel of the saddle.

Kotvich, 121.

484. He descended at the corner and gathered willow leaves.—Taking the yurt apart.

Kotvich, 49.

485. He runs fast [like falling drops], has a strong lash, sits like a khan, and has a black lambskin cap.—Needle, thread, and thimble.

Kotvich, 95.

486. A man smaller than you lifts you up and seats you.—Stirrups.

Rudnyev, 9.

487–490. *Motion Denied*

487. If I could rise, I would reach the sky./ If I could speak, I would catch the thief [by telling where he has gone].—Road.

Zhamtsaranov, 5.

488. He was unable to step over the golden spile (the Pleiades).—Serpent.

Bazarov, 17.

489. Places that cannot be reached by a person were reached by his small baby.—Mind.

Kotvich, 232.

490. Over there (Not far away) the not-walking *tekelzhin* rising high on four legs, the *tekelzhin* that eats neither camel's nor goat's meat.—The spirit (*onggon*) of the dead.

Bazarov, 113.

491–494. SEEING, LOOKING

491. A clever woman watches the house.—Lock.

Mostaert, 156.

492. Though blind, I show men's footprints.—Road.

Bazarov, 22.

493. A thin boy does not see the sun.—Core or heart of a tree.

Bazarov, 141.

494. Behind the house [persons] are crosswise/ And the back one is looking at the front one.—Ribbons of the smoke opening.

Zhamtsaranov and Rudnyev, 64.

495–499. EATING, LICKING, DRINKING

495. The fire ate the protruding black one.—Kettle on fuel.

Rudnyev, 66.

496. The son of heaven chews iron sulphur.—Bit in horse's mouth.

Bazarov, 124.

497a. Galba licked the soil.—Hob of a boot.

Gomboyev, 42.

497b. Galba licks the earth.—Sole of a boot.

Bazarov, 82.

498. He licks a tasteless thing ten times.—Threading a needle.

Kotvich, 94.

499. He does not drink, but has eight red cups./ He does not drive a car, but has a whip [made of Spiracea altaica].—Eight cow's hoofs and a tail.

Bazarov, 11.

500–521. MAKING A SOUND

500–517. *Making a Specified Sound*

500. He climbed on top of a trunk and called his uncle Adian.—Marmot.

Kotvich, 132.

501. Its sound is *khong khong*, on its hip is a quiver.—Dog and its tail.

Bazarov, 53.

502. He has a voice *khong khong*, he has a quiver on his hip.—Dog barking.

Poppe, *Aga Buriat*, 57.

503. His voice goes *khong khong*,/ On his hip has a knife.—Dog.

Gomboyev, 23.

504. *Khong-, khong*-voiced,/ With a plume on his rump.—Dog.

Mostaert, 25.

505. Its voice is *bar bar*, it has a kaftan of silk brocade, it has fire-red eyes, it is doomed to walk alone.—Eagle owl.

Bazarov, 23.

506. Its sound is *bar bar*, it has a silken brocade coat.—Frog.

Bazarov, 30.

507. It makes the sound *pot* here; it makes the sound *pot* there; near Engkhe's house it makes the sound *pot* three times.—Camel relieving itself.

Mostaert, 23.

508. Its voice goes *jing jing*; it goes to places at a year's distance.—Cart.

Rudnyev, 56.

509. He has a voice *jir jir*;/ He reads a sacred book (*Jigden Gombo*);/ He has a homeland that is years away.—A bird.

Poppe, *Aga Buriat*, 64.

510a. He has a voice *boo boo*;/ He has a sleeping place in a bent tree;/ He has two sacks of food.—Baby.

Poppe, *Aga Buriat*, 63.

510b. With a sleeping place in a hollow tree,/ With two bags of food.—Baby.
Poppe, *Aga Buriat*, 18.

511a. There is no flesh that one can pinch;/ It has a piercing sound (*tšas*).—Cymbals.
Mostaert, 62.

511b. It sounds *ching ching*./ There is no flesh when you pinch it.—Cymbals.
Mostaert, 62 var.

512. Under the earth it makes the sound *khur khur*;/ A single stick goes up and down.—Stick for stirring kumiss.
Poppe, *Barguzin*, 1.

513. Over there it made the sound *tes*/ And the tail of a camel quivered.—Lightning.
Poppe, *Aga Buriat*, 84.

514. It makes the sound *shur shur;* it has become so fat that it has a furuncle.—Spinning wool.
Poppe, *Ekhirit*, 14.

515. It makes the sound *shab shab,* it has a base of . . . felt and a hole as wide as three fingers.—Flint.
Bazarov, 145.

516. With a voice sounding like *shak shak,* with a cap of yellow fur (i.e., fox's fur).—Shakchaga.
Rudnyev, 31.

517. What has come from the north makes the sound *khon khon,*/ Two ears hang down,/ The last vertebra (i.e., the last before the pelvis) is versatile,/ A calf tail stands up.—Wolf.
Zhamtsaranov and Rudnyev, 17.

518–521. *Sound Not Specified*

518. A shouting black Tibetan who has come from Tibet.—Gong.
Zhamtsaranov and Rudnyev, 31.

519. The long one emitted a sound. Hush! Three crows scraped the ground.—Gunshot.
Kotvich, 225.

520. Ariābalo speaks from between his thighs.—Lama's bell.
Mostaert, 65.

521. Keep it an empty (or: uncrowded) place, do not let the children see it. If it emits a sound, then know that it is dead.—Porcelain.
Bazarov, 79.

522. DEAFNESS

522. A deaf oldster has ramifications in all four directions.—Corners of a wooden house.
Poppe, *Aga Buriat*, 45.

523–528. STRIKING, CLENCHING FIST

523a. He hits the Buddha with willow branches.—Eye and eyelashes.
Mostaert, 173.

523b. He lashed his Buddha with willow branches.—Closing the eyes.
Rudnyev, 74.

523c. He beat his Buddha with a withe.—Winking the eyes.
Poppe, *Aga Buriat*, 1.

524. The children of the Buddha play with willow branches.—Eyelashes.
Gomboyev, 9.

525. Someone beats his Buddha with twigs.—Eyes.
Zhamtsaranov and Rudnyev, 65.

526. They strike him on the head and kiss him on the mouth.—Smoking tobacco.
Poppe, *Dagurskoe*, 6.

527. A naked lama hits his groin.—Sound of the bell used in religious services.
Bazarov, 142.

528. Behind you he clenches his fist.—Thong fastening the wall of the yurt.
Gomboyev, 33.

529–540. OTHER ACTS

529. A man smaller than you overcomes you.—Sleep.
Rudnyev, 8.

530. A fat Russian warms his buttocks.—Kettle over the fire.
Bazarov, 25.

531. Close to the fire there sits a naughty girl.—Plug of the kettle in which alcohol is distilled.
Kotvich, 84.

532. An unborn child stands guard at a pole with a loop (?).—Grain recently sown.
Bazarov, 166.

533. A tall man measured something with his arms above his head.—Milky Way.
Gomboyev, 2.

534. He aims from an elevation; two feet sneak up.—Gunshot.
Kotvich, 224.

535. He aimed and hit the leg; he turned around and hit the nose.—Crepitus ventris (?).
Kotvich, 240.

536. A hero not slipping on rocks, a hero not to be hit by arrows, a "high" hero with an incision in the middle.—Ant.
Rudnyev, 10.

537. A thin virgin played and played and became pregnant.—Spinning wheel.

Bazarov, 140.

538a. He plowed the soil with five oxen and made a speech in Tibetan.—Writing.

Bazarov, 117.

538b. They sowed grain with five bulls. They spoke in the Tangut (Tibetan) language. They made a plowshare from the horn of a Manchurian deer. They slaked its thirst with springwater.—Writing.

Sanzheev, p. 168.

538c. He sowed seeds for five months,/ He made a tongue [of a plow] of the Tangut (Tibetan) tongue (i.e., language),/ He made a plowshare of the horn of a deer,/ He made a drink from springwater.—Writing.

Poppe, *Aga Buriat*, 90.

539. A stupid boy makes the sign of the fig to heaven. —Tentpole (*bagana*) that often sticks out of the circular opening at the top of the yurt.

Bazarov, 112.

540. A beautiful girl lost her comb.—Fox.

Zhamtsaranov and Rudnyev, 41.

541–543. A MAN AND A THING

In the following three riddles the man and the thing have no immediately obvious connection with one another. Many other riddles, which will be found in appropriate places, involve a comparison to a man using a thing for some purpose.

541. A sitting Buddha, a running tether.—Horse and rider.

Rudnyev, 51.

542. The son of earth is astonished,/ A single (or: solitary) tree is shaking.—Catching a horse with a loop attached to a pole (*urga*).

Mostaert, 192.

543. A tree without color; a young fellow without blood.—Reed in the lake and a subject of the ants' king.

Zhamtsaranov, 14.

IV. COMPARISONS TO SEVERAL PERSONS, NOS. 544–636

544–554. FORM

544–553. SIMILAR IN FORM

544. Ōnō and Chono.—Adze and ax.

Mostaert, 121.

545. A pair: Tunta and Munta.—Cover and pendant of a braid.

Kotvich, 40.

546. Older and younger sister wholly alike.—Earrings and similar ornaments worn in pairs, pendants.

Rudnyev, 34.

547a. Two sisters, the older and the younger, have equal shoulders.—Upper jambs of the door and threshold.

Kotvich, 62.

547b. The older and the younger sister are equal in respect to shoulders.—Door.

Poppe, *Aga Buriat*, 20.

547c. Two sisters of equal stature.—Wings of a gate.

Gomboyev, 30; Mostaert, 40 (equal size).

547d. Two sisters of exactly the same size.—Doors.

Whymant, p. 38, No. 4.

547e. The older and the younger brother are equal in respect to their shoulders.—Gate.

Zhamtsaranov and Rudnyev, 13.

547f. Older and younger brother of the same rank.— Two wings of a gate.

Klukine, 27.

548. Ten novices with faces backwards.—Hand and ten fingers.

Klukine, 1.

549. Old women whose yurts are full have woolen buttocks.—Logs at the unino.

Kotvich, 61.

550. The children of the northern yurt have white hips.—Rump of an antelope.

Poppe, *Aga Buriat*, 26.

551. Many thousands of warriors in a home without a door.—Seeds of a watermelon.

Kotvich, 158.

552. People who have a house full of people have no doors to go in and out.—Watermelon.

Kotvich, 265.

553. The *jarvādai* and *jirvēdei* were thrown from the bare (or: empty) vessel into a hole.—Eating.

Zhamtsaranov and Rudnyev, 99.

554. CONTRASTED IN FORM

554. The beauty this way; the bald one that way.— Pillow.

Rudnyev, 48.

555–559. DRESS

555. Four brothers have one hat.—Legs of a table.

Kotvich, 78.

556. Ten people put on something large and shaggy.— Putting on hats or caps.

Bazarov, 9.

557a. From the south there came four men, two in furs, two without furs.—Horns and ears.

Gomboyev, 17.

557b. Two with fur coats, two without fur coats.—Ears and horns of cattle.

Sanzheev, p. 169; Poppe, *Aga Buriat*, 9.

557c. Four people have come from the north, two have fur coats, two of them are naked.—Horns and ears of a cow.

Poppe, *Aga Buriat*, 82.

557d. From the south four people are coming, two in red goat-skins, two are naked.—Ears and horns of a cow.

Bazarov, 169.

558, 559. COLORS OF DRESS

558. Children of noblemen dressed in green silk.—Milt.

Gomboyev, 15.

559a. The son of a prince is dressed in black silk;/ The son of a princess is dressed in red silk.—Liver, lungs.

Mostaert, 12.

559b. The son of a king/ Is dressed in black silk;/ The son of a prince/ Is dressed in green silk;/ The two sons of the people/ Have a house of suet.—Liver; gall bladder; kidneys.

Mostaert, 11.

559c. The king's son wears a black silk kaftan; the minister's son wears a green silk kaftan.—Liver and gall bladder.

Bazarov, 60.

559d. The tsar's daughter has a belt made of black silk; the prince's daughter has a belt made of green silk. —Lungs and liver.

Kotvich, 120.

560–562. MEMBERS OF A FAMILY

560. Who is that beautiful maiden/ With the beautiful blue winter camp in the steppe,/ With the father in the blue plain,/ With the bony, empty mother?—Lily.

Rudnyev, 47.

561a. With something like iron for his father,/ And a mother who dances back and forth,/ A daughter as white as the flour of wheat,/ A son as black as jet.—Making fire under a pot: fire, ashes, poker.

Mostaert, 7.

561b. It has something branchy and tufted for its mother,/ It has Erlik Khān (Yama, the King of Hell) for its father;/ It has a son-in-law as black as lonton [seeds].—Kindling fire.

Mostaert, 117.

561c. It has something branchy and tufted for its mother;/ It has Erlik Khān for its father;/ It has a squat black son-in-law;/ It has a beautiful white daughter.—Kindling a fire and washing a kettle.

Mostaert, 118.

562. It has a father who is a hawk;/ It has a mother who is an owl or a partridge;/ It has a bent gray horse;/ It has four bloody sons;/ It has six yellow daughters.—Forequarter (*khā*) of a sheep: scapula, humerus, os femoris, os radiale, the four long ribs, the six short ribs.

Zhamtsaranov and Rudnyev, 94.

563–636. FUNCTION
563. MANNER OF LIFE

563. The daughters of Enke (Peaceful) live in harmony.—Wings of the gate.

Mostaert, 186.

564–596. MOTION

564. On an elevated river bank there is a stupid game,/ A game in which older and younger brothers are trotting,/ A game in which a silken scarf is knotted. —Archery or shooting at a mark (*sur kharbhakhu*). The leather belt is the target, the bow is bent, the arrow is inserted.

Zhamtsaranov and Rudnyev, 102.

565a. I go this way; you step that way. We shall meet at the brook called Bilȳty.—Woolen rope around the felt tent.

Bazarov, 36.

565b. I here [and you there]; we shall meet on the Bilȳty (belt) River.—Belt of a house.

Zhamtsaranov and Rudnyev, 21, 68.

565c. You go that way, I want to go this way. We meet at the Bilȳty River.—Ropes girding the felt tent.

Rudnyev, 13.

565d. You go this way, and I will go that way. On the Bilȳty road let us join each other.—Putting on a belt.

Mostaert, 105.

566a. You go there, I go here, and we shall meet at the khan's door.—Rope around the yurt.

Kotvich, 69.

566b. You can go in that direction,/ I'll go in this direction,/ And we'll meet outside the house.—Putting on a girdle.

Poppe, *Barguzin*, 14.

567. Eight girls going to a banquet; two girls coming from a banquet.—Teats of a bitch and teats of a mare.

Kotvich, 107.

568. A white-eyed youngster flies through the soldiers. —Fish.

Kotvich, 262.

569a. A hardy knight penetrates among many thousands of warriors.—Dipper.
Kotvich, 87.

569b. Among the enemies who arrive in confusion one hardy knight walks in.—Dipper.
Kotvich, 86.

570. They took each other by the hand,/ A pale and a pipe pressed against each other;/ They followed each other's trail,/ Silver pipes pressed against each other.—Plaiting clasps for a coat.
Poppe, *Barguzin*, 8.

571. Tall: four;/ Younger brothers and children: five;/ Those who move alternately to the right and left: two;/ You, poor one (i.e., scapegrace): alone.—Four legs of the camel; legs and head; two humps; the tail.
Mostaert, 5.

572a. If three black devils had not kept me back, I would have reached the Tugulchin (Herdsmen of Calves) River long ago, by now I would have reached the Mungguchin (Silversmith) River.—Hobbled horse.
Bazarov, 119.

572b. When did it go? It reached the Kherlen River,/ It went now, it reached the Orkhon River,/ Three devils in between will not let it go.—Hobble.
Zhamtsaranov and Rudnyev, 58.

573. Our folks have gone to the monastery,/ A *mad* boy watches the house.—Lock of the gate.
Zhamtsaranov and Rudnyev, 12.

574. Tushiyetu Khan comes suppressing,/ Dzasaktu Khan goes standing aside.—Grass growing.
Zhamtsaranov and Rudnyev, 46.

575–582. *Overtaking*

575. A person driving in a cart tried to overtake the rider on horseback.—Vapors rising to the sun.
Kotvich, 194.

576. A man carrying wool is chasing a man carrying iron on his back, but he cannot catch him.—Head and feathers of an arrow.
Mostaert, 82.

577. A person with a horseshoe is chasing a person with a spear.—Needle and thread.
Kotvich, 203.

578. A foolish old woman was unable to catch up with her husband.—Shadow.
Bazarov, 133.

579. Four old women trying to outrun one another came from *dobrotor*.—Four woolen ropes tied to the roofpiece at the smokehole.
Kotvich, 68.

580a. Two sisters were racing; the older could not overtake the younger.—Wheels of a cart.
Kotvich, 230.

580b. The elder and the younger brother went racing, The elder brother did not overtake the younger brother.—Carriage wheels.
Poppe, *Barguzin*, 16.

581. Two elder brothers chasing two younger brothers are unable to catch up with them.—Sled runners.
Klukine, 31.

582. The four sons of the father never meet during their lifetime.—Four wheels of a cart.
Bazarov, 177.

583–593. *A Company Moves*

583a. Twenty people put Khorkudai on his trail.—Putting on one's trousers.
Rudnyev, 69.

583b. Twenty men put a spread-out thing (*khorkodoi*) in its place.—Putting on trousers by working with the hands (ten fingers) and the feet (ten toes).
Bazarov, 70.

584. Ten men put Aksadai on his trail.—Putting on one's hat.
Rudnyev, 49.

585. Ten people helped Arzadai to start his travels.—A shirt is put on a person.
Poppe, *Aga Buriat*, 66.

586. A great vast nomad horse is approaching; loosen the bay's reins.—Loosen the belt of the trousers.
Kotvich, 185.

587. From the shores of the blue sea the infantry comes.—Eyelashes.
Kotvich, 10.

588a. Thousands of soldiers work on a space big enough to hit with a lash.—Ants.
Kotvich, 144.

588b. The entire universe was placed on a space the size of a saddlecloth.—Ants.
Kotvich, 143.

589. Three racing women arrived from the *gurbuts*.—Three legs of a tripod.
Kotvich, 81.

590. Five peasants move around in a very thick fog.—Five toes.
Kotvich, 23.

591. Five brothers ascended a snow-white mountain./ Perhaps it will snow, perhaps it will rain.—Five fingers scratching a scurvy head.
Mostaert, 123.

592. One hundred and eight novices run on the same road.—Reciting on a rosary the prayer "um mani badmai khun(g)."
Mostaert, 64.

593. When going, they jangle;/ When coming back, they weep.—Buckets carrying water.
Mostaert, 34.

594–596. *Carrying Burdens*

594a. On their backs ten old women of western countries carry ice.—Fingers and fingernails.
Mostaert, 104.

594b. Five old women loaded with ice walk about.—Toes and nails.
Kotvich, 24.

595a. Five soldiers carry ice on their shoulders.—Finger (and toe) nails.
Bazarov, 118.

595b. Ten soldiers carried ice on their backs.—Fingers.
Poppe, *Aga Buriat*, 5.

596. For his descendants he carries ice on his back.—Male camel (when in heat).
Bazarov, 4.

597, 598. SEEING, LOOKING

597. You scold (*tarixu*), I curse, we both do not look at each other's faces.—The two saddlebows.
Rudnyev, 7.

598a. Two sisters do not see each other's faces.—Saddlebows.
Gomboyev, 44.

598b. Two brothers do not see each other's faces during their whole lives.—Saddlebows.
Mostaert, 98.

599–602. WARMING SELVES

599a. Three old women warm their bellies.—Tripod for a kettle.
Bazarov, 181.

599b. Four sisters warm their livers;/ A lonely old woman cauterizes her buttocks.—The four legs of the kettle stand and the kettle.
Mostaert, 38.

599c. Four old women warming their livers.—Stand for a kettle.
Klukine, 4; Rudnyev, 43; Zhamtsaranov and Rudnyev, 36 (feet of an andiron); Mostaert, 37.

600. Helun Erentshdjen warms his liver; three muzhiks warm their legs.—Kettle and tripod (stand).
Kotvich, 82.

601. On the fire is Gatiga, close to the fire is Mortsokha.—Flat cake and griddle.
Kotvich, 249.

602. The entire population was warming itself at a fire the size of a cup.—Sun.
Kotvich, 173.

603–613. QUARRELING

Compare also the riddles that refer to a person striking, Nos. 523–529 above.

603a. A son with a felt head/ Takes his father and beats him.—Beating a drum.
Mostaert, 69.

603b. A son with a felt head/ Slaps his father's cheek.—Beating a drum.
Mostaert, 69 var.

604. Old man T'eg from heaven,/ Old man Jag from the earth/ Are beating each other; Old man with hairs of gray artemisia/ Coming in between to separate them,/ Gets his forehead scorched and leaves.—Steel for striking a light, flint, tinder.
Mostaert, 48.

605. Tolya and Bolya quarreled this side of heaven; the person who intended to separate them came out of darkness with blood.—Fire.
Kotvich, 90.

606. Kerelda and Berelda were quarreling; they were separated by a person dressed in a coat of squirrel fur.—Fire, flint, and spark.
Kotvich, 91.

607. Otso and Totso fight each other. The old man's nose that is between them glows red.—Making fire with flint.
Rudnyev, 2.

608. Ökhön and Chökhön get hold of each other mornings.—Buttoning clothes.
Mostaert, 185.

609. Husband and wife fight every morning and evening.—Pounding tea in a mortar with a pestle.
Bazarov, 103.

610. Bloodless warriors fight in a waterless place.—Chess.
Kotvich, 227.

611. On a space the size of a saddlecloth the Torguts and the Durbets are fighting.—Chess.
Kotvich, 226.

612. Soldiers without souls fight without pay.—Chess.
Mostaert, 109.

613. You are angry and I am angry, so let us not meet.—Eyes.
Kotvich, 200.

614, 615. OTHER ACTS

614. Osoi and Sosoi kneaded until dawn.—Lower jaw of a horse.

Poppe, *Ekhirit*, 16.

615. Four old women urinate into one hole.—Milking a cow.

Zhamtsaranov and Rudnyev, 52.

616–619. SEVERAL ACTS

616. Five Russians sow;/ Two Russians watch;/ One Russian chases the flies away.—Camel: its head, humps, and tail.

Bazarov, 194.

617. The straight ones are four;/ The protruding ones are three;/ The hanging-down one is single.—Camel: its legs, head and humps, and tail.

Poppe, *Aga Buriat*, 78.

618. Turned downwards, there are four novices;/ Turned upwards, there is one novice;/ From the side one novice comes and sportingly fills the novice (i.e., the novice who is turned up) and carries him off. If you look at it, it is the white juice of grass.—Milking a cow: the udder, the milk bucket, the woman who milks.

Mostaert, 59.

619. The five take it and give it to the ten,/ The ten take it and give it to the naked one,/ The naked one takes it and throws it in the hole.—Eating: the hand, teeth, and tongue.

Mostaert, 114.

620–636. ACTS CONTRASTED OR OTHERWISE CLOSELY ASSOCIATED

620a. Five peasants wanted to go out; a fat yellow girl opened the door for them.—Camel's excrement.

Kotvich, 125.

620b. When fifty blackies came close, the fat yellow one opened his door.—Sheep's excrement.

Kotvich, 255.

621. Many entering,/ One coming out.—Firewood, ashes.

Zhamtsaranov, 10.

622. Many entering,/ One coming out.—Horse's tail before and after entering river.

Zhamtsaranov, 10 var.

623. The white one says, "Let's go!"/ The black one says, "Stay!"—Snow, earth.

Zhamtsaranov, 7.

624. The sun rose and the dew dried up, they all went away, the strong ones remained.—Falling of leaves.

Sanzheev, p. 169.

625. Ten thousand have gone, the tardy ones have remained.—The leaves of a tree blown by the wind.

Poppe, *Aga Buriat*, 11.

626a. You rise, I sit down.—Gait of quadrupeds.

Bazarov, 191; Gomboyev, 55.

626b. You step forward and I will sit in your place.—Gait of cattle.

Kotvich, 126.

627. When it stands, it is short (or: low);/ When it sits, it is high.—Dog.

Zhamtsaranov and Rudnyev, 96.

628. Who walks upwards?/ Who walks downwards?/ Who walks without feet?—The blazing fire walks upwards through the air; the running water flows downwards through the tube; the snake walks on its belly.

Klukine, 51.

629. I reach (or: touch) the father; I do not reach (or: touch) the mother.—Pronouncing the word *aba* (father), the lips touch each other, but in pronouncing the word *iji* (mother), they do not touch.

Gomboyev, 60.

630. An old woman stooping;/ An old man bowing.—Churning kumiss (*airak*): a woman churning and a churning staff.

Mostaert, 189.

631. Those sneaking up toward the incautious ones,/ Those falling backwards and forwards;/ Those throwing water and snow;/ Those assembling the relatives.—Making felt.

Zhamtsaranov and Rudnyev, 39.

632. The Circassian keeps his door open; the Kirghis keeps his door closed.—Tail of a goat and tail of a sheep.

Kotvich, 114.

633. The Russian doctor exorcises weeping;/ The Mangut doctor exorcises bleating.—A he-goat pursues a she-goat.

Bazarov, 160.

634. Below at the emperor's house something makes a loud sound;/ Below at his wife's house something makes a cracking sound.—Gate.

Mostaret, 147.

635. One father, three sons;/ The one enjoys himself in summer;/ The second enjoys himself in winter;/ The third never enjoys himself.—Sleigh, cart, horse.

Zhamtsaranov, 13.

636. Four sons of a father: three are martyrs, one is at large.—Legs of a hobbled horse.

Bazarov, 179.

V. COMPARISONS TO PLANTS, NOS. 637–680

637–654. TREES

637. *Olkhon* trees grew below the summit.—Hair on the head.

Zhamtsaranov, 17.

638. Under the smaller there are really large black willows.—Mustache.

Mostaert, 100.

639. The willow of the north (or: back) is shaggy. While shaggy, it is curly; while curly, it is full of merits.—Juniper.

Mostaert, 106.

640. The tree in the north [has patterns] standing out in bold relief; the tree in the south (or: bosom) [has patterns] only slightly raised.—The back and the palm of the hand.

Rudnyev, 79.

641. Dragging a mountain by a cord, a lonely elm tree in front of a high mountain.—Halter and nose-peg of a camel.

Rudnyev, 40.

642. A hollow, curved tree.—A wooden house.

Kotvich, 48.

643–653. TREE AND BRANCHES OR LEAVES

643. A thin tree does not raise (or: put forth) its leaves.—Rope for tieing up lambs.

Rudnyev, 42.

644. At the source of the Nirbon River there is one big *raina*. Twelve branches grew on it, and on the twelve branches 360 leaves grow up.—Year, months, days.

Kotvich, 272.

645. On the top of the Altai and Khangai mountains there stands an agra scandalwood tree with twelve branches and 365 burs.—Year, months, days.

Barazarov, 1.

646a. The tree has twelve branches; each branch has thirty leaves.—Year, months, days.

Kotvich, 195.

646b. The tree has twelve branches; each branch has 360 leaves.—Year and months (*sic*).

Kotvich, 195 var.

646c. A sandalwood tree has twelve branches,/ On the twelve branches are 360 cones.—Year, months, and days.

Poppe, *Aga Buriat*, 41.

647. Eighty thousand branches on an imaginary tree, a nest on every branch, a nestling in every nest.—Grain not yet harvested.

Kotvich, 148.

648. The swaying tree has eighty thousand joints; on every joint there is a nest; in every nest an egg; in every egg a nestling.—Grain not yet harvested.

Kotvich, 259.

649. On the spreading pine there are eighty-seven limbs; on each limb there is a nest; in each nest an egg. —Stalk, ear, and grain.

Zhamtsaranov, 6.

650. A shaking tree with eighty branches. Each branch has a nest on it; each nest an egg in it.—Millet.

Mostaert, 113.

651. The *ninghnakhä* tree has eighty-one branches; each branch has a nest on it; each nest has an egg in it. —Agrophyllum, an edible grain.

Mostaert, 112.

652. The *nairaljin* tree with eight thousand branches, with a nest on each branch, and with eggs in each nest. —Cedar.

Gomboyev, 52.

653. A *nayar-nayar* tree,/ A tree with eighty branches,/ A *tör-tör* tree,/ A tree with ten thousand branches,/ Each twig has a bough,/ Each bough has an egg,/ Each egg has a white mouth.—Cedar.

Zhamtsaranov and Rudnyev, 38.

654. FUNCTION

654. The tree Tchjintchji is pacing around the fathomless abyss.—The chime of a bell.

Kotvich, 221.

655–663. PLANTS OTHER THAN TREES

655. He pulled the weeds out from the image (*burkhan*).—Pulling the main artery of a sheep.

Kotvich, 115.

656. In the back of the trunk is the thornbush.—A girl's braid; a rope.

Kotvich, 74.

657. On top is the Denji River, nearby is the Yuldui River, below is the Khuda-khuda River, grass (*bambakhai*) of the well water.—Distillation of brandy.

Rudnyev, 58.

658. The grass that flew away from here reached to Zu (Lhasa, Tibet).—The grass called "rolling stone."

Kotvich, 156.

659. At the beginning of the ford there is a single reed. —Larynx, tongue.

Kotvich, 237.

660. Reeds grew up along the shores of a round lake. —Eyelashes.

Kotvich, 11.

661. The reed of the northern (or: back) lake is beautiful; the feather grass of the southern (or: front) lake is beautiful.—Mane and tail of a horse.

Gomboyev, 18.

662. A firm reed at the connecting line of two felts.—Cord used to embroider the edges of felt.

Kotvich, 65.

663. Between two mountains weed-reed grew.—Fur growing between the animal's humps.

Kotvich, 103.

664-674. FLOWERS

664. On the summit of the northern mountain there grow six kinds of flowers. They are flowers that do not grow in summer; they grow in winter. What are they?—The Pleiades.

Mostaert, 78.

665. Without a summer/ Six flowers/ Grow in winter.—The Pleiades.

Zhamtsaranov and Rudnyev, 110.

666. On the summit of the sandalwood mountain six artemisia grow. They grow in winter; they do not grow in summer.—The Pleiades.

Mostaert, 78 var.

667. On top of the trunk is the flower *bumba;* in front of the trunk is the flower *onkho;* at the edge of the fire something is rocking; between the doors there is a poisonous snake.—Lamp in front of an ikon; an offering; a kettle stopper; a man.

Kotvich, 75.

668. A lotus flower in a small sea.—Lamp.

Whymant, p. 37, No. 2; Gomboyev, 37 (lake).

669-673. COLOR

669. Within the circular white embankment a white fig (*dumba*) flower is visible.—A lamp that has been lit.

Mostaert, 67.

670. The yellow poppy does not leave alone the poppy that eats.—A ladle.

Kotvich, 247.

671. At the foot of the Artemisia campestris (*săwak*) there is a yellow arrow.—Orobranche (*săwageen sŏjong*).

Mostaert, 132.

672. On this side of Astrakhan there is a green garlic plant with a hardly noticeable stem.—Lamp [before an ikon].

Kotvich, 19.

673. On the other side of Astrakhan there is a green garlic plant with a hardly noticeable stem—The tongue in the mouth.

Kotvich, 18.

674. FUNCTION

674. As they cannot stand the cold, they turn in the opposite direction and grow backwards.—Ears.

Mostaert, 76.

675-678. FRUITS

675. Six green ones appear in winter and disappear in summer.—The Pleiades.

Bazarov, 90.

676. One jujube reddens the whole felt tent.—Lamp.

Mostaert, 130.

677. One jujube cannot find room enough in a whole house (a house with three bays).—Light of a lamp.

Mostaert, 128.

678. A cone on a crossbeam.—Conch.

Poppe, *Ekhirit*, 3.

679, 680. TREE AND ANIMAL OR THING

679. A single tree is without branches,/ A careless sable is without bones.—Hair and louse.

Poppe, *Aga Buriat*, 47.

680. A high tree, half is its root;/ A large sea, half is its middle;/ An ox hide, one section is a half.—Handle of a pail; well, pail.

Zhamtsaranov and Rudnyev, 40.

VI. COMPARISONS TO A THING, NOS. 681-908

681-687. A LANDSCAPE

681. The Tunka steppe without vegetation.—Woman's face.

Klukine, 12.

682. At the beginning of the natural boundary of Bortin there are four objects.—Four woolen ropes tied to the end (roofpiece) of the smokehole.

Kotvich, 67.

683. Above is the Dendein River,/ Alongside is the Well River,/ There is a swimming in the well water.—Distillation of brandy.

Zhamtsaranov and Rudnyev, 112.

684. It is offended by the earth,/ It is hitched to a lonely tree,/ It is stretched from the sky,/ It is attached to that tree.—A rope attached [at the roofpiece] to the rafter.

Zhamtsaranov and Rudnyev, 106.

685. A stone wall,/ A bone trough,/ A boat of flesh.—Bellows, the head of the bellows, the nose of the bellows.

Zhamtsaranov and Rudnyev, 100.

686. A country with no characteristics,/ A building with no architecture.—Nose.

Zhamtsaranov and Rudnyev, 101.

687. The cupboard fits,/ The *khargana* (Papilionacea, a plant) makes the sound *khab*,/ A lonely tree makes the sound *shab*.—Saddle, bridle, whip.

Zhamtsaranov and Rudnyev, 104.

688–692. METEOROLOGICAL PHENOMENA

688. The earth and water are noisy; the solitary tree is shaking.—Preparation of kumiss.

Kotvich, 45.

689a. From a small sky/ Snow falls in big flakes.—Bolting of flour.

Mostaert, 138.

689b. At the higher end of the salt marsh (*tsaidam*)/ A drizzling rain slowly (or: softly) falls until sunset.—Bolting of flour.

Mostaert, 139.

690. On top of a cone-shaped mountain it snowed and rained.—Tassels (fringes) on a Mongol cap.

Rudnyev, 80.

691. On the pointed peak [of a mountain] bloody rain went down.—The red tassel on the hat worn by Buriats and other Mongols.

Bazarov, 144.

692. In a grassless cavity/ Rain falls without clouds.—Pouring water into a kettle.

Mostaert, 32.

693–697. FOG, VAPORS

693. Over/ The vapors rising to the sun/ The point of the spear!—The head of a reed.

Kotvich, 193.

694. He has kindled incense to a trusty (?) god; a fog has spread over the narrow river.—Smoking tobacco.

Bazarov, 138.

695. In the long river a mist has arisen;/ On the southern hill a fire has started.—Smoking tobacco.

Rudnyev, 25.

696. At the higher (or: western) end of the saltmarsh (*tsaidam*)/ It flutters in the wind until sunset.—Windhorse.

Mostaert, 190.

697. Its darkness has disappeared; the stump remains.—Falling of leaves.

Bazarov, 115.

698–703. POLE, NEEDLE, SPEAR

698a. An iron pole reaches heaven (or: the sky).—Smoke.

Mostaert, 179.

698b. An iron nail (or: spike) came down from heaven.—Smoke.

Zhamtsarano, 8.

698c. Gray-blue iron as high as heaven.—Smoke.

Mostaert, 180.

699a. A needle hangs down heaven.—Camel's tail.

Bazarov, 120.

699b. A thick needle suspended from the sky.—Camel's tail.

Kotvich, 215.

699c. From the sky an awl hangs down.—Camel's tail.

Poppe, *Aga Buriat*, 43; Poppe, *Barguzin*, 18.

700. Ten thousand spears are thrust into the shores of a round lake.—Smokehole (with rafters) and circular roofpiece of yurt.

Kotvich, 57.

701. Thirty poles in a ditch.—Teeth.

Whymant, p. 38, No. 3.

702. Inside the yurt is a golden stake.—Fire.

Kotvich, 100.

703. In front of the customary—a protruding pale (stave).—Candle.

Poppe, *Barguzin*, 4.

704–707. WELL, HOLLOW, LAIR

704. There is a well behind the house.—Hollow on the back of the neck.

Kotvich, 7; Whymant, p. 38, No. 1 (nape of the neck).

705a. Behind the mountain is the hare's lair.—Hollow in the nape of the neck.

Bazarov, 198; Gomboyev, 12; Rudnyev, 6.

705b. On the shadowy side of the mountain the lair of a hare.—Hollow on the nape of the neck.

Klukine, 10; Zhamtsaranov and Rudnyev, 24 (on that side of the mountain).

706. On the other side of five hills is a dog's den.—Palm of the hand; hole in the back of the thumb.

Kotvich, 30.

707a. Seven holes on a hill.—Mouth, two eyes, nose, and ears.

Kotvich, 8; Klukine, 3 (head); Gomboyev, 7 (head).

707b. There are seven holes around a hillock.—Human head.

Mostaert, 14; Poppe, *Barguzin*, 12.

708–712. MOUNTAIN, HILL

708. A strong spike on a solid hillock.—Name.

Bazarov, 146.

709a. A mountain is led by a thread.—Reins of a camel.

Kotvich, 101.

709b. A thread hangs down the mountain.—Reins of a camel.

Kotvich, 102.

710. A rare jewel on a solitary mountain.—Acorn.
Bazarov, 164.

711. A rare jewel on a solitary mountain.—Spire (*ganjir*) on a Buddhist temple.
Bazarov, 155.

712. The back one is the hill of sleeping,/ The middle one is the hill of fire,/ The front one is the hill of the pass.—House.
Poppe, *Aga Buriat*, 46.

713–718. ROAD, MOUNTAIN PASS

713. Mountainous roads, impassable roads, many, many roads, but you cannot find the [right] road.—Stomach of a sheep.
Kotvich, 117.

714. A mountain of flesh with a pass of wood,/ An iron ladder and a woolen rope.—Horse, saddle, stirrups, tether (made of hair or wool).
Mostaert, 4.

715. A crooked (bent) mountain pass and eight sinews.—Saddle and accessories (belly band, crupper, etc.).
Bazarov, 130; Poppe, *Aga Buriat*, 27.

716. The pass of celebration (carousing),/ The pass of foliation (?),/ The pass of crackling,/ The pass of desolation.—Autumn, summer, winter, spring.
Rudnyev, 62.

717a. Three mountain passes of the genius protector (*yidam*);/ Three cairns (*obō*) of abundance;/ Three icy cavities;/ Three fields of flowers.—The four seasons: spring, autumn, winter, and summer.
Mostaert, 171.

717b. Three mountain passes of the stage (*bardo*) intermediate between death and reincarnation;/ Three flowers as green as leaves;/ Three rich mountain chains;/ Three cold valleys.—Spring, summer, autumn, winter.
Mostaert, 171 var.

718. It is possible to go over many passes,/ It is not possible to go over the diamond pass.—A rosary and the end (head) of the rosary.
Zhamtsaranov and Rudnyev, 113.

719–727. STONE, ROCK, CHIP OF WOOD, PEG

719. The stone *shin* with nine holes.—Eyes, nostrils, ears, mouth.
Rudnyev, 72.

720. A beautiful stone with seven holes.—Head: eyes, nostrils, ears and mouth.
Bazarov, 185.

721. A stone from Tenggelge, water from Tenggebe, a long beautiful plume.—Flask for holy water.
Rudnyev, 15.

722. A little ball, a little stone,/ Swifter than a horse.—Bullet.
Zhamtsaranov, 22; Poppe, *Ekhirit*, 12 (A round rock is quicker than a horse).

723. The ball is quicker than a horse.—Shooting a rifle.
Poppe, *Aga Buriat*, 33.

724. A thin rock cannot be opened.—Fingernail.
Mostaert, 170.

725. The gravel rock is a wartlike protuberance,/ The cairn rock (*obō*) is a boiling spring.—Distilling alcohol.
Poppe, *Aga Buriat*, 34.

726. A chip cut here will reach the khan.—Letter.
Poppe, *Barguzin*, 15.

727. One takes (keeps) the hole,/ But throws away the peg.—Emptying the stomach.
Zhamtsaranov and Rudnyev, 82.

728–748. MEMBERS OF AN ANIMAL

The following comparisons of an object to some member of an animal are arranged according to the member in an order proceeding downwards from the head. For a comparison to a sheepskin used as a bed or blanket see No. 874 below. In comparisons of the various parts of an object to the members of several animals the point lies in the heterogeneous nature of the combination; for such riddles see Nos. 749–767.

728. Over there he buried a camel's head. Later I shall take it and eat it.—The fire covered for the night.
Bazarov, 122.

729. A rapid tongue licks the ground.—Boot.
Kotvich, 38.

730. A long red nose/ Has come from the west.—Incense stick, perfumed candle.
Zhamtsaranov and Rudnyev, 77.

731. The chest is full with the hide of a curly sheep.—Teeth.
Zhamtsaranov and Rudnyev, 50.

732. It is impossible to pierce the hide of the black sheep.—Shadow.
Kotvich, 164.

733. An eagle's hide is worthless.—Openings in the grating of a yurt.
Kotvich, 53.

734. The eagle's hide is completely torn.—Iron sieve.
Kotvich, 53 var.

735. The spread-out tail of a calf.—Stalk of a lily.
Rudnyev, 81.

736–748. BONES

736. He separated the vertebra, but was unable to break the marrow.—Manipulating the rosary.

Bazarov, 139.

737. He is unable to finish (i.e., grind off) the anklebone of a three-year old cow in three years.—Whetstone.

Bazarov, 83.

738. It is impossible to guess whether a golden anklebone lies with its convex side or its concave side turned upwards.—You cannot guess whether the baby in the womb is male or female.

Bazarov, 110.

739. In the cup there are golden ankle bones.—Eyes.

Bazarov, 3.

740. A bag full of red ankle bones.—Coals.

Bazarov, 171; Rudnyev, 37 (in a bag there are red anklebones); Poppe, *Aga Buriat,* 67 (red-hot charcoal).

741. A bag full of red ankle bones.—Fire glowing on the hearth.

Mostaert, 35.

742. A bag full of dice.—Fire.

Zhamtsaranov and Rudnyev, 71.

743. I have a basket full of ankle bones,/ And two handsome brothers.—Stars, moon, and sun.

Zhamtsaranov, 30.

744. Among the knuckle bones filling the hem [of a skirt] there are two for throwing.—Sun and moon.

Poppe, *Barguzin,* 13.

745. In a courtyard there are two red ankle bones.—Kidneys.

Bazarov, 85.

746. Bones drifted down the Yangba River.—Dog swallows bones.

Rudnyev, 24.

747. Bones of a Tungus on a mountain.—The idol (*onggon*) on the mountain.

Zhamtsaranov, 11.

748. On the top of a mountain range there is the bone of a whale.—Person's queue.

Poppe, *Aga Buriat,* 49.

749–767. MEMBERS OF SEVERAL DIFFERENT ANIMALS

749. The skin of a snake, the ears of a scared camel.—Fox.

Kotvich, 109.

750. Two feet, an empty skin.—Traveling tent.

Rudnyev, 57.

751. He has a supple, supple body like the ring with which one cleans a cannon. He has thirty-three vertebrae. He is bay-, bay-colored. He has the eyes of a screech owl.—Cat.

Mostaert, 169.

752. The shape of a mouse,/ Cloven hoofs like a cow,/ The breast of a tiger,/ The lips of a hare,/ The neck of a dragon,/ The eyes of a snake,/ The mane of a horse,/ The wool of sheep,/ The hump of an ape,/ The comb of a rooster,/ The thighs of a dog,/ The tail of a pig.—Camel.

Mostaert, 8.

753. The head of the ox is buried,/ The dog's cap is hung up.—Sarana lily and its flower.

Bazarov, 32.

754. The silken tail of a bustard;/ The wise tail of a peacock.—Writing brush.

Mostaert, 90.

755. It has the body of a python,/ It has the voice of a lion,/ It has two feet,/ It has the globular excrements of a sheep.—Gun on a two-legged support.

Mostaert, 102.

756. It has the voice of a dragon,/ It has the ear of a mule,/ It has excrements like those of a sheep,/ It has some dung taken from a paddock [for sheep].—A gun: the explosion, the cock, the powder charge.

Mostaert, 140.

757. It has the body of a frog and the bill of a magpie.—Scissors.

Mostaert, 107.

758. It has the four hoofs of a cow,/ It looks like a corpse,/ It has the ears of a male gazelle./ It has the two eyes of a wolf that roars "Oh!"/ He who guesses this/ Will have a tiger's tail for a head ornament/ And a rank button striped like a lotus./ He who does not guess this/ Will have a kite's tail for a head ornament/ And the excrement of an ass for a rank button.—Pig.

Mostaert, 168.

759. Sorrel-colored, not a horse; antelope-horned, not an ox; six-footed, without hoofs.—Cockroach.

Klukine, 34.

760. It is particolored, but is not a tiger; it is horned, but is not a bull; it can recite prayers, but is not a lama; it is in a bottle, but is not brandy.—Bee.

Mostaert, 178.

761. Drum-bellied, crow-billed.—Tea kettle.

Klukine, 19.

762. It has a drumlike abdomen/ And a crow's beak.—Fan.

Zhamtsaranov and Rudnyev, 93.

763. With a tail in the back like a lance; with ten iron spears.—Canopy.

Kotvich, 246.

764. With a *muriu* (twisted or slanting) body; with hoofs like Manjushrī; with thunderbolts on the crown of his head; he is an object of admiration for many tens of thousands.—Donkey.

Mostaert, 101.

765. From behind it looks like a camel with a collar (*khomut*); from the front it looks like a domesticated he-goat.—Winged grasshopper (*tyzhin golo*).

Bazarov, 67.

766. Horse-headed, iron-footed, man-tailed.—Plow.

Klukine, 32.

767. It has a horse cart (a light cart), a wooden body, iron feet, and human buttocks.—Man plowing.

Bazarov, 137.

768, 769. Vacant.

770-776. HOUSE, TENT

770. Two felt tents, one crutch.—Cow licking her nostrils.

Bazarov, 66.

771. Two houses (or: rooms) with one pillar.—Nose.

Mostaert, 28.

772. A red house with felt of white thread.—Heart.

Rudnyev, 63.

773. A house that has neither a door nor an opening in the roof contains many thousand objects.—Watermelon.

Kotvich, 266.

774. Thirty white tents in a ditch.—Teeth.

Kotvich, 17.

775. One large settlement has four gates; on each gate there are thirty nails.—Year, four seasons, days of the month.

Bazarov, 197.

776. A large felt tent; in the large felt tent there is a small felt tent; in the small felt tent there is a lotus flower.—Lamp.

Bazarov, 106.

777-782. PARTS OF A HOUSE OR THINGS ASSOCIATED WITH IT

777. Four pillars of equal length given by heaven;/ Three strong locks given by us.—Four legs of a horse; hobble with three arms.

Mostaert, 58.

778. Four pillars *dzing;* three locks *dzi dzu.*—Legs of horse; hobble.

Mostaert, 58 var.

779. In the yurt without a grille the lower part of the felt (*koshma*) is white.—Heart.

Kotvich, 22.

780. On the top of the smokehole is a knobby nail.—Plug of a kettle.

Rudnyev, 38.

781. The Barguzin door faces northwest.—A cupboard (*ergenek*):

Bazarov, 24.

782. Dirt under the bed.—Dirt under the fingernails.

Kotvich, 27.

783. SHIP

783. A white ship stopped in a puddle.—Teeth, tongue.

Kotvich, 201, 201 var. (shallow muddy water).

784-792. CART, SADDLE

784-787. FORM

784. In place of the buggy of the rich [man], the watchman's *solovko* is tied up.—Spigot of the kettle in which alcohol is distilled.

Kotvich, 210.

785. The pretty gold is in a covered cart.—Human mind.

Kotvich, 2.

786. The trimmings are painted; the saddlecloth is tied around.—Painting the kettle before distilling alcohol.

Kotvich, 46.

787. A golden saddle on a knotty tree.—Ring.

Kotvich, 42.

788-792. FUNCTION

788. A lama makes the sound *khur khur,*/ A one-wheeled cart makes the sound *jee joo.*—Grinding buckwheat.

Mostaert, 136.

789. The two-wheeled cart thunders, the Tungus boots gallop.—Shamanizing.

Bazarov, 196.

790. An ox cart comes rolling to the deity.—Manipulating the beads of a rosary.

Bazarov, 26.

791. From behind the mountain a golden chariot rolls.—Sun.

Bazarov, 7.

792. An iron carriage has filled the whole world.—Automobile.

Poppe, *Aga Buriat*, 50.

793–823. FOOD OR DRINK

793. There is flesh (or: meat) beneath a hollow.—Withers of a horse.
Bazarov, 50.

794. There is half a pretzel on the upper jamb of the door.—The felt that covers the opening in the roof of the yurt.
Kotvich, 64.

795a. Half a pancake on top of the yurt.—Moon.
Kotvich, 176.

795b. Half a loaf of bread on top of the yurt.—Moon.
Kotvich, 177.

796. During the day, a crust of bread; during the night, a whole loaf.—Felt used to cover the opening in the top of the yurt.
Kotvich, 245.

797. Cheese dropped from the sky has four crooked legs.—Frog.
Kotvich, 133.

798–814. FOOD OR DRINK IN A CONTAINER

798. There is water in a bottomless teapot.—Mucus.
Rudnyev, 44.

799. In a pail/ There is real cottage cheese.—Mucus.
Zhamtsaranov and Rudnyev, 53.

800. Chopped meat in a trough.—Coals.
Zhamtsaranov, 21.

801a. A cup of motley meat.—Eye.
Klukine, 6.

801b. Varicolored meat in a bowl.—Eye.
Whymant, p. 38, No. 2; Kotvich, 9.

801c. Motley meat fills the bowl.—Eye.
Zhamtsaranov and Rudnyev, 69.

802. A bowl of broth on the point of an awl.—Dew.
Kotvich, 167.

803. The vessel is gilded; the tea is shaped like a lamp before an icon.—Egg.
Kotvich, 137.

804–814. *Food in a Container and an Attendant Act*

804. There is a little copper colored pot; it is food that the prince carries with him; he holds the kettle aslant; one sucks and enjoys it.—Smoking tobacco.
Mostaert, 177.

805. A little box. Crack! Butter (or: fat) flowed out.—Cracking a nut with the teeth.
Bazarov, 123.

806. In a bulging vessel it is chopped;/ With a *khuloo* it is mixed;/ He takes it and throws it into a well.—Eating.
Mostaert, 116.

807. The kettle is small; the mush tastes very good.—Nut.
Kotvich, 261.

808a. I was unable to take the opening of the golden cup in my mouth.—Palm of the hand.
Zhamtsaranov, 1.

808b. One cannot bite the opening of the golden cup.—One cannot bite the palm of the hand.
Poppe, *Ekhirit*, 10.

809. He took the gold; the box he threw away.—Nut.
Gomboyev, 53.

810. He ate the gold and threw away the box.—He ate the brain and threw away the skull.
Kotvich, 122.

811a. The red wineskin cannot be exhausted however much is dipped out of it.—You cannot exhaust the mind that is located in the chest.
Kotvich, 1.

811b. You cannot exhaust the red wineskin by dipping.—Mind.
Kotvich, 233.

812. A black kettle boils alongside the road.—Anthill.
Kotvich, 140.

813. On the steppe yellow tea is boiling.—Ants coming out of a hole.
Mostaert, 17.

814. Having poured out his tea on the steppe,/ He goes away, taking his container with him.—Urination.
Mostaert, 53.

815, 816. COLOR OF FOOD

815. Underground there is yellow butter.—Marmot.
Whymant, p. 38, No. 3; Zhamtsaranov and Rudnyev, 30; Gomboyev, 25 (yellow fat).

816. Dried cheese from above; something ample from below; something bluish-roan that adds color; white that adds flavor; something fat [and] yellow that cares for the pleasure.—Preparing tea: tea, water, milk, malt, and butter.
Kotvich, 209.

817–823. FOOD AND AN ATTENDANT CIRCUMSTANCE

817. Among sour things one wooden thing gurgles.—Churnstaff.
Bazarov, 93.

818a. There is stinking meat in the cupboard.—Inner sole of a boot.
Kotvich, 36.

818b. There is something stinking in the lower part of the yurt.—Inner sole of a boot.
Kotvich, 37.

819. The yurt is filled with broken tea-bricks.—Openings in the grating of the yurt.
Kotvich, 54.

820a. Everybody ate the quail's liver and could not finish it.—Caressing (nursing) a child.
Kotvich, 234.

820b. The entire family cannot destroy one piece of fat the size of a cake of soap.—Mother's breast.
Kotvich, 4.

821. I fried fat on a mountain, but nothing fell into my mouth or hands.—Dream.
Kotvich, 188.

822. Balls of fat,/ A straw [container with a] narrow base and a wide opening.—Bird's nest.
Mostaert, 141.

823. A fat lump, a hay bunch.—The ruminating stomach of a cow.
Poppe, *Aga Buriat*, 6.

824–838. CONTAINERS

For comparisons to food in a container see Nos. 798–814.

824. On the hill slope a dipper with a broken edge.—Hare's lair.
Kotvich, 129.

825. A trunk on top of a trunk.—Joints of a reed.
Kotvich, 151.

826. A wooden kettle on a stand of flesh.—Drinking cup.
Bazarov, 184.

827. At the side a slanting trough.—Ear.
Rudnyev, 17.

828a. Many-colored things in cups.—Eyes.
Gomboyev, 8.

828b. In a cup there is something multicolored (*alak bulak*).—Eye.
Mostaert, 143.

829. There is no support from the bottom and no hanger from above.—Cloud.
Kotvich, 269.

830. A black bottle with a red cork.—Daw (gnat?).
Zhamtsaranov and Rudnyev, 14.

831–838. CUP, BOWL, OR SAUCER OUTDOORS

Since a cup, bowl, or saucer is properly found in a house, its appearance outdoors constitutes an enigmatic situation.

831. There is a low bucket on the wall.—Moon.
Bazarov, 114.

832. A flat pail (*kyng*) in the steppe.—Moon.
Rudnyev, 70.

833. A sandalwood eating bowl on the road;/ A silver eating bowl on the ice.—Droppings (*argal*) of animals; sun.
Rudnyev, 52.

834. On the ice there is a silver cup.—Sun.
Zhamtsaranov and Rudnyev, 89.

835. On the ice a silver bowl.—Moon in the sky.
Gomboyev, 1; Mostaert, 24 (goblet).

836. A silver cup on the ice.—Reflection of the moon.
Klukine, 18.

837. A silver cup on the ice.—Trefoil on the water.
Kotvich, 160.

838a. On the side there is a black saucer.—Ear.
Zhamtsaranov and Rudnyev, 4.

838b. On the side there is one half of a saucer.—Ear.
Zhamtsaranov and Rudnyev, 73.

839–898. ARTICLES OF COMMERCE

839. From the Tunka country/ Many ten thousands of carloads of goods have come./ The hesitant ones remained,/ Tens of thousands have gone.—Clouds.
Poppe, *Aga Buriat*, 70.

840. When it goes to Peking, it is engraved work./ When it comes to the pasture ground, it is tawny with white spots.—Silver ornaments.
Mostaert, 175.

841. The full copper ladle is good,/ The thin shank is good.—Lamp.
Bazarov, 89.

842. The earth makes a lock; the key is wool.—Mouse entering a hole.
Mostaert, 49.

843. A shaggy drum and a smooth drum.—Earth and sky.
Bazarov, 134.

844. On the ice there is a silver clasp.—Moon.
Poppe, *Aga Buriat*, 3; Zhamtsaranov and Rudnyev, 43 (silver ornament).

845. A ring is on the bow of the boat that was thrown into the ocean;/ The speech of the muzhik, who followed the Dalai Lama, is wise.—Pen.
Kotvich, 275.

846. A golden ring was put on the tree with many branches.—Ring.
Kotvich, 241.

847. A thimble on a birchtree.—Hare.
Zhamtsaranov, 25.

848. Iron tongs filled the continent.—Telegram.
Poppe, *Aga Buriat*, 42.

849. Under the earth there is a rosary.—Snake.
Zhamtsaranov and Rudnyev, 45.

850. On the road there is a sandalwood ornament.—Excrements of a cow.
Zhamtsaranov and Rudnyev, 42.

851. There is a hammer inside the yurt and a hammer outside.—Thong with which the twigs of the grating in the yurt are tied.
Kotvich, 55; Zhamtsaranov and Rudnyev, 28 (beetle for beating clothes).

852–862. CLOTH

852. Coarse cotton cloth (Chinese *ta-pu*) has come from Peking. On measuring it with outstretched arms, it measured twelve fathoms. On measuring it by folding it into equal squares, there are 360.—Months and days of the year.
Rudnyev, 21.

853. The red silk hangs; the blue silk flutters.—Carrying off the bride.
Kotvich, 6.

854. In the field a piece of silk in five colors is becoming pale,/ Neither you nor I can grasp it.—Rainbow.
Mostaert, 95.

855. A whole piece of silk that cannot be rolled up;/ Ten thousand pearls that cannot be strung.—Sky.
Mostaert, 125.

856. A whole piece of blue silk that cannot be rolled up.—Sky.
Mostaert, 124.

857. Silk that is not tattered in a closed trunk.—Omentum.
Kotvich, 118.

858. Silk still unpeeled in a closed trunk.—Core of a reed.
Kotvich, 154.

859. On that side of the mountain/ There is a red flag (*dartsok*).—Ribbons on a hat.
Zhamtsaranov and Rudnyev, 25.

860. *Cloth without a Seam*

860a. It was cut without measure, sewed without seams.—Spotted cattle.
Kotvich, 254.

860b. Connection without a seam.—Brindled cow.
Kotvich, 106.

860c. Though seamless, it is striped.—Motley cattle.
Gomboyev, 19.

860d. Something put together of shreds with no seam.—Motley cattle.
Poppe, *Aga Buriat*, 23.

861, 862. *Silk without a Border*

861a. Beautiful silk without a border,/ Small corals without holes.—Sky, stars.
Rudnyev, 23.

861b. Real silk without a border; small pearls without holes.—Sky and stars.
Klukine, 33.

861c. A beautiful silk stuff without borders; small corals without holes.—Sky and stars.
Bazarov, 182.

861d. The piece of silk has no border;/ The little pearls have no holes.—Sky.
Zhamtsaranov and Rudnyev, 103.

862. A small pearl without a hole;/ A piece of silken cloth without a border.—Star, sky.
Zhamtsaranov and Rudnyev, 19.

863–873. GARMENTS

863. The ball of Shan Datoi with seventy suits of clothes.—Onion.
Kotvich, 157.

864. At the end of a sleeve: black sable.—Vessel used for distilling milk brandy.
Gomboyev, 51.

865. Seventy thousand buttons on the white coat (*keshmet*) made of flags (*dartsok*).—Stars.
Kotvich, 178.

866. A marmot [-skin] shirt is not tattered; the Tatar's trade is without law.—Burrows of mice.
Bazarov, 121.

867. Before marriage the girl's trousers were torn.—Pillow.
Bazarov, 175.

868a. In the skirt full of *alchiks* there are also two sky-blue hoop-nets.—Sun, moon, stars.
Kotvich, 180.

868b. Among the *alchiks* that fill the skirt are two hoop-nets filled with lead.—Sun, moon, and stars.
Kotvich, 179.

868c. Two thousand *alchiks* have two sky-blue hoop-nets.—Stars.
Kotvich, 181.

869. I threw away a felt hat on the other side of the Volga; it is impossible to get there and take it.—Eagle's nest.

Kotvich 136.

870. The purse of the Dalai Lama/ With seventy double compartments.—Third stomach of ruminants.

Rudnyev, 75.

871a. On the steppe a small tobacco pouch of which half is lacking.—Camel's track.

Mostaert, 18.

871b. In the steppe there is a small tobacco pouch of which the upper part is lacking.—Camel's track.

Mostaert, 18, var. 1.

871c. On the steppe a small tobacco pouch.—Camel's track.

Mostaert, 18, var. 2.

872a. Worn-out boots at the side of a mountain.—Ears.

Rudnyev, 68; Bazarov, 42.

872b. By a rock there is a torn boot.—Ear.

Poppe, *Aga Buriat*, 4; Poppe, *Ekhirit*, 13 (On a rock).

873. At the sides there are slanting summer boots.—Ears.

Mostaert, 33.

874–878. RUG, BLANKET, CARPET

874. You cannot step over father's sheepskin; you cannot roll up mother's sheepskin.—Earth and sky.

Kotvich, 171.

875. A rug with wool and a rug without wool.—Earth and sky.

Kotvich, 172.

876. In the middle of the village a square carpet.—Well.

Poppe, *Dagurskoe*, 3.

877. The father's blanket will never end when folded again and again.—Sky.

Zhamtsaranov and Rudnyev, 18.

878. The house is full/ With the monk's (*gelyng*) carpet.—Wall.

Zhamtsaranov and Rudnyev, 61.

879–888. ROPE, RIBBON, HOBBLE

879. On the honey ridge somebody has tied a solid (or: hard) knot.—Bolt [of a door].

Bazarov, 40.

880. Braided hobbles in a deep well.—Thin intestine of a horse.

Kotvich, 111.

881. In a house there is a bundle of ropes.—Intestines.

Zhamtsaranov and Rudnyev, 79.

882. A long ribbon as white as silk reaches as far as Peking.—Road.

Mostaert, 80.

883. A lasso without an end.—Road.

Bazarov, 16.

884. The multicolored rope sliced by the mother cannot be tied together.—Road.

Gomboyev, 57.

885. A long lasso that I was unable to roll up.—Road.

Zhamtsaranov, 19.

886. The lasso thrown by the king will not be put together before death.—Road.

Poppe, *Barguzin*, 17.

887a. Behind the house/ Something dangles.—Queue.

Mostaert, 19.

887b. Something is dangling behind the felt tent.—Queue.

Rudnyev, 11.

888. One cannot step over a rope.—Snake.

Poppe, *Aga Buriat*, 44.

889–891. WEAPONS

889. A red bow, white arrows.—Udder.

Gomboyev, 20.

890. A taut (?) bow with a bony bowstring.—Shinbone.

Rudnyev, 64.

891a. A bow of *yag* wood and a bowstring of bone.—Ulna and radius in cattle.

Mostaert, 163.

891b. A short bow, a string of bone.—Ulna in cattle.

Gomboyev, 21.

892–898. BOOKS, LETTER, WRITING

892. At the top of a very high tree Russian characters are written.—Features of the head.

Kotvich, 31.

893a. A delusive letter under the pillow.—Dream.

Bazarov, 149.

893b. On the pillow there is an unrealizable letter.—Dream.

Poppe, *Aga Buriat*, 88; Poppe, *Ekhirit*, 8.

894a. A riddle that a lucky man can guess,/ A riddle that an unlucky man cannot guess.—Writing.

Bazarov, 68.

894b. An old riddle. The matchmaker cannot guess it. Only the happy man can guess it.—Writing.

Bazarov, 192.

895. A riddle of each past year,/ A riddle which a person cannot solve at all,/ A riddle of every year,/ A riddle which a person cannot solve evenly.—Writing.

Poppe, *Aga Buriat*, 12.

896. The beginning of the story (or: riddle) is in Turkish; the meaning is exponded compactly; it is dear to the author; it cannot be expounded in the present world.—The Sacred Book.

Kotvich, 197.

897. In the box there are *akhä* characters.—Brain.

Mostaert, 47.

898. In the box there are many-colored characters.—Brain.

Mostaert, 47 var.

899–903. COINS, SILVER, GOLD

899. A bronze coin sitting on the fence.—A small bird sitting on a wall.

Mostaert, 97.

900a. Half a kopeck on a cushion,/ A patch of sheepskins.—Moon.

Whymant, p. 38, No. 4.

900b. A coin on the pillow,/ A patch on the sheepskin coat.—Moon.

Kotvich, 33.

901. I have a trunk full of silver money;/ In it I have two golden coins.—Stars, sun, moon.

Poppe, *Ekhirit*, 11.

902. They loaded silver on *myixegsen*.—Answer lacking.

Poppe, *Aga Buriat*, 94.

903. In the corner there is melted (?) gold wax in the ears.—Fox.

Kotvich, 21.

904–907. AN UNIDENTIFIED OBJECT

904. A flat [thing] licked the earth.—Sole of a boot.

Poppe, *Aga Buriat*, 7.

905. A flat [thing] licked the earth.—Shovel.

Poppe, *Barguzin*, 7.

906. A long thing entered a - - - -.—Key.

Poppe, *Ekhirit*, 15.

907. It is a very strange thing,/ It is a strange and unlucky thing,/ It is a skilful and tricky thing,/ It is a thing with water and a key.—Distilling alcohol.

Zhamtsaranov and Rudnyev, 51.

908. VARIOUS OBJECTS

908. Forklike wood, strange wood,/ A sable cap, God's cross.—Felt yurt.

Poppe, *Aga Buriat*, 86.

VII. ENUMERATIONS OF COMPARISONS, NOS. 909–919

The following riddles consist of comparisons to various objects and contain the word "like" or its equivalent. They contain several such comparisons and confuse the hearer by implying that one thing is intended.

909. Bigger than a camel, smaller than a goat, whiter than snow, and blacker than coal.—Magpie.

Sanzheev, p. 168; Poppe, *Aga Buriat*, 75 (male goat . . . soot).

910. Extremely long, lower than the grass.—Road.

Mostaert, 84.

911a. With holes like a comb, round like the moon.—Wheel.

Bazarov, 80.

911b. It is dented like a comb,/ It is round like the moon.—Wheel of a carriage.

Poppe, *Aga Buriat*, 35; Poppe, *Barguzin*, 10.

912a. Feathery like a comb, round as the moon.—Smokehole in a yurt and its frame.

Klukine, 22.

912b. Round like the moon,/ Dented like a comb.—Smokehole of the yurt.

Zhamtsaranov and Rudnyev, 11.

913–916. LIKE SOMETHING FROM A DISTANT PLACE

913a. As if it had descended from heaven, as if made by a master, as if trimmed by a sharp knife.—Egg.

Bazarov, 148.

913b. Like something fallen from heaven, like something descended upon a grassy hill, like something trimmed with a sharp knife, like something washed with rain water.—Egg.

Gomboyev, 26.

913c. As if it had come down from above,/ As if it had been put on a stub,/ As if it had been washed in rain water,/ As if it had been carved with a sharp knife.—Egg.

Poppe, *Aga Buriat*, 69.

914. Like hail that has fallen down from above, like ice that has been trimmed by a knife.—Egg.

Mostaert, 165.

915. Like a hail stone fallen from above, like a flower in front [of you], like [something] washed with quicksilver (lit.: silver water), like [something] trimmed with a sharp knife.—Mandarin's button of rank.

Mostaert, 166.

916. Like a cake (*baling*) arrived from the east, the fat in the back of a mare that has not yet foaled, like the tail of an orphan lamb, like the hoofs of a three-year old cow, like the two horns of a he-goat.—Yellow cap worn by a lama.

Rudnyev, 20.

917. COMPARISON TO AN ANIMAL AND A PERSON

917a. If one is looking at it as a lama, it has a camel's halter. If one is looking at it as a camel, it has the cloak of a lama.—Stomach of a sheep.

Bazarov, 27.

917b. On looking at the peg that passes through and through, it resembles a camel; on looking at its priest's cloak, it resembles a lama. Whence did the brave fellow come?—Stomach of a sheep.

Mostaert, 20.

918. COMPARISON TO COLOR

918. Red as the flame of a camel, with six black things.—Fox with black hair on its ears and somewhat higher on its four paws.

Bazarov, 193.

919. COMPARISON TO OTHER QUALITIES

919. Sweeter than honey, but worthless on the open market.—Dream.

Kotvich, 268.

VIII. ENUMERATIONS IN TERMS OF NUMBER, FORM, OR COLOR, NOS. 920–950

920–933. FORM

920. Four wide; two widest.—Four felts (*turga*) covering the upper part of the gratings and the lower part of the roof and two felts (*deber*) covering the roof.

Kotvich, 63.

921. Curly in winter and summer.—Pine.

Bazarov, 180.

922. Behind the house cross on cross.—Braid.

Poppe, *Dagurskoe*, 2.

923. An iron hook, a crooked neck,/ A belly like a tureen, a Russian cap.—Samovar.

Zhamtsaranov, 24.

924. Something round, something square,/ Four Chinese, two Mongols.—Chinese cash as cast under the Manchu dynasty.

Mostaert, 120.

925. Three hoops, three hooks, in the middle is a god.—Tripod for a kettle and the fire.

Klukine, 5.

926. Three wheels,/ Four hooks,/ A brass statue of Buddha.—Tripod.

Zhamtsaranov and Rudnyev, 56.

927. Three hoops, twelve hooks.—Tripod for a kettle on a fire.

Rudnyev, 55.

928. It is pretty, round, and made of tallow; it is pretty, exact (or: accurate), and made of grass.—Lily.

Bazarov, 19.

929. Round, round, young hares./ How do you solve that?/ Lanterns without a rope./ How do you solve that?/ A cloak without seams./ How do you solve that?/ Ten thousand chessmen./ How do you solve that?—Cow: croup, feet, skin, hair, eyes, horns.

Mostaert, 150.

930. A thousand, thousand meshes (*minggaldak*);/ A thousand, ten thousand knots (*janggildak*); Sticks (*xonggildak*) of yellow wood;/ Twenty thousand knots.—Net for catching hares.

Mostaert, 167.

931. Little silver tweezers and a sable flatiron.—Horse browsing.

Bazarov, 132.

932. A single [piece of] copper,/ A double [piece of] copper,/ A horn of a three-year old bull,/ A tapering [piece of] copper.—Temple trumpet.

Mostaert, 61.

933. A felt lash, a straight face, with two stakes at the cliff.—Cow.

Kotvich, 104.

934, 935. COLOR

934. On top it is very white; in the middle it is as white as a conch shell; below it is wrinkled and grayish.—Boiling down cream.

Mostaert, 9.

935. The top is yellow, the center is white like a shell, the bottom is gray.—Cream, milk, sediment [obtained when the milk is boiled].

Kotvich, 242.

936–950. DETAILS CHANGE ACCORDING TO CIRCUMSTANCES

936. NUMBER

936. Four in the morning, two at midday, three in the evening.—Man.

Gomboyev, 5; Whymant, p. 37, No. 1.

937–945. FORM

937. Starting on its road: a patriarch (or: It takes a great deal of room)./ Leaving its road, it has the appearance of a rampart.—Chariot.

Mostaert, 110.

938. Square at night; triangular in the daytime.—Flap covering the smokehole of the yurt.

Rudnyev, 53.

939. In the daytime it is triangular;/ At night it is square.—Smoke opening.

Zhamtsaranov and Rudnyev, 37.

940. What has come from heaven forms a perfect square;/ What we have added makes it a complete triangle.—Hobbling horses: the four legs of the horse and the triangular hobble.

Mostaert, 57.

941. In the daytime northwards (or: backwards); at night southwards (or: forwards).—Flap covering the smokehole of the yurt.

Gomboyev, 32.

942. In the evening it went down; in the morning it went up.—Flap covering the smokehole of the yurt.

Poppe, *Aga Buriat*, 25.

943. In the daytime at home; at night outside.—Arm.

Gomboyev, 14.

944a. Gathered (or: Rolled up) in the daytime; spread out at night.—Mattress.

Klukine, 22b.

944b. In the daytime it is folded; and night it is spread out.—Bed-carpet.

Zhamtsaranov and Rudnyev, 44.

945. In the steppe a hairless brindled one;/ With us a bowlegged ambler.—Frog.

Gomboyev, 29.

946. TEMPERATURE

946. When looked at, it is cold; when one seizes it, it is warm.—Horns of a cow.

Poppe, *Aga Buriat*, 8.

947–950. COLOR

947. Black in the daytime, white at night.—Sheepfold.

Bazarov, 195.

948. It goes away, growing white;/ It comes along, growing red.—Wild goat.

Bazarov, 162.

949. If you look at it from over there, it seems to be camel-colored. If you come nearer to it, there is nothing more hideous.—A large, wingless, big-bellied grasshopper (*tyzhin golo*).

Bazarov, 125.

950. On entering the water, it tilts its rump; on leaving the water, it is red.—Lama's bird (*Casarca ferruginea*, Pall., a kind of yellow duck).

Mostaert, 99.

IX. ENUMERATIONS IN TERMS OF ACTS, NOS. 951–971

951. It looks as if it were near, but it is far [if one wants] to bite it.—Hollow of the hand.

Bazarov, 58.

952. Though near when looking at it, one cannot catch it when chasing it.—Rainbow.

Gomboyev, 6.

953a. If you set it free, it fills the steppe, they say. If you take it in your hand, it doesn't fill the hand, they say.—Eye.

Mostaert, 2.

953b. If you take it in your hand, it fills the hand. If you set it free, it fills the steppe.—Eye.

Mostaert, 2 var.; Klukine, 13.

953c. If you take it in your hand, it fills it. If you release it, it fills the whole world.—Eye.

Bazarov, 8; Gomboyev, 8a.

954. A knock here, a knock there, a knock on Perlya's door.—Camel's excrement.

Kotvich, 123.

955. He cannot enter Buddha's temple,/ He cannot eat gruel.—Fire.

Poppe, *Aga Buriat*, 96.

956. A little *ngī ngū* [sound of weeping].—A thorn has pierced the hand.

Zhamtsaranov and Rudnyev, 91.

957. In widening [it], it pops out.—Button.

Klukine, 26.

958. On being pulled asunder, it becomes round.—Button.

Gomboyev, 41.

959. When one sprawls out the legs, it gets in.—Button.

Zhamtsaranov and Rudnyev, 32.

960. By digging it becomes longer; by taking away from its sides, it becomes wider.—Digging a well.

Mostaert, 75.

961. Smaller than you, it bears you down.—Sleep.

Klukine, 25.

962. Smaller than you, but it oppresses you.—Dream, sleep.

Zhamtsaranov and Rudnyev, 49.

963. It is smaller than you, but it fooled you.—Dream.

Kotvich, 267.

964. It is smaller than you; it carries you.—Stirrup.

Mostaert, 93; Klukine, 24 (it lifts you).

965. Though smaller than you, it threw you away.—Stirrup.

Gomboyev, 45.

966. Having been ground up in the bone mill, it was sent by the Chermoyarsky road.—Eating food.

Kotvich, 208.

967. It was pounded many times, it is multiplied fifteen hundred times, it is transformed by rainwater, you pound it again two thousand times.—Manufacture of felt.

Kotvich, 228.

968. You lift and pour, and it spits out by itself.—Pouring tea from a teapot.

Rudnyev, 41.

969. Tumult behind the mountain; confusion behind the rock.—Small rope for tying up sheep and calves.

Gomboyev, 40.

970. All living things were burned, only one long-legged *sosalzhin* did not burn.—Pair of tongs.

Bazarov, 75.

971. An unholy thing has seduced all.—Tobacco.

Bazarov, 29.

X. SHREWD QUESTIONS, NOS. 972–1027

972. HOW . . . ?

972. How long is the distance between heaven and earth?—As far as human thought.

Klukine, 50.

973–980. WHAT (ADJ.) . . . ?

The questions are arranged alphabetically according to the noun following *What*.

973. What city has no lord?—The hearth (ruined city).

Klukine, 41.

974. What cow has no calf?—The ox.

Klukine, 40.

975. What fire has no smoke?—The spark springing from a flint.

Klukine, 38.

976. What hill has no game?—The dune (hill of sand).

Klukine, 43.

977. What man has no friends?—The slanderer.

Klukine, 46.

978. What person has no name?—The baby in the womb.

Klukine, 39.

979. What thing has no owner?—The animal in the steppe.

Klukine, 42.

980. What water has no fish?—The water in the well.

Klukine, 44.

981. WHERE . . . ?

981. Where does the rain start? Where does the fog start? Where do the clouds start?—The rain starts from the ocean. The fog starts from the earth. The clouds start from the ocean.

Klukine, 49.

982–985. WHO . . . ?

982a. Who made a hole?—The younger (or: youngest) one did. With what did he make a hole?—With a chisel. With what did he push?—With an awl. With what did he stop it up?—With a sinew.—Sewing boots.

Bazarov, 63.

982b. Who made the hole through?—A very thin one made the hole through. With what did he make the hole through?—He made the hole through with strength, he pushed with a pusher, he plugged with a sinew.—Tendon.

Poppe, *Aga Buriat*, 93.

983. Who are more numerous: honest people or liars?—People who speak the truth are rare. People who distort the truth and tell lies are numerous.

Klukine, 48.

984. Which are more numerous: men or women?—If you add the number of capricious men to the number of women, women are more numerous.

Klukine, 47.

985. Which are more numerous: days or nights?—If you add the number of gloomy days to the number of nights, the nights are more numerous.

Klukine, 46.

986–992. INTERPRETATIONS OF A SERIES OF NUMBERS

Although many scholars have investigated this curious series which associates numbers with religious and secular themes, a full account of the widely scattered and extremely different versions remains to be written. The nature and use of the Sanskrit versions have been made clear and the main outlines of the history of the European versions of the Carol of the Twelve Numbers have been fairly well established, but the intermediate versions need much more attention than they have received. To these intermediate versions belong the Mongolian texts printed here. It is perhaps worth saying that the survival of Celtic methods of counting as found in the so-called Anglo-Cymric score has little or no bearing on this subject. The Anglo-Cymric score, which is only a series of numerals and contains no references to religious or secular themes, shows that men are likely to remember a manner of counting with which they have become familiar. It has been mentioned along with

Villemarqué's efforts to find an origin for this series in his discredited *Barzaz Breiz*. For a bibliography of articles on the *Barzaz Breiz* see Henri Gaidoz and Paul Sébillot, *Revue celtique* 5: 308–309, 1881–1883. The distribution of the versions of the Carol of the Twelve Numbers makes a Celtic origin extremely improbable. The study of these texts demands an intimate acquaintance with the details of culture, literature, and religion in many countries. Although beset with difficulties, it is an attractive task. For references to investigations or collections of versions see Archer Taylor, *A Bibliography of Riddles*, FF Communications, 126: 149–151, Helsinki, 1939; "Formelmärchen," *Handwörterbuch des deutschen Märchens* 2: 171–174, Berlin, Walter de Gruyter, 1934–1940; and "The Carol of the Twelve Numbers Once More," *Southern Folklore Quarterly* 4: 161, 1940. See further A. N. Veselovksii, Akademiia nauk, *Zapiski* 45, "Razyskaniia v oblasti russkago dukhovnago stikha, VI-X," 78–82, 432–433, St. Petersburg, 1883; F. Ilešič, "Slovenska 'Hagada,'" *Zbornik za narodni život južnih slavena* 7: 207–219, 1902; N. G. Polites, *Laographia* 2: 137, 1910; J. S. Bystroń, "Uwagi nad dziesięu pieśnami ludowymi żydow polskich," *Archivum nauk antropologicznych* 1 (10): 5–8, Warsaw, 1923; J. Bolte and G. Polívka, *Anmerkungen zu den Kinder- und Hausmärchen* 3: 15, n. 1, Leipzig, Dieterich'sche Verlagsbuchhandlung, 1918; Leah Yoffie, "Songs of the 'Twelve Numbers' and the Hebrew Chant 'Echod mí yodea,'" *Journal of American Folklore* 62: 382–411, 1949; Alexander Schreiber, "Hungarian Parallels of the 'Twelve Numbers,'" *ibid.* 63: 465–467, 1950; I. B. Cauthier, "The Twelfth Day of December: *Twelfth Night*, II, iii, 91," *Publications of the Bibliographical Society, University of Virginia* 2: 182–185, 1949–1950; Mrs. L. L. MacDowell, "The Twelve Days of Christmas," *Bulletin of the Tennessee Folklore Society* 11: 2–3, 1945; Erich Seemann, *Jahrbuch für Volksliedforschung* 8: 160–161, No. 40 and 167, No. 58, 1951; Waldemar Liungman, *Varifrån Kommer Våra Sagor*, Sveriges Samtliga Folksagor, 3: 266–267, 414–415, Djursholm, Vald Literatur, 1952. Aurelio M. Espinosa studies many European versions and makes some comment on Oriental parallels in *Cuentos populares españoles* 2: 111–143, Madrid, Instituto Antonio de Nebrija de Filologia, 1946. Perhaps pertinent is the "graded numerical aphorism" cited in Percy W. Long (ed.), *Studies in the History of Culture* [dedicated to Waldo Gifford Leland], 50, Menasha, Wis., George Banta Publishing Co., 1942. Vicente T. Mendoza studies a somewhat similar song in "Origen de dos canciones mexicanas," *Anuario de la Sociedad folklórica de México* 2: 145–172, 1941.

These numerical series containing religious and secular materials are allied to the "Novice's Questions" in the *Khuddaka-pāṭha*, Text 2. For this see R. C. Childers, "Khuddaka Páṭha, a Páli Text with a Translation and Notes," *Journal of the Royal Asiatic Society*, N. S., 4: 309–339, especially pp. 310–311, 1870; Karl Seidenstücker, *Khuddaka-Páṭho,* Breslau, Veröffentlichungen der Pāli-Gesellschaft, 2, 1910; Mrs. Rhys-Davids, *The Minor Anthologies of the Pali Canon,* Part I. *Dhammapada and Khuddakapāṭha* (Sacred Books of the Buddhists, 7 = Pāli Text Society, Translation Series, 23, Oxford, 1931). Maurice Winternitz mentions this text without much comment; see *A History of Indian Literature* 2: 78, Calcutta, Univ. of Calcutta, 1933. His discussion of numerical series (p. 65, n. 1) is very useful and so also is his discussion (pp. 60–66) of the *Aṅguttaranikāya* (Collection of Sermons Arranged in Ascending Numerical Order). This last text contains rather little useful material for comparison and no series similar to those discussed here. See a translation by E. R. J. Cooneratne and A. D. Jayasundere, 1, Galle, Ceylon, C. Calyaneratne, 1913, 2, Madras, Vasanta Press, 1925. For these and other Sanskrit references and for the translation of a text cited below I am indebted to the kindness of Murray B. Emeneau.

In India these series served various uses. The nouns were used in inscriptions to replace numerals and thus make chronograms. For example, the eyes of Shiva signified the number three, because Shiva has three eyes. For a discussion of this procedure see Georg Bühler, *Indische Palaeographie,* Grundriss der indo-arischen Philologie, 1, Heft 11: 80–83, Strassburg, 1896, where a very full list of numerals and their equivalents may be found. Walter E. Clark has recently commented on the earliest examples; see "Hindu-Arabic Numerals," *Indian Studies in Honor of Charles Rockwell Lanman,* 225–226, Cambridge, Mass., Harvard Univ. Press, 1929. As a sample of such a list I print a translation of the following text from Cambridge University MS. Additional 1681. The Sanskrit original is printed in A. O. Ivanovskii, "K tak nazyvaemoi 'Povesti o chislakh,'" *Zapiski vostochnago otdeleniia Imperatorskago russkago arkheologicheskago obshchestva* 8: 359, n. 1, 1893–1894. The translation is as follows:

1. One earth; one moon. 2. A duo; a pair; two arms; two eyes. 3. Three eyes of Shiva; three strands of material nature; three Rāmas [Parashurāma, Rāmachandra, Balarāma]; three fires [of the Vedic three-fire sacrifice]. 4. Four oceans; four faces of Brahma; four Vedas. 5. Five arrows [of the God of Love]; five senses; five elements. 6. Six seasons; six faces of the god Skanda [Kārttikeya]; six flavors [sweet, sour, salt, pungent, bitter, astringent]. 7. Seven mountains; seven sages [seven stars in Ursa Major]; seven hells. 8. Eight Vasus [a class of gods]; eight elephants [each of the principal directions has an elephant and the eight support the earth]; eight auspicious things [lion, bull, elephant, water jar, fan, flag, trumpet, lamp; or Brahman, cow, fire, gold, ghee, sun, water, king]. 9. The nine numbers [i.e., 1–9]; the nine apertures of the human body; nine planets [Mars; Mercury; Jupiter; Venus; Saturn; the sun; the moon; Rāhu, the eclipse demon; Ketu, the body or tail of the eclipse demon, which is responsible for comets and meteors]. 10. Ten directions [four cardinal directions, four intermediate directions,

up, down]. 11. Eleven Rudras [a class of gods]. 12. Twelve Ādityas [a class of gods]. 13. All [i.e., all the gods]; the thirteen Vishve Devās. 14. Fourteen worlds [the earth, six worlds above the earth, seven hells]. 15. Fifteen lunar days in the half-month. 16. Sixteen kings [a traditional list].

Some of these are not found elsewhere. Ivanovskii cites G. H. Damant, "Notes on Hindu Chronograms," *Indian Antiquary* 6: 13-14, 1875, and P. Fouceaux, *Grammaire de la langue tibétaine*, 158-161, Paris, 1858. The general resemblance of such Oriental lists as these to the European Carol of the Twelve Numbers is as close as could be expected in view of the impossibility of translating one set of symbols into another set. The free use of these series in India as a catechetical device and as a basis for chronograms makes it plausible to derive the idea from India.

As an example of an Asiatic series I quote the Tibetan:

One demon, two teats of the she-goat, three precious treasures [Buddha, his teaching, the community of believers], four teats of the cow, five victorious races [of the Buddhas, according to the translator of the Tibetan original], six stallions, seven stars shining by night, eight petals of the lotus, nine peaks of the heavenly sphere, ten fingers, eleven teats of the sow, twelve years of the cycle, thirteen chessmen, fourteen volumes of the *Prajñāpāramitā*, the fifteenth day of the moon [full moon], sixteen senior pupils (*sthavira*) of Buddha [Ivanovskii has here emended the text], seventeen levels of water in the ocean [this is translated from the Mongolian version of the obscure Tibetan original], eighteen growths on the head of the great elk, nineteen slanders, about the twentieth thieves are not worried, twenty-one forms of the goddess Chzholm (Sanskrit Tāgā [*sic*], Mongolian Dara-ekhe).

I cannot elucidate the pertinence of all these numbers to the objects named, but note that Ivanovskii points out that nineteen and twenty have been erroneously interchanged. The *Prajñāpāramitā* is a chief text of the Mahayana sect of Buddhism. The Sanskrit name of the goddess is Tārā; see Getty, pp. 108-109, where her twenty-one names are quoted from L. A. Waddell, "The Indian Buddhist Cult of Avalokita and His Consort Tārā 'Savioress,' Illustrated from the Remains in Magadha," *Journal of the Royal Asiatic Society*, N. S., 26: 51-89, 1894, especially pp. 83-89. I am indebted to Professor G. R. Noyes for the translation of this Tibetan text from A. O. Ivanovskii's article cited above; see Ivanovskii, pp. 359-360. I have quoted it at length because it shows a mingling of religious and apparently secular themes. See further the Siberian Turkish

One, two, ... ten. What is that?—One is the wrist, two is a little needle, three is the soul of a dead man, four is manure, five is a cradle, six is a lasso, seven is land, eight is the outer garment of women, which is put on over a fur coat, nine is minced pieces of meat, ten is a pit (Katanov, p. 466, No. 534)

with an even more confusing parallel that shows some similarity in details to the Tibetan version:

Will a man who lives well forget for the second time what he remembers well? Will a man forget what he is holding with both hands? Is it possible to lose one's wool (literally: to grow bald with the wool), falling three times into a stony pit? That is not gunpowder which is scattered over the space of four months! [Five and six are lacking.] If seven men lived in harmony, then the dawn would shine forth when the Seven Tsars [a name for Ursa Major] are rising over the smokehole of the yurt! The horns of the roebuck, having eight branches, cannot eat an eight-months supply! If one says nine, then it is not a round hat but the wind! Thus conversed a youth with a maid. The youth said one thing, and the maid refuted him (Katanov, p. 634, No. 133).

Both the Turkish "Hey sir! You know what is one and what is five. A sheep gave birth to a lamb. Its mother is male, its offspring is female.—God, prayer, Adam, Eve" (Hamamizade, 5) and the Bulgarian "What is it that is forever one?—God" (Chacharov, 3) are fragmentary and contain the first element of the European Carol of the Twelve Numbers. See also Hausa: Tremearne, pp. 68-70. Mandingo: Monteil, pp. 183-185 and pp. 186-187, No. 19. Swedish: Wessman, 734. French: Montel and Lambert, "Chants populaires du Languedoc," *Revue des langues romanes*, 2d Ser., 3: 78-79, No. 31, 1877. Basque: Cerquand, pp. 243-244, No. 28. Portuguese: A. C. Pires de Lima, *Revista lusitana* 20: 30-32, 1917.

986. What is the first thing to guess?—That which one has seen once, does one forget it? What is the second thing to guess?—That which is held in two hands, does one let it escape? 3. If one hobbles [one's horse] with a three-fold hobble made of three twisted cords, does it go beyond three heights [when one pastures it in the steppe]? 4. If we work with our black bull, whose nose is pierced with a ring, we have food for four years. Variant: If we work with four cattle, harvests [covering all of] a depression in the field are ours. 5. If we unbind our five hawks, the wild beasts of the plain are ours. Variant: If we set our hunting dogs in pursuit, the wild beasts of the plain are ours. 6. If we consult our divination tables, then we know all. 7. When Ursa Major comes to stand overhead, then it is clear weather. 8. When the eighth moon [the fifth month of the Chinese lunar year] has come, then leaves and flowers open. 9. I am the father of absolutely all the world. 10. Not knowing anything else to do, you will have only to raise and spread your ten fingers. 11. You are a boy who no longer knows what to do. 12. When the twelfth month comes to an end, then one goes into the new year.

Mostaert, pp. 487-488, "Jeux d'enfants," 1.

987. What is in the number one?—How can one forget a thing once seen? What is in the number two?—What is there that a person with two eyes would be unable to see? What is in the number three?—How can a horse hobbled with three hobbles cross three mountain passes? What is in the number four? How can there exist something far away for a horse with four legs? What is in the number five? What should a man with five sons have to fear? What is in the number six?—How could it not be summer when the six stars [the Pleiades] are invisible? What is in the number seven?—How should it not be morning when the Seven Buddhas [Ursa Major] go to the zenith? What is in the number eight?—How should leaves and grass not wither in August? What is in the number nine?—How could a person not become rich on sacrificing to the nine gods [Mongolian *tengri,* Sanskrit *devas*]? What is in the number ten?—If one kills the deer with ten antlers, how could one soil the baggage straps on one's father's saddle?

Rudnyev, B 1–B 10.

988. One: an object seen once and famous. Two: an object held by both hands and not let loose. Three: a horse hobbled [i.e., having three legs] will not go far. Four: a man who killed a four-year old ox will have food for the winter. Five: a man who rides on a five-year old [i.e., a seasoned] horse will reach his destination. Six: a man who milked a six-year old mare boiled kumiss. Seven: when the Seven Buddhas [Ursa Major] will show up overhead, the years are parted (or: divide). Eight: the bitch that has eight little pups feeds the pups. Nine: the man who has nine sons is the elder of the hamlet (*khoton*). Ten: a dog licks the mouth of the man who drank ten glasses of vodka.

Kotvich, 276–285.

989. Is it possible to forget a person whom you have seen once? Two: is it possible to drop something that you hold with two hands? Three: where could a hobbled horse [having three legs] go? Four: a man who killed a four-year old black ox will not ask someone else for meat. Five: a man who rides a good seasoned five-year old horse will reach his destination. Six: a man who milks six mares, boils and drinks vodka during the summer. Seven: when the Seven Buddhas appear overhead, the years divide. Eight: a man who milks eight mares has a sufficient amount of kumiss. Nine: a man who has nine sons can live as he pleases. Ten: though a dog may lick the mouth of a man who has had ten drinks of vodka, the man does not notice it.

Kotvich, 286–295.

990. Six: a man who placed on the crown of his head [the image of] Zunkhara became six Zu, will know no sufferings. Seven: the man who loaded seven of his camels will not remain in a strange camp. Eight: a man who built a yurt with eight grates will be located in front of the hamlet (*khoton*). Nine: a man who begot nine sons will sit in the place of honor in the yurt. Ten: if you depend on the words (i.e., teachings) of ten Buddhas, you will escape the dreadfulness of hell.

Kotvich, 296–300.

991. One: rock salt for tanning sheepskins. Two: the excrement of a sheep. Three: a hearth [supported by three stones]. Four: an anvil. Five: a shelf. Six: a hole in the yard for a kettle. Seven: a burial mound. Eight: a feast. Nine: the world. Ten: a large knuckle bone.

Kotvich, 301–310.

992. The nine outstanding qualities of a man: the highest quality is harmony (agreeableness). At sea: a swimmer. In war: a hero. In books: depth (thoroughness). In a lord: lack of treachery. In work: skill. In words: wisdom. Abroad: steadfastness. In archery: marksmanship.

Rudnyev, C 1.

993–996. ARITHMETICAL RIDDLES

993. There are forty-nine chickens and hares [in all]; they have a hundred feet. How many hares, how many chickens are there?—One hare, forty-eight chickens.

Mostaert, 197.

994. One hundred lamas, one hundred flat cakes. The fully ordained lamas (*gelyng*) eat ten cakes [each], the candidates (*getsyl*) eat five cakes [each], the novices (*bandi*) eat one-half cake [each]. How many ordained lamas, candidates, and novices?—One ordained lama, nine candidates, and ninety novices.

Mostaert, 198.

995. The Buddha's mirror has one handle. The mould board has four handles. The pot has two handles. There are forty-nine utensils with one hundred handles. How many mirrors, mould boards, and pots?—Six mirrors, four mould boards, thirty-nine pots.

Mostaert, 199.

996. On the other side of the river there is a flock of sheep tended by a man. On this side of the river there is another flock of sheep tended by a man. The man from this side of the river says to the man on the other side of the river, "If you give me one of your sheep, I shall have twice as many sheep as you have." The man from the other side of the river said, "If you give me one sheep of yours, we shall have an equal number of sheep." Guess how many sheep there were in these herds.—One had seven, one five sheep.

Mostaert, 200.

997–1024. TRIADS

Triads constitute a special variety of riddle that is closely akin to the tripartite proverb. In such proverbs and riddles one element may drop out or a new element may be added and thus they may be reduced to a pair of assertions or enlarged to four assertions. I have for convenience put together in this section all groups of two, three, and four assertions. Typical examples of enigmatic triads are the Kabardin "Three unknown wonders. Give me three and I'll tell you the answer:

Who gets up the sky on a ladder? Who carries [something] in a sieve? Who cooks butter on a spit?—Rainbow, cloud, sun" (Talpa and Sokolov, 1); the Cheremis "In this world three objects are the most pleasant.—Stream, water, fire" (Porkka, 30 = Genetz, 46 = Wichmann, 172 = Sebeok, 8.2), "Three objects that are bent.—Fire, river, road" (Genetz, 45 = Sebeok, 8. 1. 3), and "In God's world there are three crooked objects.—Road, river, fence" (Porkka, 29 = Wichmann, 171 = Sebeok, 8. 1. 1) with a Russian parallel (Sadovnikov, 1341); the Chuvash "What are the three things not found in this world?—There is no ladder to climb to God, water has no branches, the horse has no horns" (Karahka and Räsänen, 104); the Turkish "An inn without a door, a bath-house without a vault, an imam without a tongue.—Earth, sea, cock" (Hamamizade, 168); and the Lithuanian "What is useless in the world for three men?—Brightness for a blind man, bells for a deaf and dumb man, a comb for a bald man" (Balys, p. 158, No. 551). For brief comment on triads see Walter Suchier, *L'Enfant sage*, 269. Professor Charles Speroni of the University of California at Los Angeles has in preparation a study of triads with special reference to the Italian examples.

997. TWO

997. Two things are lacking in this world: a ladder to ascend to heaven, a lid to cover the ocean.

Rudnyev, N 12.

998–1019. THREE

998. The three months of a tramp.—The periods of a bitch.

Bazarov, 81.

999–1003. *Colors*

999. Three black (or: dark) things in life: that which is called the fifteenth of the month is dark; the shadow (*segdyr*) of that which is decorated with gold and silver; no matter how much you scrub a kettle, it remains black.

Rudnyev, F 4.

1000. There are three red things in the world. Guess, what are they?—Red cheeks of a healthy woman, the red horizon before cold sets in, the red eyes of a sick person.

Bazarov, 154.

1001. Only three things are red in the world.—Red is the red woolen belt (*toroka*) of a young brave; red are the cheeks of a beautiful woman; red is the view of the sunset.

Kotvich, 191.

1002. Three red things in the world.—When the wind (*jabar*) blows, the horizon is red; when she is enjoying herself, the lady's cheeks are red; the eyes of an angry person are red.

Rudnyev, E 3.

1003a. Three white things in the world.—While growing, white teeth; while aging, white hair; when dead, white bones.

Rudnyev, D 2.

1003b. Only three things in the world that are white.—White are the bones of the dead; the teeth of the laughing; the hair of the aged.

Kotvich, 190.

1004–1009. *Defects*

1004. Three causes for regret in the world.—Coming to a hunt without arrows; a lama coming to a religious service without sacred texts; a girl without luck given in marriage.

Rudnyev, L 10.

1005. Three empty things in life.—In sleep, a dream; when shouting, an echo; in a mirage, the image.

Rudnyev, C 13.

1006. Three without's in life.—The Sumeru (Cosmic) mountain is without a belt; the Milk Ocean (surrounding Sumeru) is without a lid; Heaven is without a pillar.

Rudnyev, M 11.

1007. In the world three things are lacking. What are they?—Supports for the sky; a lid for the ocean; a belt for the mountains.

Bazarov, 116.

1008. Three things are lacking in the world.—The bird has no teats; the sea has no bottom; the sky has no rim.

Kotvich, 192.

1009. The horse has three drawbacks. What are they?—It has no horn; it has no gall; it doesn't chew the cud.

Bazarov, 5.

1010–1015. *Emotional Qualities*

1010. There are only three gloomy things in the world.—Gloomy is the soul of a muzhik who does not know the law; gloomy is the hamlet (*khoton*) that has no sheep; gloomy is the soul of a woman who has no children.

Kotvich, 189.

1011. A variant of the third element in No. 1010: Gloomy is the prince who has no subjects.

Kotvich, 189.

1012. Three thee's (i.e., threats) in the world.—Without skill, the frog—thee; without a caul, the hare—thee; the nose of a burrow (*asamay*)—thee.

Rudnyev, T 18.

1013. Three raging things in life.—A woman growling at her husband rages; a horse throwing its saddle under its belly rages; a spark falling into the hay rages.

Rudnyev, U 19.

1014. Three annoying things in life.—A mettlesome horse when hunting; a capricious woman for her neighbors; a nagging traveling companion.

Rudnyev, K 9.

1015. Three nice things in life.—A child when leaping; a puppy when starting to walk; a foal when completing its flesh (growing in the womb?) are nice.

Rudnyev, J 8.

1016–1019. *Physical Qualities*

1016. The strength of a dark brown horse is good./ The solidity of a pigskin is good./ Its goodness is very good.—Iron hobble.

Zhamtsaranov and Rudnyev, 74.

1017. Three swift things in life.—A horse galloping over the steppe; a lama counting (i.e., reciting) his spells; the winged ones (i.e., the birds) flying over the sky.

Rudnyev, R 16.

1018. Three rough (or: cruel) things in life.—To be an envoy to a country is rough; a hedgehog in a dry lake is rough; for iron, a file is rough.

Rudnyev, H 6.

1019. Three *in*'s in the world.—When separating from your ship, you are in the ocean; when separating from your quiver and bow, you are in (or: among) enemies; when separating from your good horse, you are in the steppe.

Rudnyev, S 17.

1020–1024. FOUR
1020–1022. *Form*

1020. Four rough things in life.—To walk on a road and step on a hedgehog is rough; to be an emissary (or: express messenger) is rough; to be a dog ignorant of its birth (or: rebirth, life) is rough; to be a file ignorant of [the hardness of] iron is rough.

Rudnyev, I 7.

1021. Four links (or: supports, relationships, ties) in life.—The prince for the people; the bank for the water (or: river); the circular roofpiece for the felt tent; the intestine (peritoneum, Mongolian *oziryai*) for the belly.

Rudnyev, Q 15.

1022. Four knots in life.—The Dalai Lama ties a knot in silk. The King of Hell ties a knot in sins. In government affairs the emperor ties a knot. The Nepalese craftsman ties a knot in iron.

Rudnyev, F 4.

1023–1024. *Color*

1023. Four black things in life.—A house without a lamp is black (i.e., dark); unsown (or: unprepared) millet is black; tea without milk is black; a heart without religious faith is black.

Rudnyev, G 5.

1024. Four green things in the world.—Vegetables; growth; the turquoise stuck in the hair; bile (lit.: blood) in the belly.

Rudnyev, V 20.

1025. PUNS

1025. Things were called mother (*akhai*) that were not mothers.—The many words containing the phoneme *akhai*, e.g., *tsur gakhai* (pig), *tsur akhai* (pike), *bolchis akhai* (gland), *zara akhai* (small fish), *manggut akhai* (vermin).

Gomboyev, 59.

1026, 1027. QUEER NAMES

1026. It has the name of a domestic animal, but the color of a wild animal.—Jerboa (*alak dagan*).

Bazarov, 136.

1027. On the other side of the flowing, under a growing, the howling devoured the bleating.—On the other side of the water (or: river), under a tree, a wolf devoured a lamb.

Kotvich, 110.

COMPARATIVE NOTES

The numbers in bold face introducing the paragraphs refer to the riddles in the preceding section. These numbers are not to be confused with those in ordinary type which, unless preceded by the abbreviation "p." for page, refer to the number assigned by the collector. In citing parallels, I have not repeated the solutions that are identical with the solutions of the Mongolian riddles under discussion.

1, 2. Riddlers often use the related idea of teeth that cannot eat to describe a toothed tool, especially a saw, a comb, or a rake. For examples see the headnote to Taylor, *English,* 297–300. Although the enigmatic descriptions of a pair of scissors vary greatly in their fundamental conceptions they do not often employ the obvious comparison to jaws that open and close and do not often mention biting. Compare, however, the Yakut "Two bears bite; if anything comes [between], they cut" (Popov, p. 289), the Annamese "Two bamboo leaves that strike together" (Dumoutier, p. 201), and the Turkish "Riddle me, riddle me ree, the tongue moves, the palate cuts" (Bahaeddin, 35).

3, 4. Compare the Arabic "It is as big as a hazelnut, it has a thousand protruding eyes" (Bauer, p. 222, No. 2; Löhr, p. 108, No. 25; Littmann, 95). Somewhat similar is the description of a thimble as a supposed creature that has abnormally numerous eyes and lacks a nose; see Taylor, *English,* 13 with the note.

5. The translation of *moilokhon* is uncertain. A native speaker cites a tree called *moil* that has an edible fruit. Compare the Bulgarian "John is riding on nine vines; God Himself wonders how he rides" (Chacharov, 93. See also Gubov, 269). This has Serbian parallels; see Novaković, p. 162, Nos. 6, 7. There some similar ideas in other riddles for a spider's web. The Kashmiri say, "Silver branches stretched across a golden ceiling. Árif (Arabic: the wise one) said to Kárif (Arabic: the witty one), 'Who tied them?'" (Knowles, 29; Koul, 40). The Armenian "It pitches a tent without any rope" (Grigorov, 2) involves a seeming impossibility. Another contradiction appears in the Polish "Upwards with its roots; when it climbs, it [stands] upside down" (Kopernicki, 66). For comment on the idea of growing upside down see the headnotes to Taylor, *English,* 544, § 5 and 1055–1057. Among the rather remote African parallels the most similar is perhaps the Pangwe "There is a tree there: Bokobo and Ada (men's names) climb on it" (Tessmann, 33). For riddles describing a spider crossing a river see No. 100 below.

6. The first clause occurs again in a riddle for saltwort; see No. 30 below. Words that describe the sound made by an actor are numerous in Mongolian riddles. For a somewhat similar conception of a rabbit see Taylor, *English,* 220.

7. Hungarian: *Magyar Nyelvör* 5: 89 (1876) (It walks in the mountains, it jumps in the valley, it has ears like spoons, and it wears leather pants, it's the butcher himself).

8. The meaning of the allusion to Barguzin is obscure. It concerns a region east of Lake Baikal. For other references to this region see No. 781 below and the wood of Bargusi (a variation in dialect or transcription) in No. 298 below. For a similar conception see No. 966 below.

9. Compare the Yakut "Has wings, yet does not fly. It is without legs, yet it walks (moves)" (Popov, p. 284; Iastremskii, 127); the Kashmiri "It is a tree-bird; it does not sit on a tree. It has young without number; it never hatches them" (Knowles, 24; Koul, 15); the Chuvash "It has wings, it cannot fly; it has no feet, one cannot overtake it" (Karahka and Räsänen, p. 103, No. 112); and the Russian version (Sadovnikov, 1616), which is the same as the Chuvash riddle. The fins have suggested the Kashmiri, Chuvash, and Russian references to wings. Note also a curious Russian version in narrative form: "Noblemen had a meal at a handsome maiden's. Having eaten, they prayed to God, saying: 'Oh! We thank you, O handsome maiden, for your bread and salt, and we invite you to be our guest.' The maiden replied: 'I do not walk over the ground, nor do I look heavenwards. I do not make me a nest, but I do rear children'" (Sadovnikov, 1617). The themes of the Mongolian riddle appear here and in the Russian variant, "Does not walk on the earth, does not look skywards, does not make a nest, yet does give birth to children" (Sadovnikov, 1617c). See also the Algerian Arabic "It is a company of beaters hunting game and flies from all men; it does not fly in the air, it does not walk on the earth" (Giacobetti, 209). There are novel themes in the Icelandic "I saw a boy today whom snowstorms do not make downcast. He doesn't walk and doesn't fly, and yet there is life in his body" (Arnason, 61) and "There is a very swift girl of whom the devil got neither hide nor hair. She has no feet, but dances all over the sea. No one knows where she stays at rest unless it be in the net in the sea" (Arnason, 149). For references to the devil's pursuit of the haddock alluded to in the last riddle see Oskar Dähnhardt, *Natursagen* 1: 201, Leipzig, Teubner, 1907. Andrew Lang tells another story about the marks on a haddock; see *Myth, ritual, and religion* 1: 140, London, 1887. Walloon: Colson, *Wallonia* 4, 62, No. 64 (Who does not talk and cannot talk, who does not walk and cannot walk, who does not fly and cannot fly, and yet is alive like you and me?).

10. The Mongolian *bultai* means "to appear with one end hidden from sight." For parallels see Nos. 11, 957, 958 below.

11, 12. A comparison to a person spreading his legs occurs also in riddles for a gun and its rest; see Nos. 196, 414, 519 (crows scrape the ground), 534 (two legs sneak up), and 755 below. A quite different *tertium quid comparationis* is implied in No. 959. The Yakut comparison of a button to a person in "Only as large as a finger, but people rely on him" (Priklonskii, 52) has perhaps been modelled on the riddle for scales (see the note to No. 410 below).

13, 14. Turcoman: Samojlovich, 30 (Something small and nimble and it won't let itself be caught by the tail). An animal is more clearly suggested in No. 50 below.

15. For parallels see the headnote to Taylor, *English,* 227, nn. 12–19. Samoyede: Lehtisalo, 145 (The traveler travels, he always covers up his trail), 225 (One does not see his trail), 280 (A man, if he goes, there is no trace of him; if one cuts through him, he has no blood). Yakut: Ionova, 41 (A gray horse has passed by without leaving a trace). Mordvin: Paasonen and Ravila, p. 680, No. 4. Nagaibak: Vitevskii, p. 276, No. 2 (It goes but there is no trace). Compare the Dschagga "I cut it but it is nevertheless not divided.—Water" (Stamberg, 206). The Svanians describe fire in a similar way: "It cuts, it cuts, yet nothing comes out" (Y. Nizheradze, p. 66, No. 9).

15c. The Mongolian text contains a jingle: *xaixodo* (looking) rhymes with *xatxodo* (pricking). As in Nos. 15a and 15b, the pricking is the cutting or stabbing of the oars in water.

16. This riddle and No. 15 are based on the same comparison but have different answers. For other pairs of riddles employing the same comparison and having different answers see the note to No. 476–478. For parallels to the notion that a shadow cannot be cut see the headnote to

Taylor, *English,* 1665–1666, § 2. See Nos. 142, 193, and 732 below for similar themes and compare further the Zyrian "If you strike with an ax, there is everywhere a mark; in one place [only] none is left" (Wichmann, 204) and the Javanese "There is a man. When one shoots a cannon at him, he doesn't die. When one strikes him with a sword, he is not injured. When one leaves him, he follows everywhere" (Ranneft, *Proza,* p. 13, No. 60. See also his Nos. 59a, 61).

17. For a remote parallel see the headnote to Taylor, *English,* 240, § 12.

18. Mongolian *sēr* means the place between the back and the croup, especially the spot where the yoke is put. The first three of the four Mongolian words in this riddle alliterate. Compare No. 628 below, the Kashmiri "Neither with hands nor with feet,/By its power it goes on" (Knowles, 110), the Yakut "Has neither legs nor wings, but goes more quickly than anyone" (Iastremskii, 125), the Kosi "It has no feet and yet climbs a palm" (Ittmann, 83), and the Wanamwezi "Who has no legs?" (Dahl, 87). The Toda call a snake a "jungle creature without legs" (Rivers, p. 599).

19, 20. For parallels see the headnotes to Taylor, *English,* 260–265, § 5 and 365–366, § 3. See further the Yakut "It flies without wings, it walks without legs" (Iastremskii, 36) and the Lithuanian "What flies without wings?" (Jurgelionis, 96) and "What flies without wings, walks without feet?" (Jurgelionis, 97; Basanavicius, p. 190, No. 31). In "What has no wheels, yet moves?" (Popov, p. 283) the Yakut conceive a cloud in terms of a wagon rather than a bird.

21. Muria: Elwin, p. 592, No. 40 (The deer goes to and fro without feet). Compare the Arabic steamer riddle: "A bird flies over the sea. It lives without feathers and accompanies the dervishes" (Ruoff, p. 21, No. 9a). The dervishes are pilgrims to Mecca. For additional parallels see Zhamtsaranov's note; Taylor, *English,* 372; and compare Taylor, *Ainu,* 2. For parallels to the notion of a creature without a neck see the note to No. 148 below.

22. The feet and wings are names for parts of the vertebra. For other riddles that employ words possible of being understood in two senses see the note to No. 661. Compare a Swedish nose riddle, "Root up and wings down between two lakes" (Ström, p. 81, "Näsan," 1). Here "root" signifies, as in English, the base of the nose and the wings are the nostrils.

23. The door is a tent flap blown open by the wind. See Turkish: Hamamizade, 575 (A handless and footless fellow opens the door). Cherekessian: Tambiev, p. 61, No. 94 (Who opens doors without hands?). Russian: Sadovnikov, 1902a (Without arms, without legs, yet opens gates), 1902b. Welsh: Hull and Taylor, 283, citing Lithuanian, Zyrian, and Votyak parallels. See further the headnotes to Taylor, *English,* 260–265, § 9 and 365–366, § 1.

24. Chuvash: Mészáros, 127 (Lives without a body, speaks without a tongue. Nobody sees it, everybody hears it.—Voice), which should probably have the answer "echo." Lithuanian: Mickevicius, p. 586, No. 209 (I have no tongue, but I give correct answers. No one sees me, but all hear me); Jurgelionis, 1098 (Lives without a body, speaks without a tongue, no one sees him but everyone hears him). French: Rolland, 20 (Who lives without a body, hears without an ear, speaks without a mouth, and [is one] whom the air causes to be born?); Carmeau, p. 35 (Who lives without having a body and talks without having a tongue, [is one] whom no one has seen and whom all the world hears?). Bakongo: Peschuël-Loesche, p. 100 (Who speaks without a tongue?). See also the headnote to Taylor, *English,* 259–265.

24b. The Mongolian *aldar* (fame), which is used in polite address, is also the name of the person addressed in this riddle. The second clause, therefore, contains an untranslatable pun. For riddles employing puns see the note to No. 661 below.

25. Riddlers often mention the jerky hopping of a magpie; see No. 456 below and Taylor, *English,* 1379 through 1382 with the notes to Nos. 1379 and 1380. Siberian Turkish: Katanov, p. 93, No. 790 (Walks by jumps, clad in black and yellow boots). Compare the Turcoman jay riddle, "With a swaying gait, motley swords at its sides" (Samojlovich, 44). For parallels to the magpie's shagreen or goatskin boots see Nos. 26 and 456b below. Compare the Turkish stork riddle, "The right specialist comes from Bagdad, the engineer with yellow boots" (Bahaeddin, 7). For other riddles describing a magpie see the Index of Solutions.

26. An adaptation of the preceding riddle. For riddles employing the same comparison but having different answers see the note to Nos. 476–478 below.

27. The riddler probably has a magpie in mind; see No. 25 above. The contrast of high and low often occurs in riddles for a road and a saddle; see the note to No. 910 below.

28. The meaning of *yā yā* is obscure.

30. Golstunskii, 2 : 87a translates *khamkhak* as artemisia. For a personification of saltwort see No. 479 below. Compare such riddles as the Welsh description of a fern, "What goes swifter after its legs are cut?" (Hull and Taylor, *Welsh,* 10) with a Scotch Gaelic parallel, "It is faster after breaking its leg.—Broken bracken blown by the wind" (Nicolson, p. 35).

31. The Arabic "As big as a hornet, it fights horses in the field" (Bauer, p. 29, No. 51) contains a similar reference to the small size of a bullet. See also Taylor, *English,* 801, § 1. For comparisons to a man speaking see the headnote to Taylor, *English,* 755.

32, 33. The answer "cicada" seems to be correct. Compare the Malayalam "Little man, strong voice.—Cricket" (Schmolck, 24) and the Algerian Arabic "It is as big as a fingernail and it neighs like a foal.—Grasshopper" (Giacobetti, 227). The Yakut "The noise of scissors of Chinese girls is clearly heard.—Crickets" (Ionova, 132. See also Piekarski, 89; Popov, p. 284) is also used to describe a mare (Iastremskii, 148). Presumably a mare eating grass is intended. The Yakut locust riddle "A king's daughter rings her scissors" (Popov, p. 284) is analogous. Like these riddles, the Mordvin cricket riddles—"In the moss an old woman is crying out" and "Russian women wander over the field, singing songs of mourning" (Paasonen, 214, 215)—mention the sound that the insect makes but do not contrast the small creature and the loud noise. This contrast is the subject of Nos. 31–35, 406 in this collection. See also the Shor "In size a handful; in voice loud enough to be heard over a day's journey.—Nightingale" (Dyrenkova, 5) and an English nightingale riddle (Taylor, *English,* 336). For comparisons to a creature that is small but remarkably strong see the note to No. 52 below.

34, 35. Yakut: Iastremskii, 128 (In a coat [?] of silk and leather a short tail-less shaman hums.—Bumblebee), 134 (With songs, with tunes, a singer with a short neck, with a head plunged into his shoulders.—Fly). In No. 343 the comparison to a lama is ingeniously developed with special mention of his reading the scriptures aloud.

36. When the steelyard "counts its years," the marker is indicating the weight of the object laid in the scales.

37. The pot evidently has the shape of the Chinese *yehhu* (night-tiger). Compare Hungarian: *Magyar Nyelvör* 3 : 329, 1874 (A kettle of wood, a cover of leather. If you guess what it is, I shall give you what is cooked in it), 4: 180, 424, 1875.

38. See a more elaborate version in No. 134 below. For parallels to the formula "at the mouth (or: source) of the river" see Nos. 97, 134, 644.

39. The riddler is too specific; one would expect the answer "fish." The Ainu "What is in the river and burns with light?—Old salmon or trout" (Taylor, 34) involves the paradox of fire in water, a theme often used to describe a samovar (for references see the headnote to Taylor, *English*, 1440–1441, nn. 3, 4). See also the Ainu "What moves its burning tail in the water?—Old salmon or trout" (Taylor, 17), "What runs in the river with a torch?—Salmon" (Taylor, 30a), and Taylor, *Ainu*, 29. The Albanian "Something living that is rubbed with gold.—Fish" (Hahn, p. 162, No. 62) implies a paradoxical combination of a living creature and a metal. See also Kolarian: Wagner, 52 (In the rivers white *hisir*-necklaces are swimming.—The eyes of the fish.) The meaning of *hisir* is not given. Mordvin: Paasonen, 398 (In the water blue pestles).

40–42. Riddles for frogs vary greatly in the choice of themes. Note such comparisons to persons as the Yakut "To the wonder of all there is a speckled child, so they say" (Piekarski, 97), the Baiga "He sits weeping in the river" (Elwin and Archer, p. 273, No. 32), and the Turkish "She comes from below, croaking [and] opening wide her eyes" (Kowalski, *Zagadki*, 11). See other riddles for a frog in the Index of Solutions, the note to No. 797 below, and the headnote and note to Taylor, *English*, 347.

40. The meaning of *dendžin* is obscure. This word or one much like it occurs in Nos. 337a, 440 (Denzen), 654 (Tchjintchji), 657 (Denji), 683 (Dendein). According to Rinchene's Mongolian-Russian dictionary (p. 85a), *dendž* signifies a hillock or steep slope. A native speaker believes that it refers to Ulan Bator, capital of Outer Mongolia, where the Soviet consulate is called *konsulin denzdži*. For references to the four feet of a frog see also Nos. 440 and 797.

44. A hobble consists of three wooden sticks with loops for the horse's legs. Compare the Altai Turkish "Gaily colored wooden block over which no horse can leap" (Menges, p. 78, No. 53) and the Yakut "'A silver bracelet hinders me from freeing myself,' says someone.—Hobbled horse" (Iastremskii, 63); "'I would find the road into the wide world, if this noisy 'clapper' would not hold me,'" (Iastremskii, 64), and "'If there were not this pretty woman, I would go to the Aldanski station,' he says" (Iastremskii, 65). See also his No. 66).

45. The meaning of *mogdoe* is obscure. The orifice of the abomasum is closed with a wooden plug and the whole is wrapped in a small intestine. For an entirely different description of a stuffed stomach see No. 917 below.

49. This riddle occurs in the fourteenth-century *Codex cumanicus* in virtually the same form: "He eats and drinks and goes into his den" (Németh, 29). Many parallels are reported in modern eastern European and Siberian tradition. See the Votyak "Eats, eats, then goes into a pit" (Wichmann, 41) and "Eats and goes back again into its bed" (Buch, 31) and the Altai Turkish "He has eaten and eaten and has gone into his hole" (Menges, p. 78, No. 59. See Katanov, p. 160, No. 1321 and p. 242, No. 94. See also Katanov, *Urianchai*, 35 (Ate the whole time, then disappeared in his yurt). These somewhat vaguely conceived riddles do not specify the nature of the actor.

In Nos. 309 and 310 below the actor, who represents the knife, is called a wolf or polecat. For other comparisons to animals see the notes to these riddles and the Cheremis "My gelding eats and eats and just lies down in the manger" (Sebeok, 2. 12. 15. 3), the Russian "Having eaten, the horse fell into the manger" (Sadovnikov, 435) and "The little lamb will eat, will eat. Then—into the little manger" (Sadovnikov, 435b), and the Polish "A worm goes along the table and what it comes upon it maims" (Saloni, *Rzeshów*, 157). The Cherekessian "A freshly shaved head jumps into the manger" (Tambiev, p. 57, No. 51) seems to be disordered.

Some similar comparisons do not concern animals. See an Icelandic comparison to a man: "I was hurt by the stern steward who divides men's food and afterwards enters into himself to rest" (Arnason, 78). The allusion to entering into himself implies a folding pocket knife. A curious Bengali riddle makes a comparison to a plant: "A black thorny plant [*Argemone mexicana*] eats black grass. When night comes, the thorny tree goes into a refuge.—Razor" (Mitra, *Chittagong*, p. 852, No. 16). For additional discussion see the headnote to Taylor, *English*, 1042–1044, nn. 13–24.

A rare variation of the theme is seen in the Togo "My father has a ram, its head does not go into its stable" (Schönhärl, p. 100, No. 2). Since the Javanese kris is curved, it can be compared to a snake: "A poisonous snake is put into dead wood" (Ranneft, *Proza*, p. 41, No. 13). The sheath of a kris is made of wood. This resembles a Kashmiri sword riddle: "A snake came out from under a green stone, and [after] killing thousands of people went back again" (Knowles, 98).

The Poles use the comparison of an animal crawling into a hole to describe a key: "It creeps, creeps over iron. Should there be a hole, it crawls into it" (Gustawicz, 138. See also his No. 139). For a similar description of putting on a shoe see No. 470 below. For comparisons to a hollow tree see the note to Nos. 308b, 308c.

50. Siberian Turkish: Katanov, p. 238, No. 35 (If you seize him by the head, he's wild. If you seize him by the arse, he's gentle). Cheremis: Sebeok, 1.7. 18. 1 (Only small but very heavy, it can't even be held.—Embers), 1. 7. 18. 2, 7. 7 (It is small, it is hard to carry, I cannot carry it at all); Sebeok-Beke, 2. 12. 9 (a comparison to horses). Uraon: Archer, 197 (A jack-of-all-trades, but no one can hold him). The Chuvash "Easy to look at, difficult to lift up.—Hot embers" (Mészáros, 120) is a vaguely conceived contrast. The Uraon "A blossoming flower that cannot be picked" (Archer, 79) is a comparison in terms of a plant rather than an animal. Comparisons of fire, flame, or a lamp to a flower are rather numerous (see Nos. 667–669, 776, and the note to No. 667 below), but allusions to the difficulty of plucking the flower are rare. Such allusions occur more frequently in the use of these comparisons to describe the stars; see the headnote to Taylor, *English*, 1071, nn. 9–18. For a related Mongolian conception of a firebrand see Nos. 13, 14 above. Compare also Quechua: Quijada Jara, p. 184, No. 24.

52. For comparisons to a small creature or thing with great strength see Nos. 204, 366, 397, 486, 489, 527, 961–964. See also the Mordvin "It is small but rules a city.—Lock of a city gate" (Paasonen, 289) and the Breton "What is as small as a little finger and contains all the king's horses?—Lock" (Sébillot, *Côtes du Nord*, 62a). A flea is small but moves a king or a log (the log is the enigmatic equivalent of a sleeping man); see the headnote to Taylor, *English*, 344, nn. 8, 9. See additional examples of the flea riddle in Mordvin: Paasonen and Ravila, p. 622, No. 3. Cheremis: Sebeok, 1.7.3.1–1.7.3.4. Russian: Preobrazhenskii, p. 170. Polish: Kopernicki, 12; Saloni, *Rzeshów*, 132.

53. For a description of these seven cups see Getty, p. xlix.

54. A Mongolian pillow has a leather cover and is stuffed with horsehair. One of its wooden ends is ornamented with five silver buttons. The riddler calls the wooden end a shelf and the ornamental buttons flies.

56. See another reference to the eight sinews or bands attached to the saddle in No. 715. In No. 56a the Russian translator has added the word "eight," which is lacking in the Mongolian original.

57. Compare a Vogul riddle for a pole (perhaps more correctly, a rope) lying on a haystack: "The cow stands below, her tail lies on the roof" (Ahlqvist, 26), which has a Mordvin parallel (Ahlqvist, *Moksha Mordvin,* p. 145, No. 78).

58. These skin-worms infest sheep and make the hides useless by eating holes in them. The holes in the hides are compared to the holes in the lattice wall.

59. The wooden foot is the support on which the gun rests when it is fired.

60. Like the Chinese *ch'ung,* the Mongolian *xorxöi* is a generic term for animals other than fish, insects, birds, and mammals. For a survey of the Mongolian comparisons of the eyes to parti-colored animals and things see the notes to Nos. 801 and 828.

61. Virtually the same comparison serves to describe an inkwell and pen; see No. 62. For other comparisons used to describe two entirely different objects see the note to Nos. 476–478. For parallels to the formula "in a well" see Nos. 69, 173 (in a ditch), 342, 363, 365 (in a hole), 393, 394, 783 (in a puddle), 880, and a Georgian riddle quoted in the note to Nos. 309, 310. The formula often occurs in riddles for the moon. It is akin to the formula "in a grassless hollow," which is discussed in the note to No. 692 below, and the Turkish formula "in a dark place." For the Turkish formula see Kowalski, *Asia Minor,* 71, 77, 83; Kowalski, *Zagadki,* 75, 129; Kúnos, p. 165, Nos. 164, 165; Boratav, 8, 9, 85, 115, 116. See also a Turcoman riddle quoted in the note to No. 69 below and the Turkish formula "in a dark valley" (Kowalski, *Zagadki,* 49, 50).

62. See the note to No. 61. Mongolians ordinarily write with a reed (*kalan*) and rarely, if ever, use a goose quill. This riddle is probably of foreign origin.

64. For comparisons describing a candle that consumes itself see Taylor, *English,* 779 and the note.

66. Riddles for waves are rare. See a comparison to eagles fighting (Taylor, *English,* headnote to No. 397, n. 12). This is an adaptation of a riddle for grinding flour. See also comparisons to a girl opening a kerchief (Taylor, *English,* 713); to neighbors who do not greet one another (Taylor, *English,* headnote to Nos. 966–968, § 9); and to brothers who cannot overtake one another (Taylor, *English,* 1000).

69. For comparisons of the heart to an animal see the Turcoman "In the midst of the darkness a tiger roars" (Samojlovich, 143) and the SeSuto "The mouse has gone to our big pot" (Norton and Velaphe, 60). For similar comparisons used to describe a mill see the headnote and note to Taylor, *English,* 387. For a comparison of the heart to a person see the Siberian Turkish "In Kaspal land a shaman is conjuring" (Katanov, p. 97, No. 836; Katanov, *Urianchai,* 21). For a comparison of the heart to a thing see the Votyak "At the bottom of the chest a thinking button" (Buch, 22).

71, 72. Compare the riddle for the human mind, No. 489 below. The significance of Kurulda, the bird's name, is obscure. It may be connected with Kerelda, a person's name, in No. 606.

72. The import of the riddle is obscure.

73. The various comparisons of a lamp to a bird, especially to a bird drinking water, seem perhaps to be independent inventions rather than derivatives of a single inventive act. See the headnote to Taylor, *English,* 413; the Uraon "The golden parrot with the silver beak drinks water through its tail" (Elwin and Archer, p. 294, No. 33); and a riddle current among the Moslems in India: "There is a bird. It sits along a river, drinks water with its claws, holds communion with God" (Elwin and Archer, p. 308, No. 6). Mongolians use many widely varying comparisons to describe a lamp; see the Index of Solutions. The similarity of the Uraon and Moslem riddle for a lamp to a widely known riddle for writing or a pen is curious; see the note to No. 87 below.

74, 75. Compare French and Breton leek riddles cited in the headnote to Taylor, *English,* 1273–1274. Cheremis: Sebeok, 2. 1. 5.

76. Cheremis: Genetz, 39 = Sebeok, 2. 8. 2 (On the stove a big wolf howls.—Ringing of a bell). Serbian: Novaković, p. 59, No. 10 (God's rooster is singing outside. Whenever it starts to sing, everyone goes to it) and p. 60, Nos. 1, 2 (bull). For comparisons of a bell to a bird with a single wing see Taylor, *English,* 472 and to a cock with a long tail see Taylor, *English,* 1326.

77. The "fast black duck" is the puff of smoke that follows the bullet or, less probably, the wadding. Riddlers have often called a bullet a flying bird; see the headnote to Taylor, *English,* 379–380. Lithuanian: Sabaliauskas, p. 319, Nos. 81, 82; Mickevicius, p. 583, No. 24 (A wingless bird came flying and [although it was] without teeth, it bit a man). The last of these riddles is obviously related to the comparison of a snowflake to a wingless bird that a handless or mouthless maiden devours. For discussion of this snowflake riddle see the headnote to Taylor, *English,* 367–369.

78. I can cite no parallel to this riddle, which is an adaptation of No. 77 to a new theme. In this riddle the "fast black duck" seems to be the eye. For examples of a comparison used to describe two entirely different things see the note to No. 476–478.

79. For the comparison of a cow's teats to geese see Nos. 83, 84, 321, 322. The *tertium quid comparationis* is the white color.

80. Compare the Georgian "*Kakha, kakha,* a cherry tree (*kakhambali*), in it five seeds grew, one can neither eat nor drink [them] nor even climb to the top" (Glushakov, p. 22, No. 7) and "A crooked tree and a real tree, five grains grew on it" (Glushakov, p. 32, No. 67). See the discussion in the headnote to Taylor, *English,* 1040–1041.

81. A goose and a plow are similar in shape, and both dig in the ground. Compare also the riddle for writing discussed in the headnote to Taylor, *English,* 1063.

82. The aptness of the comparison to a goose is not obvious. See a survey of the Mongolian comparisons used to describe a louse in the note to No. 105. For comment on the adjective "voiceless" see the note to No. 299.

83, 84. For parallels to the comparison of a cow's teats to geese see the note to No. 79. For a survey of Mongolian riddles for milking a cow see the note to No. 889.

85. For parallels see the headnote to Taylor, *English,* 1042–1044.

86. The same scene serves to describe spinning in No. 91 and drawing water in No. 92. For other examples of a scene used in riddles having entirely different answers see the note to No. 476–478.

87. Siberian Turkish: Katanov, p. 93, No. 783 (Nine birds drank water from Hua-Kem.—Dipping a pen into ink). See similar references to a parrot in No. 93, a swan in No. 98, and a camel in No. 155. Compare also the note to No. 73.

88. Comparisons of the sun or moon to an animal with horns, tail, or reins projecting into a house (see the headnote to Taylor, *English,* 412–413, § 9) or to a person whose hair similarly projects (see the headnote to Taylor, *English,*

544, § 10) are numerous. Comparisons of this sort to a bird are rather rare.

89. In this Mongolian text the mouse is the tongue. In an Aandonga riddle, "The mouse ran along the trail" (Pettinen, p. 227, No. 5), the mouse is the food. This Mongolian riddle is expressed in terms of two animals. In No. 262 below the description is in terms of two horses, in No. 332 in terms of a person and a mouse, in No. 553 in terms of two persons, in No. 806 in terms of unspecified actors, and in No. 966 in terms of a thing. For the many different comparisons of eating to threshing or grinding see the headnote to Taylor, *English*, 841, §§ 4, 5. For comparisons naming several persons see the headnote to Taylor, *English*, 980–982. See also Modern Greek: Polites, 17. Kuanyama Ambo: Loeb, 13 (A dove runs along a branch, —Ball of porridge runs down the throat).

90. Siberian Turkish: Katanov, p. 143, No. 1173 (On the top of Poshtag there is a hill like a camel foal at which a golden magpie is pecking). See a different description of a mandarin's button in No. 915 below.

For parallels to the formula "on the top of the Alkhanai" see Nos. 53 (on a hill), 68 (on an undefiled dune), 96 (on the top of a black hillock), 164 (on a hill), 201, 333 (on a white dune), 347 (on the summit of the eastern mountain), 414 (on the saddle-like pass), 645 (on the top of the Altai and Khangai mountains), 664 (on the summit of the northern mountain), 666 (on the summit of the sandalwood mountain), 690 (on top of a cone-shaped mountain), 691 (on the pointed peak), 708 (on a solid hillock), 710 and 711 (on a solitary mountain), 747 (on the mountain), 748 (on the top of a mountain range), 821 (on a mountain), 879 (on the honey ridge). For the formula "behind the mountain" or "from behind the mountain" see the note to No. 112.

91, 92. See No. 86 and the note. For other examples of a comparison used to describe entirely different things see the note to Nos. 476–478.

93. See the note to No. 87.

94. Compare a Lappish riddle cited in the note to No. 177. Turkish: Bahaeddin, 83 (Riddle me, riddle me ree, sons [and] servants twelve, the spade of the twelve, their arse grows on the earth.—Tent). Nandi: Hollis, p. 142, No. 39 (I despatched the advisers, and they entered the earth.—Poles of a house).

96. For parallels to the formula "on the top of a black hillock" see the note to No. 90.

97. A Lithuanian description of beer foaming in a vessel mentions a bird: "A pine forest, beneath it a hazelnut tree, under it a pond, in the pond a white goose" (Daukantas, 2). Although the general meaning of both the Mongolian and the Lithuanian riddle is clear, the explanation of the details is difficult. For a survey of Mongolian riddles for alcoholic liquors and distilling see the note to No. 337. For parallels to the formula "at the source (or: mouth) of the black river" see the note to No. 38.

98. The swan is the pen imported from the south (China); see the note to No. 274. The canal is the inkwell or the Chinese ink-slab. The interpretation of the eternal mountain is obscure. One thinks of the mythical mountain Sumeru, but there is no obvious pertinence in a reference to it. For similar riddles describing writing or the instruments used in writing see the note to No. 87.

99. The Ölöt are Kalmucks living between Lake Kuku-Nor and Volga and the Don. Comparisons of a lock to a bird are not numerous, but see the Mordvin "A sparrow hold an ox" (Paasonen, 212; Ahlqvist, p. 41, No. 11 = Ahlqvist, *Koksha Mordvin*, 37). This has a Cheremis parallel in Porkka, 67 = Sebeok, 2.2.7.1. See further the Mordvin "A sparrow sleeps by the door" (Paasonen and Ravila, p. 630, No. 1); the Votyak "A little bird protects the house" (Wichmann, 172); the Serbian "A sparrow rides on a she-bear.—Padlock on a chest" (Novaković, p. 85, No. 6); and a Turkish riddle quoted in the note to No. 418 below.

100. I can cite only parallels that have the answer spider. See the Bulgarian "A cricket swam across the sea, neither did it die nor did the sea stir" (Ikonomov, 44. See also Bozhov, 92). This conception is allied to the one discussed in the note to No. 140 below and to the Irish "A bobbed trimmed brown little gelding would traverse Ireland and not wet its feet" (De Bhaldraithe, 26 = Hull and Taylor, *Irish*, 105). See also the Taveta "[That which] reaches the other bank [of the river]" (Hollis, 3) and the Yao "Spin string that we may cross the river" (Werner, p. 213 = Werner, *Nyassa*, p. 82, No. 5). The notion of crossing water without wetting the feet is also used to describe a fly; see the headnote to Taylor, *English*, 431–432, § 2. It serves also to describe the sun and the moon; see Taylor, *English*, 165–173, § 2 and 431.

102. The Basque version in a comparison in terms of a person: "Who dresses himself in the evening and undresses in the morning?" (Cerquand, 40). Compare also the note to No. 191 below.

103. Compare also the Siberian Turkish riddle for a balalaika: "In the forest they cut a log. From above they stretch (?) strings. They don't say thus and so. They stretch its ears" (Moshkov, p. 271, No. 84). This has Turkish parallels: "They cut down a pine tree (hollowed it out), inside they put a *tin ton dan din*, my resounder doesn't cry, they twist your ears.—Fiddle-bow, lyre, remence" (Hamamizade, 374. See also his No. 375). In these riddles the speaker wavers between a comparison to a thing and a comparison to an animal. See also the Uraon riddle for locking a lock: "Go if you must but twist your ear as you go" (Archer, 206).

104. Snivel is ordinarily compared to a person or persons as in Nos. 324, 377, and 378 below, but note the comparison to a wolf in No. 306.

105. The creature to which the louse is compared varies. It is a goose in No. 82, a pig in No. 105, and a dog without a voice in No. 299. See also the Samoyede "The wild reindeer wanders in the dark forest" (Lehtisalo, 168) and "In a dense forest without an open place there wanders a six-footed elk with difficulty and distress" (Lehtisalo, 198). Cheremis: Sebeok, 2.5.1.1.–3 (pig). For additional parallels see the headnote to Taylor, *English*, 488.

106. Muria: Elwin and Archer, p. 269, No. 30 (A little pig has a cord in its bottom). The animals mentioned in parallels to this riddle vary greatly. The Estonian "An iron cat, a woolen tail" (Wiedemann, p. 285) is a rare version. For additional parallels see the note to No. 197 below and the headnote and note to Taylor, *English*, 386.

108. See the Siberian Turkish "My black sheep is capacious, my big whip is bent, the top side is moist, the end of my horn is moist.—Kettle, pipes, lid, and trough used for distilling" (Katanov, p. 466, No. 35). For a survey of Mongolian riddles for distilling and for alcoholic liquors see the note to No. 337 below.

109. For riddles making a comparison to an animal, man, or thing having an unusual number of wrappings or garments see Nos. 226 and 227 (horse), 449 and 450 (man), and 863 (ball). For parallels see the headnote to Taylor, *English*, 1439. Surinam: Penard and Penard, 30, 31.

Western European riddles usually employ a comparison to a person; eastern European riddles employ comparisons to a person or an animal and, more rarely, to a thing. I do not understand the appropriateness of the comparison in describing a cricket or grasshopper: "A girl bred in the swamp, dressed in nine layers of silk" (Dyrenkova, 25).

111. For parallels see the headnote to Taylor, *English*, 48–55, § 7. The comparison of a crab to a sheep is appropriate only because both creatures have legs and can be eaten. A Neo-Latin versifier describes a species of crab that has eight and not six feet and says that it can be eaten: "Brachia bina, pedes octo, testamque rubentem Qui gero, regales saepius orno dapes" (Buchler, *Gnomologia*, 3d ed., 477, Mainz, 1614). The Hawaiians say of a squid, "My little animal with eight hands" (Judd, 72. See also his No. 70).

112. Comparisons of the celestial bodies, especially the stars, to sheep are numerous; see the note to No. 120, and the headnote to Taylor, *English*, 484–486 and the note to 484.

For the formula "behind the mountain" or "from behind the mountain" see Nos. 222c, 259 (from behind a rock), 281 (on the other side of the mountain), 706a, 707 (on the other side of five hills), 791, 969.

113. The sheep is the mitten covering the jug. For parallels to the notion of a creature exhibiting wounds or lacking an essential member see Nos. 1 (creature without a throat), 100 (jerboa without bones), 113 (sheep without lower jaw), 114 (sheep [cow?] without front leg), 115 (sheep with a hole in its navel), 116 (ram with torn belly), 135 (earless sheep), 152 (camel without chin), 171 (camel without jaws), 188 (hornless calf), 189 (ox without ribs), 191 (swollen side of black cow), 299 (dog without voice), 734 (torn eagle's hide). I have not included in this list riddles in which the creature functions satisfactorily in spite of the defect (flies without wings or the like). References to a camel without a neck are collected in the note to No. 148. Descriptions of this sort seem to be especially popular among the Mongols, but compare the Yakut riddle for a house and a door, "A brownish bull stands with his flank torn apart" (Ionova, 57), and the Russian riddle for a chest by the wall, "There runs the little wolf, his side is torn out" (Sadovnikov, 237). An Armenian riddle for a fireplace, "A black hen with a ripped belly" (Zielinski, p. 57, No. 13), resembles a Turkish riddle cited in the note to No. 418 below and has another Turkish parallel in Bahaeddin, 75. Comparisons to a person having a defect are collected in the note to No. 363. For comparisons to a thing having a defect see the note to No. 779.

114. Compare the Turkish jacket riddle, "It has hands but no legs, its belly is torn, it has no blood" (Hamamizade, 87). For parallels to the notion of an animal with a defect see the note to No. 113.

115. Mongolian riddlers describe a lock in many different ways; see the Index of Solutions. For parallels to the notion of an animal with a defect see the note to No. 113 and compare the examples of a man with a hole in his body collected in the note to No. 434.

118. Siberian Turkish: Katanov, p. 286, No. 210 (Among my ten thousand sheep runs a shaggy ram.—Mixer that stirs toasting barley). See also the comment in the note to No. 125 below and the texts collected in the headnote to Taylor, *English*, 489–490.

120. For parallels see Nos. 112, 122, and 123 and the note to No. 112.

121. Siberian Turkish: Katanov, *Urianchai*, 5 (I drove my thousand black sheep with an iron stick).

122. The riddler has adapted this riddle to the answer "sun" by the adjective "golden."

123. The answer is usually "moon"; see No. 120 and the note.

124. Although there are many lambs and cattle (i.e., many colored objects in the fields), there is no food (i.e., these lambs and cattle are not edible). Compare the Scotch Gaelic "A shaggy, shaggy clump, ever haunting the mountain; whiter it is than the goats of the hills, whiter than sheep, the shaggy clump.—Bog cotton" (Nicolson, p. 35).

For comment on Manjushrī see the note to No. 764. The pertinence of this reference to him is obscure. For parallels to the formula "on the southern mountains" see the note to No. 90.

125. Mongolians mix tea with salt and pound it in a mortar. The comparison used here is used in No. 118 to describe rye pounded in a mortar. The tea riddle seems to have been suggested by the writing riddle, Nos. 126–129. For other examples of a theme used to describe two different objects see the note to Nos. 476–478.

126–129. Although the answers to these riddles differ somewhat, they all deal with the act of writing or its results. For parallels see Soqotri: Müller, 15 (My enclosure is white, black sheep are in it, a fine little staff is in it. If the staff moves quickly, there will be many black sheep. —Writing). Palestinian Arabic: Ruoff, p. 22, No. 17 (Black sheep, whose herdsman is a stick. As often as the stick is broken, it increases). Ruoff's interpretation of the last sentence is not entirely clear. Probably the riddler means much the same thing as the Soqotri riddler. For additional parallels see the headnote and notes to Taylor, *English*, 1063, nn. 1, 13. The comparison used in this riddle occurs also in No. 125, which has an entirely different answer. For other examples of comparisons used to describe different objects see the note to Nos. 476–478 below.

130. Gomboyev's reference to his No. 35 should be to his No. 36, which is in this collection No. 131. For comparisons of a spindle to a colt see No. 260 and to a dog see No. 301. For other comparisons see No. 133 and the note below and the headnote to Taylor, *English*, 1455–1457, § 2. The comparison used in this riddle is used in Nos. 131, 132 to describe a different object. For other examples of a comparison used to describe different objects see the note to Nos. 476–478.

131, 132. See also the Mongolian comparisons of ashes to a grayish bull (No. 181) and a colt (No. 261). See further the Tungus "The he-goat gets fat on one spot" (Poppe, 14) and the Siberian Turkish "A crooked sheep grows fat while lying down" (Radlov, 1: 261, No. 10). No doubt the Yakut "They say that someone who remains lying down takes on weight.—Sweepings or garbage" (Ionova, 108) is the same riddle. The comparison used here to describe ashes is used in No. 130 to describe a spindle. For other examples of a comparison used to describe different objects see the note to Nos. 476–478.

133. See the general remarks on the comparison used in this riddle in the note to No. 130. For parallels to the specific comparison to a sheep that grows fat see Mordvin: Paasonen and Ravila, p. 650, No. 2. Altai Turkish: Menges, p. 86, No. 116 (My gray sheep has grown fat in running continuously). Lithuanian: Sabaliauskas, 24 (A pretty little sheep eats to satiation, whenever it runs); Basanavicius, p. 196, No. 160 ("Be gone, you gray one [i.e., sheep], you grow fat while running"). It is uncertain what creature the speaker had in mind in the Greek "It rises and falls and grows fat without eating; it only spins around and fills its tummy" (Stathes, p. 303, No. 7; Polites, p. 215, No. 127); the Hungarian "It runs and that is its way of filling its belly" (*Magyar Nyelvör* 9: 37, No. 3, [1880] and 40: 334, No. 39, [1911]); and the Russian "The more I turn, the more I grow" (Sadovnikov, 576).

134. Compare No. 38 above, in which the species of animal intended is uncertain. The import of the riddle is obscure. For parallels to the formula "at the source of the river" see the note to No. 38.

135. For parallels to the notion of an animal with a defect see the note to No. 113.

136, 139. The black ram in No. 136 and the buxom woman in No. 139 represent the pestle. For parallels see the note to Taylor, *English*, 397 and compare the Santal

"The hobby horse from the jungle on whom the women soldiers canter" (Elwin and Archer, p. 306, No. 29).

140. Serbian: Novaković, p. 226, No. 1 (The rabbit jumped into the sea, the sea got tired of it, but not the rabbit.—Splinter). As the parallels show, the riddler is referring to a splinter in the eye. The confused Bulgarian "A board fell into the sea. Neither did the sea stir nor did the board drown.—Rustle on the water" (Gubov, 416) has a new and not entirely appropriate solution. Better versions are the Russian "An oak fell into the sea, the sea weeps but the oak does not.—Dust in the eye" (Sadovnikov, 1784) and the Mordvin "A fallen tree fell across the sea. The fallen tree did not suffer, but the sea suffers.—Eye and a particle of dirt" (Paasonen and Ravila, p. 652, No. 8. Compare also Paasonen, 243). This comparison is used for both dust in the eye and flesh between the teeth. In No. 157 the animal is a camel, in No. 265 it is a colt, and in No. 305 it is a fox. For additional parallels see a riddle for a spider cited in the note to No. 100 above and the note to Taylor, *English*, 1176.

141. The Lapps express a similar conception in terms of a man: "Do you know the man who bends with every breeze and never wearies?—Protection over the smokehole" (Qvigstad, 21). For other descriptions of the flap over the smokehole see the Index of Solutions.

142. For comparisons of a shadow to something that cannot be cut see the note to No. 16. Note also the comparisons to something that falls and is not broken cited in the headnote to Taylor, *English*, 1192–1196, § 3.

143. The long hairs under a wolf's chin resemble, when it runs, the undulations of the hairs on a camel's neck. For riddles describing something, usually an animal, as being composed of the members of several different animals see the note to No. 472. See Nos. 408 and 409 below.

144, 145. The same comparison serves to describe two entirely different objects. For other examples of the use of the same comparison to describe different objects see the note to Nos. 476–478.

144. The significance of the red silk is not clear. For parallels see the headnote and note to Taylor, *English*, 484.

145. The appropriateness of the various comparisons is obscure.

146. The Mongolians use a similar comparison to describe a file (No. 218 below) and a thimble (No. 231 below). For the conventional use of eighty thousand as a very large number see Nos. 218, 231, 647, and 648.

147. See a similar comparison for a pine in No. 921 below.

148. See also the Korean "What is it that carries a load day and night?—Shelf" (Bernheisel, p. 62), the Yakut "Every day they ride on a tireless steed.—Bench" (Priklonskii, 94), and the Abyssinian "An ass that does not cry, 'Yah!'—Bench" (Littmann, Tigriña, 51). The theme of these riddles is closely related to texts discussed in the headnote to Taylor, *English*, 138–140, nn. 29, 31, 32. For parallels to the notion of a creature, usually a camel, without a neck, a notion which is not altogether intelligible in the present connection, see Nos. 21, 149, 150, 151, 153, 154.

149. The aptness of the comparison of a road to a camel without a neck is not obvious. For parallels to such a camel see the note to No. 148.

151. For an African parallel see the headnote to Taylor, *English*, 1643–1654, § 8.

153. For a similar comparison to colts that cannot be caught see the headnote to Taylor, *English*, 1643–1654, n. 6. See also the Cherekessian "Gallops better than you, gallops better than I; should you start after it, you will not catch it" (Tambiev, p. 61, No. 95). Russian: Sadovnikov, 1907 (Brother's horse cannot be caught).

154. For parallels see Taylor, *English*, 339 and the note.

155. The Mongols, and especially the lamas, usually write Tibetan and not Mongolian, if they write at all. For somewhat similar comparisons see the note to No. 87.

156. Compare the Lamba "A huge patch of felled trees and the corn may be caught in the hand.—The head. Is it not big? When one puts the hair in one's hand, one doesn't bring a basket and let it get full, no!" (Doke, 74). See also the parallels cited by Doke and those in the headnote to Taylor, *English*, 1042–1044. A similar Mongolian riddle (No. 170 below) makes a reference to the camel grinding its teeth.

157. For parallels see the note to No. 140 above.

158, 159. Siberian Turkish: Katanov, p. 615, No. 70 (Fire flashed from a lasso). See the parallels collected in the note to Taylor, *English*, 436, and compare Nos. 212, 243, and 513 in this collection.

160, 161. Compare the Yakut "When the son of God is waving his golden belt, the earth is trembling" (Ionova, 29) and "He stands and waves his golden belt" (Piekarski, 50). Several versions of the not entirely intelligible Irish "I see coming towards me along the road a young mare whinnying, a lustrous spot on her forehead and the rest of her in the fire" (Ó Dálaigh, 158 = Hull and Taylor, 110) have been reported. For parallels from various countries to the Lithuanian "Neighing in Turkey, the bridle flashes on the other side" (Basanavicius, p. 191, No. 41) see the headnotes to Taylor, *English*, 398, nn. 6, 7 and 436, nn. 19–21. For a similar comparison of a braying donkey or horse to shooting a gun see the note to Nos. 158, 159 above.

For entirely different conceptions of thunder or thunder and lightning see the Kxatla "Tell me: the bottle broke and twenty pieces came out" and "Tell me: down below, down below at Moxalakwena [signifying any place 'down the river'] where a troop of boys are playing with axes" (Schapera, 7, 8).

162. The pertinence of the solution is not clear. The same comparison is used for entirely different objects in Nos. 159–161 and 163. For other examples of a comparison used to describe entirely different objects see the note to Nos. 476–478.

163. The solution should be "flint and steel."

164, 165. See the comparisons to two different animals in No. 318 and to two persons in No. 608 and the survey of riddles for buttons in the note to No. 608. For parallels see Siberian Turkish: Katanov, p. 238, No. 150 (Beyond the mountains a bear is being choked) and p. 239, No. 56 (Between ridges a boundary mark [?] is squeezed). Shor: Dyrenkova, 12 (In the forest the bear crushed himself). Russian: Sadovnikov, 630 (Little Danilo choked himself in a noose). Albanian: Hahn, p. 160, No. 13 (The sister seizes the brother by the throat). Compare also the Cheremis description of the strings used to tie a shirt: "Two barren women struggle together all day" (Sebeok, 3. 8. 15. 1). For parallels to the formula "on a hill" see the note to No. 90.

166, 167. The center post holds the rafters together and can therefore be said to be biting them. Compare the Munda "The snake feeds her children from many breasts. —Central beam of house" (Elwin and Archer, p. 290, No. 21) and the Turkish "I have many children, a pillow is at the point of their heads.—Columns supporting the ceiling" (Orhan, 1: 4). For other descriptions of rafters see Nos. 177 (with the note), 223, 282, and 312.

170. The similar comparison in No. 156 does not involve a reference to the noise made by the supposed camel.

171. Compare Nagaibak: Vitevskii, p. 276, Nos. 12 (Small, crook-backed, finishes [or: goes over] all the field. —Sickle), 13 (Flashes, flashes, and having licked, swallows it). For comparisons to an animal having a defect see the note to No. 113.

172. For parallels and discussion see the note to Taylor, *English*, 396 and Archer Taylor, "Attila in Modern Riddles," *Journal of American Folklore* **56**: 136–137, 1943. See further No. 207 below and the Siberian Turkish "A winged black horse ran off, but the saddle cloth and *kechin* remained.—Prairie fire in forest and the ashes left behind" (Katanov, p. 369, No. 339). The meaning of *kechin* is obscure. Serbian: Novaković, p. 15, Nos. 4–6 and p. 16, Nos. 1–4. A Serbian riddle for a still, "Where my ox lay last year, that place can be recognized this year" (Novaković, p. 82, No. 3) is a specialization of the usual answer. A rare variation occurs in a Yakut riddle for a spot burned by tinder: "Where a man beating a tambourine strikes, the place will not disappear in nine centuries" (Iastremskii, 202).

In Africa riddlers express this idea in a very different way; see the Wanamwezi "A old woman died and left her backbone" (Dahl, 3), the Lamba "That which does not become effaced.—Ash heap" (Doke, 57), and the Ewe "On the resting place of the animals one still finds hairs.—Ashes" (Spieth, p. 598, No. 11).

173. For parallels to the comparison of teeth to cattle see the headnote to Taylor, *English*, 499–501. For parallels to the formula "in a ditch (well)" see the note to No. 61 above.

174. For parallels see Taylor, *Ainu*, 18 and the note.

175. Mordvin: Paasonen and Ravila, p. 661, No. 2 (It has three legs, no rump). Turkish: Zavarin, *Brusa*, 34 (A something with three legs. Whoever doesn't know it is an ass). Lithuanian: Mickevicius, p. 577, Nos. 29 (Three little sisters wear a garland), 30 (Three boys wear a cap). Compare the Siberian Turkish "Three lads girt with one belt" (Katanov, p. 241, No. 91).

176. For parallels see the headnote to Taylor, *English*, 1455–1457, § 1 and compare No. 593 below.

177. For a comparison of the poles that meet at the smokehole to a herd of camels and a biting camel see Nos. 166, 167 above and the note. See also the comparison to a tiger in No. 312. The Lappish "Four sisters peep into a hole.—Tips of tent poles" (Donner, 20; Qvigstad, 96) is probably a variation of a riddle for a cow's teats; see the note to No. 889 below. It resembles No. 94 above, which describes the lower ends of the lattice. Compare the Samoyede riddle for rafters, "Two old women cling together by their hair" (Lehtisalo, 150. See also his Nos. 156, 203, 253), the Chuvash riddle for the poles of the barn in which grain is dried, "Thirty pine trees have one crown (or: tip)" (Mészáros, 72). A Lamba comparison to birds is curious: "The larks from here, there, and everywhere gathered in one place" (Doke, 142). See also the headnote to Taylor, *English*, 1027–1028, § 3.

179. The large steelyard is called täloor. The small steelyard, which is called chingnoor, is used for weighing silver. For other comparisons to animals of contrasting colors see No. 262 and the note.

180. The pertinence of the riverbank is obscure. For comparisons to rams in a courtyard see Nos. 118, 119.

181. See the note to No. 131.

184, 185. For parallels see the headnote to Taylor, *English*, 632–644, but comparisons to an animal are rare. See, however, the comparison to a chamois (No. 275) and note the curious comparison to a thing in a Bihari lentil riddle: "A fat little queen as stone [*sic*]; if you break her, she is then a small box of vermillion" (Mitra, *Bihar*, 23).

186. The striped cow is the felt tent and the shovel is the flap or door.

187. Compare the note to Taylor, *English*, 353.

191. See the comparisons to a hare (No. 102) and to burying a camel's head (No. 728). For parallels to the notion of an animal with a defect see the note to No. 113.

192. Compare Nos. 223, 272, and 522.

193. See the note to No. 16.

196. The brindled ox that spreads its legs is a gun rest rather than the trigger. For parallels see the note to Nos. 11, 12 above.

197. The Buriats attach a peg to a hair halter that pierces the bull's nose. In order to keep the halter from dragging on the ground, it is thrown over the horns. For parallels see Nos. 106 (peg), 278 (she-goat), and 307 (wolf) in this collection; the headnote to Taylor, *English*, 394–404 and the note to No. 437.

198. See No. 266. For comparisons of the eye to a particolored animal see the note to No. 801.

199. For comparisons of the tongue to a bull or calf see the headnote to Taylor, *English*, 499–501. Yakut: Iastremskii, 173 (In a meadow covered with birch trees a brown cow is fastened); Ionova, 4 (A reddish cow is peeping out of a birch grove). Kosi: Ittmann, 117 (Large stones encircle a squirrel, it hides among them).

Comparisons of the tongue to an animal that lives in water are not nuumerous. See the Uraon "A fish jumps in a cup of water" (Elwin and Archer, p. 294, No. 34) and "A fish that sports in a drop of water" (Archer, 32), the Gondi "A well-cleaned and polished house, the home of a frog" (Elwin and Archer, p. 276, No. 16) and "A fish swims between two shells, one above and one below" (Elwin and Archer, p. 276, No. 11), the Baiga "The walls of the well are made of wood. In the water swims a crocodile" (Elwin and Archer, p. 272, No. 18), and the headnote to Taylor, *English*, 497–510, § 6.

200. This riddle has been suggested by the tongue and teeth riddle (No. 199). For other examples of riddles employing the same means of comparison but having different answers see the note to Nos. 476–478 below. Note the comparison of the eyes to a particolored horse in No. 338 and the survey of the comparisons of the eyes to something particolored in the note to No. 828.

201. For parallels to the formula "on the mountain" see the note to No. 90. Here, as is often the case, the supposed mountain is the human head.

202. A Mongolian lock is opened by thrusting in the key. The cry "Tchoo!" is used in driving an animal.

207. Estonian: Wiedmann, p. 264 (An ox lies on the ground, the spot remains for seven years) and pp. 273, 286. For parallels naming animals other than an ox see the note to No. 172 above.

209. Yakut: Priklonskii, 87 (You can't hold it on the palm of the hand, you can't pick it up with your hand). Ila: Smith and Dale, **2**: 330 (You who are so clever: you can't tie water in a lump) and a variant on the same page. See also the headnote to Taylor, *English*, 1643–1654, § 7 and the Irish "I would take it in my grasp, and the king can't put a withe on it.—A handful of sand" (Ó Máile, 50 = Hull and Taylor, *Irish*, 452).

210. Comparisons for distilling and for alcoholic liquors are surveyed in the note to No. 337. The comparison for alcoholic liquor found in this riddle resembles the comparison of wine or brandy to a foolish person, for which see the headnote to Taylor, *English*, 1017–1035, nn. 13, 15, 23.

211. Baluchi: Dames, *Panjab Notes and Queries* **2**: 70, § 423, No. 3, 1885 (The black mare is saddled and the children's hearts are glad.—Putting the griddle on the fire). For parallels to the second clause see the note to No. 341 below. Compare Irish: Hull and Taylor, *Irish*, 132 (A black sheep with a white fleece).

212. See Nos. 158 and 159 for a similar comparison to a camel.

213. For parallels see the headnote to Taylor, *English,* 871–877 (especially p. 327) and the note to Taylor, *Ainu,* 21. Chuvash: Karahka and Räsänen, 36 (A red cow licks the rump of a black cow), 37 (A black dog is hung up, a red dog barks at it). Note also a picturesque SeSuto description of a fire under a black pot and the white milk boiling over: "The red ox hits the black, the black the white, which jumps out of the kraal" (Norton and Velaphe, 49).

216. Comparisons of the stars to a herd of cattle are not as numerous as comparisons to a herd of horses and especially to a herd of sheep.

218. Compare No. 146 above with the note, the Yakut "A naked child suffering from the itch is lying in the corner" (Ionova, 106) and "They say there is a child in a rash" (Iastremskii, 325), and "On the end of the bench lies a pimply old man, they say" (Popov, p. 289). See also the texts cited in the headnote to Taylor, *English,* 576–577, nn. 9, 10. For the conventional use of the number eighty thousand see the note to No. 146.

219. The Mongolians think that an ant works with the upper part of its body. See another version of this riddle in No. 230 below, the riddles for an ant cited in the Index of Solutions, and the Uraon "Big-headed but not an elephant, thin-waisted but not a leopard, digs a hole but is not a mouse, climbs a tree but is not a snake" (Archer, 232). This Uraon riddle has some similarity to a Mongolian cockroach riddle, No. 759 below. For references to the pacing legs of an animal see the note to No. 373 below.

220, 221. The bones of the legs contain marrow, and the skull contains the brain. The riddler compares the marrow and the brain to unborn foals.

221. The Mongolian *yil* may be I-li in Chinese Turkestan, the home of a famous breed of horses. Golstunskii translates: "The mares are not pregnant." In the light of No. 220, we should expect: "The mares are with foal."

222. Compare the Samoyede "When evening comes, he lets his reindeer go individually. By daybreak not a single reindeer, nothing is there" (Lehtisalo, 227), the Mordvin "The field has not been measured, the sheep have not been counted" (Paasonen and Ravila, p. 657, No. 10), the Juang "At night they wander everywhere. They go nowhere by day. What Gaur [a demon] grazes them that there is no dung?" (Elwin and Archer, p. 278, No. 9), and the Serbian "As large as the unmeasured field, it is full of uncounted sheep; in front of them is Ogran, the shepherd; behind them is Lasak, the dog.—Sun, stars, and moon" and "A measureless field; Marche, the shepherd boy; behind them a mad Bulgarian" (Novaković, p. 217, Nos. 6, 7). For the comparison of stars to sheep see Taylor, *English,* 484 with the headnote and note.

223. The circular roofpiece permits light to enter and smoke to escape. The poles attached to it support the felt that forms the roof of the tent. Compare the riddles for the roof and rafters cited in the headnote to Taylor, *English,* 993 and in this collection Nos. 166, 167, and 192 with the notes.

224. Yakut: Piekarski, 53 (They say that a white mare forced her tail through the window). Mordvin: Paasonen and Ravila, p. 616, No. 7 (A gray stallion looks in at the chimney). Cheremis: Seboek, 2. 12. 14. 1 (A white foreheaded gelding looks through the fence.—Moon), 2. 12. 14. 2. For additional parallels see Taylor, *English,* 413 with the headnote and note.

226. This use of the comparison is rare. Its ordinary use appears in the following riddle, No. 227. For other examples of a comparison used to describe entirely different things see the note to Nos. 476–478.

227. For Mongolian riddles based on a similar comparison see the note to No. 109. For parallels to this riddle, which usually has the solution "onion," see Taylor, *English,* 1439 and the note.

230. Compare No. 219 above and the note.

231. Compare No. 218 (file) with the note and the Russian "A sow comes from Petersburg, all full of holes" (Preobrazhenskii, p. 173) and the headnote to Taylor, *English,* 1333, n. 2. For references to the conventional use of the number eighty thousand see the note to No. 146 above.

232. The answer should probably be "earring"; see Nos. 233, 234.

233, 234. Siberian Turkish: Radlov, I, 261, No. 1 (A yellow colt is beside the hearer); Katanov, p. 91, No. 762 (Outside that with which I hear is my roan steed, as red as blood).

The animals or objects used in these comparisons for earrings vary greatly. For comparisons to living creatures see the Cheremis "A white goose sits upon iron wire.—An ear ornament made of fluff" (Seboek, 2. 2. 4. 2. 1 and 2. 2. 4. 2. 2) and "A white pigeon sits glistening" (Sebeok, 2. 2. 5. 1), the Mordvin "A forest, the forest is dark, in the protection of the forest two falcons hop back and forth" (Paasonen, 410), and the Russian "Beyond dark forests the swans danced" (Sadovinkov, 673. See also his No. 672). Compare also the Chuvash riddle for an ornament hanging from a head-dress: "It waves and dangles, a beaked animal is dancing" (Karahka and Räsänen, p. 94, No. 10). For comparisons to things see the Baiga "On the fence a drum is hanging" (Elwin and Archer, p. 272, No. 22 = Elwin, p. 471, No. 69); the Kolarian "The newly bought things they throw behind the house" (Wagner, 53), the Chuvash "Behind the room hangs a lid" (Karahka and Räsänen, p. 100, No. 86); the Turkish "A stone for weighing is on meat; gold swings" (Hamamizade, 435. See also his No. 453 and Bahaeddin, 38), "I hang a sieve on a rock; I put fat in it" (Boratav, 139), and "In raw meat a hook is hung" (Hamamizade, 436, 454). See further the Russian "Under the forest, the forest, bright wheels are hanging, they beautify young girls, they ensnare young men"(Sadovnikov, 671) and "Under a forest, a forest, wheels hang" (Arkhangel'skii, p. 76). This comparison to wheels is also used to describe the ears; see the Lithuanian parallels in the note to No. 872 below.

235, 236. Comparisons of the tongue to a horse are not numerous. See Nos. 246, 314, and 328 below and a few parallels with a discussion of related comparisons in the note to Taylor, *English,* 1149 and the headnote to 1151.

237. Compare No. 241 below. See an entirely different conception of a whetstone in No. 737 below.

240. For comment on the Mongolian windhorse see the note to No. 696.

241. Compare No. 237 above.

242. Turkish: Kowalski, *Zagadki,* 124 (I have a sheep. It grazes on the other slope of the hill; it grazes on this slope [also] and is not satiated).

243. For parallels see the note to Nos. 158, 159 above.

245. The Mongolian *k'yreleng* signifies an enclosure, a courtyard, a walled town, or a monastery and in this riddle probably represents the pool from which the vapors rise. Because the vapors move with the wind the riddler compares them to an ambling horse. For the comparison of a mirage to a gazelle that cannot be caught see No. 280.

246. See Nos. 235, 236 above and the note.

247. The black felt tent is ground that has been burned over. The riddler is perhaps thinking of a tent that has been spread out rather than of one that has been erected. Compare a Yakut riddle for piles of dry grass that are burned in the fields: "A roan mare runs at a trot, a black one lags behind" (Iastremskii, 343). This resembles the Turkish "The yellow ox is lying down and does not rise again; the black ox went away and does not return"

(Boratav, 13). In the Yakut riddle the lagging black mare may be the black ashes left behind; in the Turkish riddle the black ox that goes and does not return is smoke. The Yakut riddle has something in common with the comparison of the seasons to horses; see the texts quoted in the note to No. 716, 717. A curious variation of this theme that I do not fully understand: "Here is the way a roan mare once vanished. First of all its mane vanished" (Iastremskii, 373). Perhaps a bathroom with a fireplace is intended and the vanishing mane is the smoke.

248. The Mongolian words here translated "left" and "right" mean also "wrong" and "correct" and the riddle involves a play on the two meanings. Mongolians usually believe the right to be the correct or proper side and the left to be the wrong side. They button clothes on the right and endeavor, when pouring tea into a cup, to have the stream flow on the right hand side.

I have noted no close parallel to this riddle but compare the Turkish "The hand lies down, the world lies down, the hero (lit.: lion) stretches out his arm" (Hamamizade, 323), the Lappish "The horse stands still, its shoulder moves" (Koskimies and Itkonen, 6), the Russian "A walker walks but would not walk into the house" (Sadovnikov, 73), and the Serbian "A dead donkey hangs on two feathers" (or: lappets of a kerchief) and "The brown horse is lying down while its shoulder walks" (Novaković, p. 23, No. 6, 7). The feathers or lappets (*pero*) in the Serbian riddle are parts of the hinge that holds the door.

249. Compare No. 692. Washing a kettle is somewhat similar to churning. It is here described in terms appropriate to an animal. In No. 393 it is described in terms appropriate to a man.

253. The first two clauses are found also in the gunshot riddle, No. 169 (see also No. 168). For comment on the *joodak khorkoi* see the note to No. 357 below. The last descriptive clause contains nothing enigmatic. Compare the Svanian description in terms of human beings: "There are four brothers. All four work, yet only one receives thanks.—Blacksmith, anvil, hammer, tongs" (W. Nizheradze, p. 1, No. 2). For parallels to the formula "in (or: on) the steppe" see Nos. 318, 461, 479, 560, 813, 814, 832, 854 (in the field), 871, and 945 below.

254. This may be connected with the Irish "I see [coming] from the west towards me three horses, three bridles, three golden pack-saddles, and three wild thistles.—Wind and storm, thunder and flashes of lightning" (Delargy, 58 = Hull and Taylor, *Irish*, 96a) and "I see coming towards me from the west three mares, three bridles, three golden saddles, and three hunting beagles.—A shadow coming wildly through the air on a stormy day" (Ó Dálaigh, 159 = Hull and Taylor, *Irish*, 96b). Compare further the Nandi "A tree fell in Lumbwa, and its branches reached to Nandi. What was the tree?—A great noise" (Hollis, 52). This riddle, which might seem to be particularly appropriate for thunder, is used by the Bantu to describe a word; see Tardy, 22.

254b. According to Mostaert, the Mongolian *jigde-wēr* signifies "one after another"; according to Golstunskii, it signifies "at the same time," which fits the meaning better here.

257. The tsepa is a large migratory bird that flies on the Kalmuck steppes. It is white; the tips of its wings are black; and its voice is very pleasant.

260. See the Chuvash "I have a little horse, it grows fat at the end of a rope" (Karahka and Räsänen, p. 100, No. 79), the Votyak "A hitched horse grows fat" (Wichmann, 5), and the Vogul "A horse turns around" (Ahlqvist, 22. The collector could not translate the adjective applied to the horse). Hungarian: Arany and Gyulai, p. 295, No. 14 = *Magyar Nyelvör* 9: 37, No. 4, 1880 (I have two colts. One runs around and gains weight. The other is resting in *sarju* and nevertheless loses weight). The meaning of *sarju* is obscure. For parallels see the comparison to a maiden in No. 537 below and the texts collected in the headnote to Taylor, *English*, 1455–1457, § 2.

261. See the note to No. 131.

262. For a survey of the various Mongolian versions of this riddle see the note to No. 89 above. Compare the somewhat different Irish "I drove my very little white sheep up to Baile na gCrann [Valley of the Trees] and there was not a stone of a fence that was above that did not fall on my little white sheep.—A piece of bread or potato that you would put into your mouth" (O Máile, 42 = Hull and Taylor, *Irish*, 136). For riddles making a comparison to two animals of contrasting colors see Nos. 179, 183, 196, 213, 214, 255, 263, 283.

263. The colored colt seems to be the kidneys. The renal blood vessels connect the kidneys and the heart.

265. For parallels and discussion see the note to No. 140.

266. See No. 198.

267. Bulgarian: Gubov, 280 (I have a little donkey. Whoever lives steps over it and I, too, step over it). Lithuanian: Mickevicius, p. 590, No. 378 (A little horse is ridden day and night); Jurgelionis, 302 (A small mare ridden day and night), 303 (On a little golden horse everyone rides). Note such Lithuanian variations as "A little foal, a low man; it is ridden during the day and does not always rest at night" (Mickevicius, p. 582, No. 53a) and "All ride [it] and no one feeds [it]" (Jurgelionis, 304 = Basanavicius, 138 = Mickevicius, p. 573, No. 45 and p. 582, No. 37 = Balys, *Fifty Riddles*, p. 327, No. 49). Rumanian: Papahagi, 75 (An outstretched horse is mounted by all who pass). Swedish: Wessman, 395.

A different manner of describing a threshold appears in the Ainu "What is that which peeks from below at any person who comes in any direction?" (Taylor, *Ainu*, 40, citing parallels). See further Siberian Turkish: Moshkov, p. 270, No. 72. Russian: Sadovnikov, 87. Bulgarian: Gubov, 281 (Cut down in the forest, dragged home, and it saw everybody's buttocks). Polish: Kopernicki, 8 (Grandpa sits at home, gaping into everybody's buttocks); Siarkowski, 45. Lithuanian: Basanavicius, 137; Mickevicius, p. 582, No. 53 (A little man from the lowlands looks into everybody's backside); Jurgelionis, 300, 301. The point is obscured in the Breton "Who is the most curious man in the household?" (Sauvé, 108; Sébillot, *Côtes-du-Nord*, 61). See finally the Wamajame "Why do you jump over me, jump over me after all?" (Ovir, 33) and the Kuanyama Ambo "What greets visitors?—The kraal entrance" (Loeb, 31).

268. For parallels see the comparison to sheep in No. 314 above and the texts collected in the note to Taylor, *English*, 497.

269. Note the reference to eight cups in No. 499 and the description of the eight sacrifices on a Buddhist altar in Getty, p. xlviii.

270. Kudara, a village at the mouth of the Selongga River in Transbaikalia, is inhabited by Buriats of the Irkutsk government. Since they are nearer to China and Mongolia than to Russia, they import Chinese and Mongolian merchandise. See also the note to No. 274 below.

Compare the Votyak "The rump of a she-goat becomes hot.—Kettle on the fire" (Wichmann, 42) and the texts collected in the headnote to Taylor, *English*, 871–877.

272. See No. 522 below and compare the note to No. 192.

273. The hobbling refers to the tying of willow branches with leather thongs to make a basket.

274. The adjective Chinese refers to the fact that the object is made in China. See the notes to Nos. 270 and

284. In No. 98 above, "from the South" means "from China." The horn is the handle by which the mill is turned. Compare the Kashmiri "An ass is dancing and the door is shut" (Koul, 11). Uraon: Archer, 131 (The cow with one horn that feeds on its master's food.—Grindstone [of a mill]).

275. For parallels see the note to Nos. 184, 185.

278. For parallels see the note to No. 197.

279. The cloud is steam. For parallels see the note to Nos. 419, 420.

280. For a parallel see No. 245 and compare the headnote to Taylor, *English*, 1643-1654. For references to the fact that one cannot seize a rainbow see Nos. 854, 952 below.

281. Compare No. 318. The word *zirum*, which is here translated "loop," is not in the dictionaries.

282. Compare the Muria and Gondi "A hundred dogs bite a lizard" (Elwin and Archer, p. 268, No. 22 and p. 321). For discussion of this riddle see the note to Nos. 166, 167 above.

283. See the comparisons to a dog and a snake in No. 319 and to a sosalzhin in No. 965.

284. As in No. 274, the adjective Chinese refers to the place where the object is made. See a comparison to a person in No. 521 below.

286. The full meaning of this curious riddle is not entirely clear. Since riddlers have not understood it, they have given varying and conflicting answers. The riddle has enjoyed a surprisingly wide currency. See the Votyak "The emperor Matthias cries aloud, the golden kettle bursts, the worms move.—The cock crows, the sun rises, men stir" (Wichmann, 69), the Cheremis "The silver flute resounds, the royal gate opens, a hairy worm begins to stir.—The cock, daylight, man" (Porkka, 85 = Sebeok, 5. 2. 9. 2) and "A silver flute resounds, the emperor's gate opens" (Wichmann, 206 = Sebeok, 5. 2. 9. 3); the Chuvash "A golden wall board splits, insects of all kinds bestir themselves" (Karahka and Räsänen, 23), the Hungarian "They blow the horn made of bone, golden boards break, the worms of the earth move around" (Kriza, p. 296); *Magyar Nyelvör* 9: 37, No. 1, 1880, and 11: 527, 1882. The Serbians give the answer "Lambs rising when ewes bleat" to the riddle, "The bridle rang, the earth groaned, all the angels rose to their feet" (Novaković, p. 73 and p. 149, No. 6), which seems to be a variation of this theme. Even wider variation is seen in the White Russian "A peahen flies, it fell on a stone, it smashed the stone and woke up the corpses, the corpses stood up and played on little trumpets.—Chickens" (Wasilewski, 41). In "They [the winds] blew on the village, dogs bark, cocks crow, but the people don't get up.—Graves" (Wasilewski, 41) the White Russians seem to have adapted the riddle to a new answer, which seems however to be associated with conceptions characteristic of this riddle. The Serbian dawn riddle, "The thrush sang on the top of the field and announced it to the entire world" (Novaković, p. 64, No. 6) and the Yakut "They say that when you leave the western station, a silver bird sings.—Waning of night and coming of dawn" (Piekarski, 31) may perhaps have a different origin.

Perhaps this notion of worms stirring has some connection with a queer riddle for a house. See the headnote to Taylor, *English*, 906, nn. 12, 13 and the Juang "There stands the elephant. Into its vent the flies go one by one.—Village dormitory" (Elwin and Archer, 277, No. 3), the Kolarian "Grumbling in the stomach of an elephant" (Wagner, 34). Kashmiri: Koul, 30 (Live intestines in a dead female elephant). Munda: Elwin and Archer, p. 289, No. 19. Uraon: Archer, 24 = Elwin and Archer, p. 292, No. 10 (In the belly of the elephant the mainas [starlings] chirp). Serbian: Novaković, p. 108, No. 13 (There is a mare in the middle of a field, living colts are jumping out of her), and p. 109, Nos. 2-8. Samoyede: Lehtisalo, 178. Ila: Smith and Dale, 2: 326, No. 13 (An elephant that swallows something which speaks in its stomach). The resemblance of this African riddle to the Indian versions is noteworthy. For a parallel to the waving elephant in the Mongolian riddle see No. 331 below.

287. A *d'est'in* is somewhat larger than a hectare.

289. Compare the Surinam "A horse with a broken foot runs in the house" (Penard and Penard, 55).

290. I have found no parallel to this comparison of flowing water to a dog. For the many comparisons of flowing water to a running horse see the headnote to Taylor, *English*, 114-118.

291. Yakut: Ionova, 23 (Traces of the jumps of a young man in a clean field are not effaced). This seems to have been suggested by the riddle for a spot where fire has burned as discussed in the note to No. 172 above. For comparisons of writing to making tracks see Nos. 87 (patterns) and 93. A few texts cited in the headnote to Taylor, *English*, 1063 refer to making tracks as equivalent to writing.

292, 293. Yakut: Iastremskii, 92 (Between Khamystakh and Khamagaččaia a white horsehair stretches, they say.—Spinal column of cattle). Samoyede: Lehtisalo, 180 (It penetrates a mountain chain of bone. It is very slim). Togo: Schönhärl, p. 120, No. 161 (The road to Wlawa is crooked.—Intestines). In the Mongolian and Samoyede riddles the mountain is the vertebra, but in a Letsoalo riddle for the temporal vein the mountain represents the head: "The road that winds its way up the mountain" (Krüger, 44). For a comparison of the back to a ridge see the Samoyede "The feet of the man are hanging in the slope of a hairy ridge of earth.—A hook of bone in the lumbar vertebrae of the reindeer" (Lehtisalo, 140). See also the Korean "What is a white stone embedded beyond three elevations?—The fingernail" (Bernheisel, p. 60). The elevations are the joints.

293. The adjective translated "fawning" suggests the twisting of the spinal cord.

294. The reed is the barrel of the gun. For comparisons of a gun to a barking dog see Taylor, *English*, 438, 439. A *khoton* is a hamlet in which a group of closely related Kalmucks live.

295-297. Siberian Turkish: Katanov, *Urianchai*, 15 (Leaving for a grove, the short-legged dog started barking at a tree). Munda: Roy, p. 506, No. 2 (A certain individual keeps quiet while going along, but makes noise [when] he reaches the wood). Kolarian: Wagner, 87. Cheremis: Sebeok, 2. 14. 3. 1-2. Zyrian: Wichmann, 185; Fokos-Fuchs, 2 (In a dark forest a deaf dog barks). Rumanian: Papahagi, 91 (What is that: a mad bear that cries out in the forest?). Modern Greek: Polites, p. 229, Nos. 203, 204. Hungarian: *Magyar Nyelvör* 5: 89, 1876 (A dog without a head is barking in the wood). Note a reversal of the theme in the Kolarian "The trees are being cut, the land [is resounding from] the noise [of the ax].—Dog" (Wagner, 44). For additional parallels to the ax riddle see the headnote to Taylor, *English*, 438-444, § 7.

298. For comment on Bargusi see the note to No. 8.

299. For parallels see the headnotes to Taylor, *English*, 459-460 and 488. For riddles mentioning an animal with a defect see the note to No. 113. For parallels to the comparison of hair to a tree, twig, or reed without a joint see No. 679 below; the headnote to Taylor, *English*, 1116, n. 21; the Yakut "A twig without knots.—Horse's tail" (Iastremskii, 57) and "They say that reeds growing in the south have no nodes.—Horse's tail" (Piekarski, 138); the Siberian Turkish "His tree has no heart-wood and his dog has no voice" (Katanov, p. 369, No. 335); the Asur "On a hard hill is a bamboo without a joint" (Elwin and Archer,

p. 279, No. 2); the Uraon "A bamboo without a joint" (Archer, 79); and a Filipino version communicated to me in manuscript (I have a cane field on my head and the cane has no joints). Since a louse is silent, I do not understand the Samoyede "In the middle of the forest one hears a man crying out" (Lehtisalo, 271), which resembles rather the ax riddle discussed in the note to Nos. 295-297 above. For another Mongolian reference to the louse as a voiceless creature see No. 82.

300. Taylor, *English*, 772. Planing wood is often compared to excreting see Taylor, *English*, 240.

301. Compare Nos. 131 and 133 above.

303. Riddlers have often elaborated intelligently and ingeniously the comparison of a lock to a watchdog. See Yakut: Iastremskii, 367. Zyrian: Wichmann, 192 (A wholly middle-sized dog, it does not bark or growl, but it admits no one). Votyak: Fuchs, p. 243, No. 27. Cheremis: Wichmann, 103 = Wichmann, 223 = Sebeok, 2. 14. 5 (A small dog lies in front of the door. It does not bite, it does not bark, it lets no one enter); Sebeok, 2. 14. 8; Sebeok-Beke, 2. 14. 8. Crimean Tatar: Filonenko, 41 (There is just one cur around, yet the house is closed). Turkish: Hamamizade, 389 (At the door there lies a black dog, he doesn't growl, he doesn't bite, he doesn't go inside himself). Russian: Sadovnikov, 98 (A silent dog guards the entire house), 98a-98d, 99 (A little black doggie lies curled up, she does not bark, she does not bite, yet she does not let anyone enter the house). Lithuanian: Jurgelionis, 310 (Neither barks nor bites, but does not allow entrance to the house). Note also the somewhat different and ingeniously enlarged Lithuanian "A little bitch with curled tail, she does not bark at strangers, she opens the door only to members of the household" (Mickevicius, p. 584, No. 77. See also his p. 585, No. 121 and p. 586, No. 186) and "A bitch was hanged, and her tongue was frozen on her side" (Balys, *Fifty Riddles*, p. 327, No. 42). Albanian: Hahn, p. 162, No. 9 (A black dog watches its door). Variations may be seen in the Serbian "A flea guards the house" (Novaković, p. 85, No. 7) and the Chuvash "It squeaked, it hid in its hole" (Mészáros, 148), which last may be intended to suggest a mouse. The Mongolian riddles for a lock and key vary greatly in the choice of the means of comparison; see the Index of Solutions.

304. See the more usual comparison to a person in Nos. 445 and 451 below and for parallels see the headnote to Taylor, *English*, 946-950. For comparisons to persons making ceremonial acts see the note to No. 363 below.

305. For parallels see the note to No. 140 above.

306. Yakut: Ionova, 2 (Between two lakes a fallen tree is lying, young wolves are peeping out of it.—On the face: eyes; the nose: a piece of wood; and the wolf cubs: mucus). The scene described here is the landscape in which the Yakuts live. See further Piekarski, 115 (Two wolves do nothing all their lives but look out of a den), 176 (Two gray wolves are racing with each other in a straight line); Iastremskii, 187-190; Popov, p. 286 (From a hollowed-out stump a gray ermine peeks, it is said). Siberian Turkish: Katanov, p. 91, No. 767 (A calf was tethered on the steppe and ran away) and p. 180, No. 1403 (Down the steppe went a calf on a long lasso). Turkish: Kowalski, *Asia Minor*, 81 (A blue goat peeped out of a hole). Chivash: Karahka and Räsänen, 39 (Under the haystack an ermine goes out and in). For an unusual comparison to a bird see Russian: Sadovnikov, 1759 (In the fleshy mountains martins make their nests [and] then peep out from there.—Mucus). See also the Chilean Spanish riddle for saliva (probably mucus is intended): "A dove in its dovecote, all see it come out and no one sees it go in" (Laval, p. 91, No. 8). See also the comparisons of mucus in the nose to persons as surveyed in the note to Nos. 377, 378 below and compare No. 104 above.

For parallels to the formula "in (or: through) a valley" see Nos. 7, 364, and the note to Hull and Taylor, *Welsh*, 6. For references to a grassless hollow see the note to No. 692 below.

307. For parallels see the note to No. 197 and Taylor, *English*, 437 with the note. Chuvash: Mészáros, 181 = Karahka and Räsänen, p. 104, No. 132 (Iron dog and oakum tail). Compare the curious Polish "It creeps, it creeps in its fetters. When it reaches the top, it crawls out" (Gustawicz, 63). This is a borrowing of a riddle for a poppy and the seeds falling from the ripe poppyhead; it is discussed in the headnote to Taylor, *English*, 668-680, nn. 16-18.

308b, 308c. Mongolian riddlers use the formula "in a hollow tree" in various ways. Here it is a chimney; in No. 49a it is the wooden sheath for a knife; in No. 510b it is a cradle; and in No. 642 it is a house.

309, 310. In riddles for a knife, like those for a sword, the creature represented as creeping into a hole varies greatly; see the note to No. 49 above. The Dard say, "Darkness from the house, the female demons coming out.— Sword" (Leitner, *Indian Antiquary* 1: 91, No. 6, [1872]), which is not entirely grammatical. For comparisons to a snake see the Bulgarian "Little ash tree, little ash tree, under the little ash tree there is a little hole, in the little hole there is a little snake" (Gubov, 307) and the Hungarian "*Ittyös, fittyös, fittyföllerös*, with a bright tail, a big lawful one. It crawls into holes but is no serpent.— Sword" (*Magyar Nyelvör* 3: 234, No. 13, [1874]). The Bulgarian reference to an ash tree probably implies that the sheath is of ash. For comparisons to other creatures see the Armenian "I hollowed the rotten limb. I buried a lion therein" (Wingate, 13); the Vogul "The mouse gnaws, gnaws, hops back into your room" (Ahlqvist, 24); and the Rumanian "A mad bitch sleeps in a dry block.—Sword" (Papahagi, 5). The curious variation in the Georgian "A dark pit, in it a calf can turn only with difficulty" (Blechsteiner, pp. 12-13, No. 6 = Glushakov, p. 27, No. 33) has a parallel in the Mongolian pestle riddle, No. 474 below.

The comparison to a wolf describes a rifle bullet in the Siberian Turkish "In the hollow there lies a bluish wolf" (Radlov, 1: 261, No. 8). The notion of a creature creeping into a hole is used of a person putting on a shoe in No. 470 and of a key entering the lock in a Polish riddle cited in the note to No. 49.

311. Serbian: Novaković, p. 7, No. 5 (A black cat guards the house). In the Serbian "A little black thing is guarding the house" (Novaković, p. 7, No. 6. See also his p. 85, Nos. 8, 9) the riddlers speak in vague general terms. For discussion of riddles making a comparison of a lock to a dog that guards the house see the note to No. 303.

312. The conception somewhat resembles the Togo "We have killed a pig and make knots with its intestines.—Grass house roof tied with long strands of grass" (Schönhärl, 81). See the discussion in the notes to Nos. 166, 167, and 177 above.

313. The import of the riddle is obscure. It may concern a tale or a myth. See, however, No. 821 below.

314. Kurd: Lescot, p. 347, No. 285 (It is a cavern full of white sheep, a red dog stays near the entrance). Turcoman: Samojlovich, 5 (A corral full of white lambs). See the comparison of teeth to goats in No. 268 above and the discussion of the theme in the headnote to Taylor, *English*, 497-498 and the note to No. 498.

315, 316. The fundamental conception is perhaps most clearly apparent in No. 316, in which the riddler suggests that a hare has the mouth of a camel, the breast of a horse, and the hind legs of a goat. A similar conception is intended in No. 315, but I cannot interpret all the details. See such other hare riddles as the Georgian "The head is like an owl's head, the feet are like straw. Whoever guesses it will get a kopeck from me" (Glushakov, p. 31, No. 62) and the Scotch Gaelic "I see yonder on the ben a dun gray one with a slit under its nose, two long teeth in its head, and a blanket of linen around its buttocks" with a variant, "I see across the headland a jaunty handsome one, the skirt of her shirt under her girdle, and the step of the golden ghost in her foot" (Nicolson, p. 23). For other riddles describing a heterogeneous combination of the members of various animals or the parts of several objects see the note to No. 472.

317. The parallels to riddles of this sort that are collected in the headnote to Taylor, *English*, 397 usually refer to grinding flour. See also the Kashmiri mill riddle, "Shutting the door, the ass dances" (Knowles, 23), and the Russian riddle for buttermilk or cottage cheese, "A ram fought with a goat, there was turmoil between water and sand" (Sadovnikov, 524, 536). See also the comparison of a mill to a goat in No. 274 above.

318. Yakut: Iastremskii, 284 (Two birds kiss). Turkish: Kowalski, *Zagadki*, 1. Bulgarian: Gubov, 159 (One little sparrow chirps from there, another from here, pecking at each other's eyes). For versions mentioning a single animal and for a survey of the themes used see Nos. 164, 165 with the note and especially No. 281. For parallels to the conventional scene "on the steppe" see the note to No. 253.

319. The interpretation of the details is obscure.

321, 322. For the comparison of teats to geese see No. 79 and the note.

323. The man is a plowman and the glittering object is a mould board.

324. For parallels to the comparison of mucus flowing from the nose to persons see Nos. 377, 378, and the note. For a parallel to the comparison to curds or cottage cheese see No. 799.

326. In No. 447 the horse does not appear. Here the riddler has either described the woodpecker twice or has failed to give a complete solution.

328. For a comparison of the tongue to a horse see the note to Nos. 235, 236.

330. The appropriateness of the comparison of roots to horses is not obvious. See also No. 866.

331. The sound *khurī* suggests its use in a shamanist ceremony. The shaman takes an arrow and some brightly colored pieces of cloth, goes into the steppe, and calls the spirits. After each strophe of his song, he shouts *ā khurī, ā khurī*. Compare the reference to a waving elephant in No. 286.

332. For similar riddles see the note to No. 89.

333. The white dune is the tray of the scales, the white bird is the silver ingot, and the southern hills are the arm of the scales. The invented name Dungkhulā rhymes with *unghulā* (resembling a cup). The Mongolian *barūn shil* means "righthand or southern glass, crystal, mirror, form, appearance, exterior." The assertion that the mirror looks into the distance may mean that the beam of the steelyard points upward until it is adjusted. The giver (seller) is a wise man because he will succeed in deceiving the buyer. The adjective "wise" may mean, in this context, "skilled in the art of mining." For parallels to the formula "on a white dune" see the note to No. 90.

335. Compare the Asur "The woman who early in the morning wears a white cloth.—The pot in which rice is boiled and the rice scum which boils up over it" (Elwin and Archer, p. 281, No. 20), the Kharia "The old woman who sits down with a turban" (Elwin and Archer, p. 286, No. 21) with the same answer, and the Estonian riddle for fermenting beer cited in the note to No. 337 below.

336. Kanawari: Joshi, 17 (A handsome whip which cannot be lifted). Uraon: Archer, 80 (A fallen ploughstick that cannot be picked up). Baiga: Elwin, p. 465, No. 10 (A king's stick that no one will lift). Gondi: Hivale and Elwin, p. 149, No. 20 (A golden stick that cannot be handled). Kurd: Lescot, 300 (The fresh branch on the ground). Votyak: Buch, 28 (A good whip and yet you dare not take it in your hand); Wichmann, 242. For additional parallels see the note to Taylor, *English*, 1466. Note a curious African parallel: "The stick of the chief is very slippery" (Kiniramba: F. Johnson, p. 355, No. 1).

Variations on the theme of the stick or whip that cannot be picked up are rare but note the Santal "The raja's plate which you cannot wash" (Elwin and Archer, p. 304, No. 10); the Russian "In the forest, the forest there lies a piece of iron. You can neither take it nor lift it nor place it on your cart" (Sadovnikov, 1603); and the Scotch Gaelic "On St. Bride's Day the maid comes from the tuft; I will not touch the maid, and the maid will not touch me. Who is she?" (Nicolson, p. 21). Another Russian version, "There stands a black horse. You can neither touch its mane nor pet it" (Sadovnikov, 1605), has perhaps some connection with the riddles discussed in the next paragraph.

The comparison of a snake to a stick or a whip occurs in some riddles that describe several animals or things. Compare the Baiga "The marigolds are blossoming; there is none to pick them. The goldenstick is on the ground; there is none to pick it up. The big horse is standing ready; there is none to ride him.—Sun, snake, tiger" (Elwin, p. 473, No. 90). Here the marigolds should be the stars, as we see in a parallel current among the Moslems in India: "Spread is the mat:/ There is none to sleep./ Pierced is the King:/ There is none to weep./ The flowers are in bloom:/ There is none to pick [them].—Water, cobra, stars" (Elwin and Archer, p. 309, No. 16). Unfortunately the collector does not interpret the reference to the king or cobra. See also Elwin, *Muria*, p. 591, No. 11 (sun, tiger, snake). In central Asia this tripartite riddle is represented by such texts as the Cheremis "A stallion that cannot be attached to a wagon, a bent wood that cannot be bent together, a whip with which one cannot strike.—Bear, rainbow, snake" (Porkka, 89 = Sebeok, 2. 13. 1) and the Siberian Turkish "I should like to mount my young horse, but I am afraid. I should like to take the whip in my hands, but I am afraid.—Bear, snake" (Katanov, p. 93, No. 780). For other examples of this tripartite riddle see the note to Taylor, *English*, 1466.

Riddlers have used the notion of an object that cannot be touched in various ways. For illustrations see the headnote to Taylor, *English*, 1655–1657. Note also two Baiga riddles: "No one can touch the stars in the sky and no one can touch this golden pendant.—A hanging wasp's nest" and "You can't lift this royal necklace and put it in your hair.—A procession of ants" (Elwin and Archer, pp. 270–271, Nos. 1, 9). In some Magyar and South Slavic ballads similar to the English "The Maid Freed From the Gallows" a snake creeps on a sleeping man's or woman's breast. All the relatives refuse in turn to pick it up. Only the lover picks it up and in his hands it turns into coins or a pearl necklace. See N. F. S. Grundtvig, *Danmarks gamle Folkeviser* 8: 462, No. 486, Copenhagen, Gyldendal, 1919.

337. A galtar mule is a white-muzzled mule with a dark body. The parts of the apparatus described here are (1) the receiver of the alembic, (2) the cucurbit in which the buttermilk is boiled, (3) the brandy, (4) the head of the alembic, (5) the boiling buttermilk.

Compare the Serbian riddles for a still: "The tsar is sitting on his throne, his cap is a mitre, along his right hand fragrant ointment flows"; "An old man is still (quiet) on a log and is crying"; "The Iron One (*Gvozden*) is sitting in a grove with an iron hat; his tears are dripping down into the fir vat"; "An old man is sitting in a grove; he has an iron cap; his tears are dripping into the iron cap"; "An iron kitten cries before God; its tears are dripping into a wooden cap"; "The Copper One (*Bakren*) is sitting in the grove in an earthen cap; his tears are dripping into the earthen cap" (Novaković, p. 81, Nos. 3-8). The Estonians say of fermenting beer: "It stands in a wooden container, it has a white cap on its head" (Wiedemann, p. 286); this resembles the riddles cited in the note to No. 335 above. A Swedish description of a still is a scene from nature: "It stands on living rock, it runs through the copper mountains, it runs through both tree and water" (Ström, p. 149 and compare another conception of a still on p. 198). A Swedish description of a beer bottle has very little in common with the preceding riddles: "There is a prison of glass. A man of bark watches over it. A man of iron attacks him and carries him away and throws him to one side. The prisoners are roasted and are locked up anew in many prisons of skin and bone" (Ström, p. 149, "Ölflaskan"). Note a Dhanwar narrative description of distilling that resembles somewhat the Mongolian riddles; see Verrier Elwin, *Myths of middle India*, 338-339, No. 4, London, Oxford Univ. Press, Indian Branch, [1949], and a Kamar story on p. 341. For other Mongolian descriptions of distilling or utensils used in distilling see Nos. 97 (comparison to a swallow), 108 (pig), 210 (cow), 531 (naughty girl), 628 (men walking), 657 and 683 (rivers), 725 (rocks and spring), 784 and 786 (cart), 864 (sleeve of garment), 907 (thing with water and key) and perhaps the comparison of a fountain to shamans in No. 364. See also Swedish: Wessman, 126, 377. Albanian: Hahn, p. 159, No. 7.

For Monoglian parallels to the formula "from above" and its synonyms see Nos. 440, 604, 698b, 699 (with the note), 777, 797, 816, 829, 913-915, 940. Since it occurs in the fourteenth-century Cuman riddles (Németh, 41), it is a very old formula in Asiatic riddling. See such modern examples as Turkish: Bahaeddin, 40. Shor: Dyrenkova, 21 (Falling from heaven, snow hanging on the tree, all four paws crooked.—Hare). The formula is understood literally in some instances and in the sense of "made by God, natural" in others. The hearer of a riddle is therefore likely to be confused. In No. 689a "from a small sky" refers to the sieve from which the flour falls.

337a. For comment on *Dendžin* see the note to No. 40 above.

337b. The mule is milk brandy (*ariki*) and the flat cake is buttermilk (*tsagān*). For another reference to a sleeve in this connection see No. 864.

338. The scene of an animal or a person behind a fence or trees usually describes the tongue and the teeth; see No. 199 and the headnote to Taylor, *English*, 1151. For references to the eye as a particolored object see the note to No. 801.

338b. The white birches are an appropriate comparison for the teeth but are less appropriate for the eyelashes.

339. The import of the riddle is obscure. For another description of human features see No. 681.

340. The riddler compares the whirling leaden beads attached to the thongs to dancing lamas. See a description of a Mongolian drum in the note to No. 351.

341. For parallels see No. 211 above and Yakut: Ionova, 39 (A hundred people are thinking of the same thing); Piekarski, 360 (They say that a hundred people have one and the same thought); Popov, p. 288; Priklonskii, 2; Iastremskii, 203. Turcoman: Samojlovich, 85 (Karaja Khan mounted his horse and our hopes grew strong). Mordvin: Paasonen, 291. Georgian: Kapanadze, p. 144, No. 2 (I sit in the middle; I have no value, yet everyone looks at me.—Fire). Russian: Sadovnikov, 335. Modern Greek: Dieterich, *Sporades*, 27 (A pregnant sow, a company awaits her). Note the picturesquely conceived Turkish "A crowd of people stood around and a brown stallion ran at an amble.—Men around a fire and boiling tea" (Katanov, p. 108, No. 933). Much to the same effect as the Mongolian riddle are the African parallels: SeSuto: Norton and Velaphe, 26 (Mother of Wan-hope weeps in the reeds and says people must come and see her.—Kaffir beer). Kxatla: Schapera (Tell me: baboon, squat on your haunches so that the children may rejoice). Lamba: Doke, 39 (The important thing to the Lamba people.—Cooking pot), which has parallels with different answers like "The important thing with people.—Heart" (Doke, 40) and "The important thing with white men.—Money" (Doke, 41). The answer "Waiting for evening" to the Yakut "A hundred people have one thought" (Piekarski, 361) refers to the serving of the evening meal. The Kosi say, "Even if the house is full of people and I come in, they nevertheless give me a place to sit.—Bowl of food" (Ittmann, 103) and "I am broad, yet I get a place to sit.—Calabash of palm wine" (Ittmann, 108. See also Kundu, Ittmann, 263). A Muria riddle for people gathered about liquor is expressed in terms of birds: "On a burnt tree vultures sit" (Elwin and Archer, p. 269, No. 38), which has curiously enough a Tlokoa parallel, "I cut a tree and birds swarmed on it.— People coming to drink beer" (Nakene, p. 138, No. 38). See further a Dschagga riddle for a market place: "A tall hollow tree attracts birds [from their flight in the air]" (Stamberg, 26). Compare a Togo riddle for the foam of palm wine: "The white top of the sobes [a palm] pleases the Wenyi people" (Schönhärl, p. 100, No. 3). See also a Bengali comparison to a plant: "The mallika [jasmine] flowers are in bloom and all the children are running for them.—Rice" (Elwin and Archer, p. 314, No. 3) and a Baluchi parallel cited in the note to No. 211 above. The notion of being sought by all occurs also in a Rumanian riddle for a road: "Long, long, crooked, crooked, but all seek me" (Papahagi, 33).

342. A somewhat different conception is seen in the Surinam "Bald-head rolls in a well" (Penard and Penard, 38). For parallels to the formula "in a well" see the note to No. 61 above.

343. The riddler suggests a lama by his description. The reading of the scriptures resembles the drone of a bee. For parallels to this conception see Nos. 369, 509, and 760 below and compare Nos. 34, 35 with the note as well as the headnote to Taylor, *English*, 649. The Rumanians conceive the droning of a bee in a different fashion: "Drunken wedding guests are singing around a block of wood" (Papahagi, 3).

344. Both the drum and the hand bell are used in lamaist rites. According to Mostaert, *chomoge* means a tubular bone and also the stone or seed of a fruit. Here it refers to the two globular objects attached by thongs to the drum (*damaru*). When the drum is shaken vigorously, these objects strike against it. For further discussion of the chomoge see the note to No. 891a. For a description of the drum see the note to No. 351.

345. The connection between the riddle and its solution is obscure. The solution "The Four Teachers" (Mongolian *tumbaši;* Tibetan *ston pa bzhi*) refers to a story of the election of a bird as a leader by the elephant, hare, and monkey. This story teaches human beings to live in harmony. For a picture of the Four Teachers, who are represented as standing on one another, see Charles A. Bell, *Portrait of the Dalai Lama*, pl. 184, London, Collins, 1946. For a different arrangement see Giuseppe Tucci, *Tibetan painted scrolls*, pl. 124, Rome, Libreria dello Stato, 1949. The Four Teachers are depicted on the walls of the temple Dörbed (or: Durbet) Wang in Inner Mongolia. For versions of the story see Avadāna-kalpalatā, No. 86, which is summarized in Tucci, p. 520 and E. Chavannes, *Cinq cents* *contes et apologues du Tripitaka chinois* **3**: 273, Paris, Leroux, 1911.

346. The interpretation of the details, which are chosen to suggest a lama, is not entirely clear. Compare the Arabic "A serpent in the mouth of a dragon; for nine months it conceals itself; and for three months it is apparent.—Foam of a camel" (Giacobetti, 135).

347, 348. The usual answer to this riddle is cock or rooster, as in No. 349. The answer "peewit" is, however, more suitable because the three seasons of the church rite refer to the three months that the peewit stays in Mongolia. For examples of a comparison used to describe two entirely different things see the note to Nos. 476–478.

349. See the note to Nos. 347, 348. The application of the last statement in the riddle to a rooster is somewhat obscure. The riddle deals with familiar objects in lamaist ritual. In its conception it resembles No. 453 below, which suggests a prince or general rather than a lama. For parallels to the comparison of a cock to a religious or secular dignitary see the note to No. 453.

350. The *panchen shva ser*, a cap worn in certain lamaist rites, is explained as follows: Tibetan *pan* (scholar), *chen* (great), *zhva* (cap), *ser* (yellow). In Mongolian *zhva* is pronounced *shva* or *sha*. For a picture of this cap and comment on it see Waddell, *The Buddhism of Tibet*, pp. 194–199. The Bandida Lama is the spiritual ruler of Tsang (western Tibet). Bandida is the Mongolian pronunciation of Sanskrit *pandita* (scholar, pundit). This Sanskrit word is the source of Tibetan *pan*.

351. Mongolian *xambō*, which the Russian translator treats as a proper name, is Tibetan *mkhan-po* (abbot, priest). The riddler uses it to alliterate with *xoino* (north) and *xojar* (two). The *damaru* is a small hand drum. Instead of a drumstick it has two leaden beads fastened by little leather thongs to a cylinder. The drum is made either of wood or, as in No. 344, of the calottes of two human skulls touching at their tips and covered with a tight deerskin. Human skin is also said to be used. The damaru is seized by the thumb, forefinger, and middle finger of the right hand and is sounded by rapidly turning the wrist back and forth to make the beads hit the drumhead. The loud rattle thus produced is supposed to announce the appearance of the Terrible Ones (*Dokshid*. Tibetan *Drag gçed*). See the comment on these figures in the note to No. 406 below. The rite and the name are of Indian origin. The peacock's tail refers to the long embroidered silk ribbons with which the damaru is decorated.

For other Mongolian comparisons of a drum to a man see Nos. 340 above and 603 below. The Turkish drum riddle, "Ishmael bent to his name wears a leather shirt, his ears are of iron" (Bahaeddin, 5) is not completely intelligible.

352. Riddlers often compare the fingers to ten men. See the riddles for putting on a hat, shirt, or trousers (Nos. 556, 583–585 below), the discussion in the headnotes to Taylor, *English*, 976–982 and 980–982, and the Kanawari "Ten men cause a man to fall.—Bread" (Joshi, 13).

353. The bowls are placed in front of an idol. Dondok is the Tibetan Don-sgrub, a translation of the Sanskrit Siddhārtha (He who has reached his goal), the personal name of the Buddha Sakyamuni.

354. The *ochir* or *ochire* (Sanskrit *vajra*), a short rod of special shape, is used by lamaist monks in religious services. Calves are tied by a rope fastened to the ground by a peg while their mothers are milked. The peg is driven into the ground with a special hammer. Colts tied to this rope wear a special halter. Calves are tied with an ordinary rope.

355. The stinkbug is probably a bedbug. Compare Polish: Gustawicz, 12 (It is black, but is not a raven. It has horns, but is not an ox. It has six legs without any hoofs.—Cockroach).

356. For another reference to serving a sheep to a guest see No. 429.

357. The tufts (*manchuk*) hang from the front of the harness. In this riddle they represent the six legs of the insect. The insect has a disagreeable odor. According to Mostaert, the reference to the odor of resin and sandalwood is ironical. For a reference to the pincers of this insect see No. 253 above.

358. For a description of the Buddhist novice see Getty, pp. xxxiv–xxxv.

359. Compare the picturesque Swahili "The locks of the good lady flutter" (Büttner, p. 201).

360. For a description of this sacred vessel see Getty, p. xxxix.

362. The vessel is the alms bowl used by a mendicant priest. Compare the Kxatla hare riddle, "Tell me: the small boy who never loses his sleeping mat" (Schapera, 37). The sleeping mat is the earth. See also No. 824 below.

363. Similar comparisons to the acts of a shaman are found in the Yakut "Shaman beating-squeaking, when he shamanizes, those having legs get together, those having heels crowd together.—Food stirred with a stick in a pot, eating" (Iastremskii, 388. See also his Nos. 389, 390). I suspect that the answer of the Yakut "In a pantry a shaman tells fortunes, it is said.—Rattling a rattle" (Popov, p. 288) should be "shaking a sieve" or "stirring a churn." See also a Siberian Turkish riddle for a mill quoted in the note to No. 69 above; the Rajput Kayesth "River on this side, river on that side, eddies in the middle, inside a yogi is stretching and the eddies dance around.—Churn" (Elwin and Archer, p. 299, No. 24); and the Irish "My *mu-mhu-maidén* set for *glug-ghlug-ghlagaidén*, the head of a tallyho, and she will return it in the morning.—Churn" (Ó Dálaigh, 75 = Hull and Taylor, *Irish*, 693*b*). This Irish riddle is one of the riddles describing the borrowing and return of a churn that are discussed in the note to No. 1027, § 3 below. See also the Irish weaver riddle, "A wee little man *tilling, tolling* (meaning uncertain) and he sets the wood to shaking" (Ó Dálaigh, 77 = Hull and Taylor, *Irish*, 227). The Aandinga describe a pestle in a similar way: "There is dancing by him and he does not laugh" (Pettinen, 19); and so, too, do the Kharia in "The girl who danced a lot and went to sleep in a corner" (Elwin and Archer, p. 286, No. 31). For parallels to the formula "in a well" in the Mongolian riddle see the note to No. 61 above.

This description of churning is one of many comparisons to persons bowing or praying. See the Mordvin wellsweep riddle, "It is the young wife of the house there, she bows frequently (Paasonen, 350), and the Zyrian parallel, "A tall, tall man bows day and night" (Wichmann, 133. See also his No. 243). The Zyrian "A beautiful, beautiful woman bows day and night" (Wichmann, 144) refers to a cradle. See also the Mongolian descriptions of washing a kettle (No. 249), waving grass (No. 445), and churning kumiss (No. 630). For the conventional scene "in a well" see the note to No. 61. For comparisons to a man with a defect see Nos. 355 (six hands), 356 (six feet), 363 (earless), 394 (hornless devil), 400 (girl with sores and wounds), 415 (twisted feet and swollen head), 416 (tongueless), 417 (hole in head or cheek), 424 (one eye), 425 and 426 (cross-eyed), 427 (one ear), 428 (cannot smell), 429 (toothless), 434 (boy with hole), 435 (belly behind), 440 (four legs), 472 (calf's face), 511 (without flesh).

364. Compare riddles describing distillation surveyed in the note to No. 337. For riddles making a comparison to ritual acts see the note to No. 363.

365. For parallels to the formula "in a hole" see the note to No. 61.

366. Precious Thunderbolt, which is translated through Tibetan from the Sanskrit Ratnavajra, is here the name of a man representing a medicine bottle. For other personifications of a medicine bottle or bag see No. 403 and the notes to Taylor, *English,* 6 and 514. See further the Chinese "From the South comes a little dwarf. With one grasp I take him by the neck.—The Chinese wine-pot, which is like two cones, a long one and a short one, put together at the tops" (Serruys, 33) and the Irish riddle for a bottle: "Black Donald on the dresser and a bone in his mouth" (Ó Máile, 10 = Hull and Taylor, *Irish,* 81).

367. The Mongolian *sabari* is a borrowing of Tibetan *č'abril*. This bowl has a round bottom with a button, is girdled with a leather belt, and is carried in a cloth belt. See Getty, p. xxxviii.

368. A Baljing Shaser cap worn by Buddhist monks is conical and has a tassel on its tip. The tassel resembles the tuft on a hoopoe's head. See Getty, pp. xxxi, xxxvii, and the note to No. 350 above. The words *Badan Sadan* seem to be meaningless.

369. For other comparisons of the sounds made by insects or animals to reading the scriptures see the note to No. 343.

370. This musical instrument consists of three parts, the middle being made of strong wood or horn and the two other parts of copper or brass. The mouthpiece resembles the king's or chief's double button, which was worn as an insignia of rank under the Manchu dynasty and is still in use among the Mongols. The eight double-petalled lotuses seem to be the holes in the instrument.

371. The button is a badge of rank; see the note to No. 370. The Mongolian *shȳsy* means also the whole cooked sheep that is offered to an honored guest; see the note to No. 429.

373. For other references to an animal whose legs pace see Nos. 219, 230, 438.

374. *Abai beile* is a Manchurian and Mongolian title of nobility.

376. *Dzangi* are chiefs of a *somon*, the smallest administrative unit in Mongolia; *boshko* are servants in an office. For parallels to the comparison of fire to mist rising see the note to Nos. 419, 420.

377, 378. The Mongolian *amban* signifies a high dignitary, minister, or envoy. For parallels describing mucus in the nose in human terms see the Chuvash "Two soil, three gather it up" (Mészáros, 32) and "Two run out, five lift [them] up and throw [them] away" (Karahka and Räsänen, 15), the Zyrian "Two jugglers appear, something with five ends (or: tips) seizes them" (Wichmann, 103), the Rajput-Kayesth "The Muslim who comes out of the mosque with two doors" (Elwin and Archer, p. 301, No. 40), the Kashmiri "'O Padmán, you came by way of the lake, and I laid hold of you and threw you down.'—To blow one's nose" (Knowles, 45), the Turkish "From a very narrow street a beautiful bride comes" (Hamamizade, 636), and the Modern Greek "A maiden came out of the place that is pierced with holes, five held her for shame's sake" (Dieterich, *Sporades,* 13). The Albanian "The five sons of the *hander* take the daughter of the *noser* and throw her back of the threshold" (Hahn, p. 161, No. 35) uses whimsically formed nouns. See also the comparison of mucus in the nose to maidens in No. 324 and the parallels collected in the headnote to Taylor, 970–975, § 4. The Uraon "An old woman knocks a white hen down" (Archer, 22) is an unusual variation. For parallels in which the actors are animals see No. 306 above and the note. See further the comparison of mucus to a thing in the Bengali "Anguldatta received Nakadatta's treasure" (Mitra, *Sylhet,* p. 125, No. 36) and the Kashmiri "Taking it out of a large earthen jar and dashing it against the wall" (Knowles, 63). See also No. 104 above.

Comparisons to five persons seizing another person or an object serve to describe other things than mucus. See, as examples, the Lithuanian "In Juoditskio's marsh a little colt was drowned, five women pulled at it, two hawks waited. —Bowl, fingers, eyes" and "In Apvalaina's pond a mare was drowned, five pulled at it, ten waited.—Pot, spoon, fingers, teeth" (Jurgelionis, 189, 190. See also his No. 191). The translation of these two riddles is not altogether certain.

379. See a different description of a horse's tail in No. 622.

381, 382. The Mongolians often use an incense stick to pick their teeth. For parallels see the headnote to Taylor, *English,* 970–975, § 8.

383. When sleeping, a dog thrusts its muzzle (the master) under its tail (the servant). See a fuller version of this comparison in the Yakut "One is sweeping, two are sewing, two are giving light, two are sniffing, four are preparing a bed, the chief of them lies down, placing his head near the servant" (Ionova, 14) and a less elaborated version "Two torch bearers, four chamberlains, one sweeper" (Iastremskii, 95), in which the master and servant are not mentioned. For additional versions and discussion see the headnote to Taylor, *English,* 1476–1494, § 10.

384. In the Mongolian text zandarγ-a seems to be a misprint for zarulγ-a (older brother). Compare Taylor, *English,* 781 and the texts cited in the headnote to that riddle and in the headnote to No. 801, § 4.

387. Compare the headnotes to Taylor, *English,* 412–413, § 6 and 544, § 7.

389. The meaning of Yankhal is obscure. It may be the Mongolian *yangxan* (prostitute). The Chinese *wang-pa* (tortoise) is an objurgation equivalent to the English bastard, whoreson.

390. Siberian Turkish: Katanov, *Urianchai,* 6 (In a large yurt there is a small yurt and in the small yurt there are the cheeks of a stag.—Footgear, socks, human feet). Compare the Zyrian riddle for a baby in a cradle: "On a wooden city is a straw city, on the straw city is a rag city, on the rag city a silent voivode" (Wichmann, 172). For riddles of similar construction see the riddle for a lamp below (No. 776) and the headnotes to Taylor, *English,* 1156–1164 and 1156–1160. For another description of legs and stockings see No. 441 below.

391. The riddler seems to be employing the symbolism of convex (Chinese *yang*) and concave (Chinese *yin*) for male and female. For another reference to this symbolism see No. 738 below and the note. The symbolism is very old. Huai-nan-tzu (d. 122 B.C.) refers to it as "ancient." For a reference to a bow as a symbol for a boy see H Maspéro, *Les Ivoires religieux et médicaux chinois d'après la collection Lucien Lion,* 15–16, Paris, Les Editions d'art et d'histoire, 1933.

For riddles dealing with our ignorance of the sex of an unborn child see the Mordvin "Enclosed in a box, one does not know whether it is gold or silver" (Paasonen and Ravila, p. 614, No. 9 and compare his p. 621, No. 7) and "It is in the midst of the great water, one cannot see whether it is a forest strawberry or a garden strawberry" (Paasonen and Ravila, p. 619, No. 7 and p. 620, No. 1. See also Ahlqvist, *Moksha Mordvin,* 68); the Nandi "Which would you prefer, to drink from a calabash which has a wide mouth or from one which has a narrow mouth?—I will drink from neither. The narrow mouth is male, the wide mouth is female" (Hollis, 19); the Bakongo "It is a problem as complicated as the goat's horn.—Cannot guess the sex of an unborn child" (Denis, 13); the Ila "You who have grown so clever! Can you tell whether the woman is pregnant of a male or a female?" (Smith and Dale, 2: 331); and the texts collected in the note to Taylor, *English,* 373.

393. See No. 630, in which there are two actors, and the parallels collected in the note to that riddle. See also

Yakut: Iastremskii, 387 (A disorderly head, a long [or: tall] blockhead), 389 (There is a Modut girl, a girl shaman with disheveled hair.—Churnstaff). Baiga: Elwin, p. 467, No. 32 = Elwin and Archer, p. 272, No. 13 (White water in a black tank. In it dances a queen). Kashmiri: Knowles, 10 (Mother Phát is sitting down, and the daughter Phatah is dancing.—Pot and stick). Nagaibak: Vitevskii, p. 276, No. 6 (In a deep basement [or: hole] a Russian fool sits and brawls). For parallels making a comparison to a person who performs ritualistic acts see the note to No. 363 above. In the Polish "There is wild music in the well and a boiling mass at the top" (Kopernicki, 45), where the boiling mass is either milk that is being strained or the foam that rises from the milk as it is churned, there is no reference to a person. For comparisons in animal terms see the Yakut "A white deer digging in a snowdrift" (Popov, p. 289), the Turkish "On a very narrow roof a colt kicks," "On a high roof a horse whinnies," and "A remarkable well, its water has a voice" (Hamamizade, 719–721, respectively); and the Letsoalo "Our cow stepped into the depression, I stayed and seized her by the tail.—Stick used to stir boiling meal" (Krüger, 15). For comparisons of a churn to a thing rather than an animal or a person see No. 817 below. For parallels to the conventional scene "in a well" see the note to No. 61.

Similar comparisons to a person are used to describe a mortar and pestle; see, as examples, the Javanese "There is a princess who goes to combat. When she is overwhelmed by the multitude of enemies, she seizes a weapon. Then the enemies scatter" (Ranneft, *Proza*, p. 4, No. 16. See also Ranneft, *Poëzie*, pp. 40–41, Nos. 1–3); the Turcoman "A woman with a child walks about the village" (Samojlovich, 83); the Turkish "It comes from the mountain with a tapping sound, its eyes are like knots in wood, it bends to drink water, it cries out like a courier" (Hamamizade, 679) and "That side a wall, this side a wall, inside [of them] a horseman drives about" (Hamamizade, 722); and the Makua "A naughty girl eats standing up.—Mortar." The answer should probably be "pestle" (Harries, *Song riddles*, p. 45, No. 7). Compare the SeSuto "The madman dances in the thorns.—Mealies in the pot" (Norton and Velaphe, 25), in which the thorns refer to the thorn bushes used for firewood, and the Ten'a drill riddle: "I make myself shake" (Jetté, 58).

394. The word translated "well" usually means "well-bucket" and the word translated "hornless" is not in the dictionaries. For the comparison of a gun to a well see the headnote to Taylor, *English*, 801, § 10. For parallels to the formula "in a well" see the note to No. 61 above.

395. Siberian Turkish: Katanov, p. 181, No. 1407 (in the forest lies a devil.—Bow). The Mongolian and Siberian Turkish comparisons resemble somewhat a European riddle for a nettle; see Taylor, *English*, 342 with the headnote and footnote.

398. See No. 549 and the note.

399. See the Arabic "Something is very long. It does not reach to the udder of the she-ass" (Ruoff, p. 40, No. 103) and the Masai "What does your mother resemble? She is long and yet she does not reach up to a sheep's udder" (Hollis, 8). For a somewhat different conception of a road as both very high (i.e., long) and yet lower than grass see No. 910 below. For comparisons of a road to a rope or ribbon see Nos. 882–886.

400. Chinese: Serruys, 21 (Not tall, not tall, and the body full of holes). Tungus: Poppe, 1 (An old woman's stomach is rough). Russian: Sadovnikov, 615. For other descriptions of a thimble as a rough or scabby person see the headnotes to Taylor, *English*, 576–577, nn. 6–8 and 1263–1265, n. 6.

401. An arshin (Mongolian *aršam*) is almost twenty-eight inches long. I cannot interpret all the details of this riddle.

402. An edible lily with a red flower.

403. See a somewhat similar description of a medicine bag in No. 366. Possibly the name is that of the Buddha Gung gurwā.

405. A tall conical pot without lid or spout.

406. Cymbals are especially used in the worship of the Terrible Ones (*Dokshid*). Mahākāla (The Great Black One or The Great Time, i.e., Death), a form of Shiva, is the most formidable of them. See Getty, pp. 130, 140, 143–145, and the note to No. 351 above. For another description of cymbals see No. 511 below. For riddles describing an object as small but strong or possessed of a loud voice see the note to Nos. 32, 33.

407. See the note to No. 685.

408, 409. A somewhat similar riddle for an eagle owl mentions its cries; see No. 505. The horned owl is supposed to be a magician who drives away evil spirits that are visible to him, even in the darkness of night. A riddle almost identically the same is used to describe a wolf; see No. 143.

410, 411. The "eyes" or dots on the rod mark the weights, and the strands are the ropes by which the scales are suspended when weighing.

410. The assertion "respected by the people," which has a parallel in No. 465, appears in various forms in riddles for scales. Note the Cheremis "Only an ell long (or: tall), it nevertheless administers the law" (Porkka, 24 = Sebeok, 1. 7. 14) and the Breton "Who is just and equal toward all things?" (Le Pennec, 3).

412. The red eyes are markings on the balalaika or one of its parts. For the twisted ears signifying the keys of the instrument see No. 103 and compare the crop-eared colt in Nos. 257, 258.

413. The glossy nape of the neck is the thumbnail. For comment on riddles for the fingernails see the note to No. 548.

414. For other references to the spreading legs of a gun rest see the note to Nos. 11, 12. For a formula similar to the phrase "on a saddlelike pass" see the note to No. 90.

417. Arabic: Löhr, 19 (A Negro woman, a plug in her hole.—Loaded rifle). Hungarian: *Magyar Nyelvör* 5: 127, No. 26, 1876 (In the forest one carries a young woman with a hole.—Gun). Norwegian: Brox, 37b (What is it that goes over the stream with a round hole in the neck?—Gun). For other comparisons to a person with a hole in his body see the note to No. 434.

418. The Mongolians ask many different riddles for a lock or a lock and key; see the Index of Solutions. For parallels to the notion of a person with a defect see the note to No. 363 and to the notion of a person with a hole in his body see the note to No. 434. For descriptions of a lock that are more or less similar to this riddle see the Turkish "A black chicken, its belly is a cleft" (Hamamizade, 338), which also is used to describe a hearth (see Hamamizade, 537 and an Armenian parallel in the note to No. 113 above). See a variation of this comparison in the Yakut riddle for a window, "Mrs. —, they say, has a seal in the middle of her breast" (Popov, p. 288). Sexual implications are frequently found in riddles for a lock; see Modern Greek: Stathes, p. 354, No. 101. Russian: Sadovnikov, 105–107. Polish: Gustawicz, 141, 379, 380. Lithuanian: Sabaliauskas, 40.

419, 420. See another personification of a pipe in No. 526 below and not the comparisons to a person with fire on his head that are cited in the headnote to Taylor, *English*, 1440–1441, nn. 6, 8, 9, 16. See further the Modern Greek "A long [i.e., tall], long monk with a hole in the middle, he's apt to burn his beard wearing that kind of hat" (Polites, p. 233, No. 230) and the Togo "One lights his head and the smoke comes out of his leg" (Schönhärl, 97). Compare a Kxatla riddle for a train: "Tell me: the cow that comes from Buluwayo and sends smoke out of its head" (Schapera, 129). See also the cresset riddle cited in the note to Nos. 421, 422 below. For the comparison of fire or steam to mist rising see Nos. 279 (cloud) and 376 above.

421, 422. The Russians introduced candles into Mongolia. Compare the Yakut "The good man vanished and started vanishing from the top" (Iastremskii, 352). Russian: Sadovnikov, 198 (Dron son of Dron, Ivan son of Ivan walked through fire, carried fire on his head.—Cresset). For other riddles about candles see Taylor, *English*, 631 with the note.

424. Compare Taylor, *English*, 36, 281, 486, 528–534, 931 and the notes.

425. A very different conception of a fish appears in the Bengali "My eyes are open when I sleep" (Elwin and Archer, p. 314, No. 6).

426. Kiakhta is a town on the border of Mongolia and the U. S. S. R.

429. This riddle is widely known in Asia and in countries where some Arabic or Moslem influence has been present. See Uraon: Archer, 214 (Two goats are slaughtered for a stranger. The stranger has no teeth, and the goats have no bones). The Turkish "A pasha arrives without a tongue, he ate two lambs without bones, he mounted a lifeless horse" (Kúnos, p. 150, No. 74) offers some curious variations in details. The lack of a tongue refers to the baby's inability to speak and the lifeless horse is the cradle. Arabic: Ruoff, p. 18, No. 19 (A guest came to us from a land without earth, we put two sheep without bones before him). Some versions refer to a single article of food as in the Kabardin "A toothless guest arrived; they feed him meat without bones" (Talpa and Sokolov, 17), the Turkish "A guest came from God, we put some *yahni* [a dish of boiled meat and onions] before him, the guest had no teeth, the *yahni* had no bones" (Hamamizade, 123; Boratav, 235), the Cherekessian "He comes as a toothless guest, the meat that he is served is boneless" (Tambiev, p. 53, No. 4), and the Arabic "A guest has arrived from a country without earth, we have brought him a riding animal without bones" (Giacobetti, 307). See also Littmann, 119. West of the sphere of Mohammedan and Arabic influence I have found this riddle only in Russian (Sadovnikov, 1715); the Serbian "A guest came and we killed the boneless sheep" (Novaković, p. 41, No. 6), in which Mohammedan influence may be present; and the Lithuanian "There comes a guest without teeth, there is slaughtered a ram without bones. What is that?" (Schleicher, p. 202) and "A toothless guest came and tortured a boneless ram" (Mickevicius, p. 579, No. 118). For another reference of the custom of serving an honored guest a whole sheep see the note to No. 356 above.

A perhaps independent riddle refers to this mysterious food as something that does not appear on a table. See the Yakut "They say that there is food which is never put on the table but which is fed to Russian and Yakut alike" (Piekarski, 166), "What is eaten without being placed on the table?" (Poppe, p. 286), "Some people do not place their food on the table" (Ionova, 113), and "Without a table there is exquisite food, they say" (Iastremskii, 162); the Georgian "A guest has come to visit me, and his food is such as is not served on the table" (Y. Kapanadze, p. 145, No. 10 = Blechsteiner, p. 16, No. 32) and "A strange guest has called on me, I served him with strange food that is impossible to serve on a table" (Glushakov, p. 28, No. 39); the Abchaz "It is indispensable to both prince and serf, yet you cannot cut it with a knife and you cannot put it on a table" (Guliia, p. 68, No. 15); the Mordvin "One has eaten of it, one has drunk of it, but one has not put it on the table" (Paasonen, 58), "Everyone drinks and eats it; it is not suited to be laid on the table" (Paasonen and Ravila, p. 619, No. 2), and Ahlqvist, p. 42, No. 20 = Ahlqvist, *Moksha Mordvin*, 76; the Estonian "The king, the nobility, the peasant,—all eat it but never put it on the table, never cut it with the knife" (Wiedemann, p. 272; see also his p. 282); the many Russian parallels in Sadovnikov, 1787; the Lithuanian "Neither boiled nor roasted, one never puts it on the table, yet everyone eats it" (Balys, p. 155, No. 479); Swedish parallels (Ström, p. 84, Nos. 3, 4; Wessman, 75); and the Icelandic "Kings and prelates, poor and rich have eaten it, and yet it has never been on anyone's table" (Arnason, 816). See also German: Wossidlo, 423. This riddle seems to have suggested a Gypsy riddle for cards: "What is brought to the table and cut, but none ate it?" (Sampson, 36) with a Serbian parallel (Novaković, p. 85, No. 4).

Somewhat different conceptions appear in Nos. 820 and 821 below and in the Arabic "White and soft, O you people! All the kings bowed before it, even Jesus bowed and kissed [it]" (Ruoff, p. 17, No. 14). See further Serbian: Novaković, p. 132, Nos. 5, 6; the Modern Greek "The food, the food that has not been touched by a knife. All the world has eaten of it, king and ruler" (Polites, 345); the Lithuanian "A living creature ate living food on a living table. What is that?" (Schleicher, p. 202) and "An animal eats on a living table" (Balys, *Fifty riddles*, p. 327, No. 31); and the Irish "A gold cap (*sic*. It should be *cup*) with a foot, a king's son drank a drop from it. It is not a stump or a tree top, and neither smith nor mechanic made it" (Ó Dálaigh, 5 = Hull and Taylor, *Irish*, 353); Swedish: Ström, p. 84, Nos. 3, 4. Makua: Harries, *Riddles*, p. 288, No. 16. Ila: Smith and Dale, 2: 325, No. 3 (There is nobody who has not tasted the little bone of Ntite).

432. Arji Borji is a mythical king. Compare Nos. 147 and 921.

433. The thongs (*ydēr*) are made of raw camel's hide. They pass through the lattice wall of the felt tent and are knotted to hold the wall in place. They are compared to hammers or beetles in Nos. 223, 272, and 529. See also the note to No. 192. Siberian Turkish: Radlov, 1: 261, No. 5 (At the back your father has folded his hands.—Holes in the yurt lattice); Katanov, p. 93, No. 793 (Behind him stuck out father's fist.—Rope knotted into a ball at the end and tying the grating of a yurt). Compare the Russian door riddle, "A woman stands crosswise: one hand in the house, the other in the yard" (Sadovnikov, 78). For other riddles involving the notion of being both inside and outside see the headnote to Taylor, *English*, 1423 and compare No. 851 below.

434. For other uses of the notion of a person with a hole in his body see the gun riddle (No. 417), the lock riddle (No. 418), a Kiniramba riddle for a pad put on the head when carrying a load: "The grave of the chief is circular and has a hole in it" (Johnson, 6). See also No. 115 above, a Modern Greek pipe riddle cited in the note to Nos. 419, 420, Votyak riddles for the hole in a chimney, "There is a hole in the side of a Russian woman" (Wichmann, 58) and a drinking cup, "A man's mouth is at the top of his head" (Wichmann, 404); and a Turkish riddle for a musical instrument (Bahaeddin, 36).

435. For parallels see the headnote to Taylor, *English*, 191, § 8. Muria: Elwin, p. 591, No. 9. Makua: Harries, *Riddles*, p. 285, No. 16. Surinam: Penard and Penard, 37.

438. For references to a pacing animal see the note to No. 373.

440. A noyon is a prince or ruler. For parallels to the formula "coming from above," which here signifies "of natural origin," see the note to No. 337.

441. See a somewhat different conception in No. 390. The humor of this riddle lies in the use of adjectives having the special form applicable to female animals. The Mongolian *xamniγān*, which is not in the dictionaries, is here translated "Tungus."

442. In this context the word translated "Forgive!" probably means "Goodby!" See parallels in the headnotes to Taylor, *English*, 365–366, § 2 and 941–942. Yakut: Piekarski, 247 (They say that there are *Bukuruja* hunting upon an elk and a *kȳrājda*.—Smoke and spark). The words *bukur* (bent, hunchbacked) and *kȳrai* (to leap up into the air) are used as the bases of nouns. Siberian Turkish: Katanov, p. 291, No. 242 (A handsome man is going in answer to a call.—Spark). Swedish: Ström, p. 224.

443. See the headnotes to Taylor, *English*, 952–957, § 8 and 1643–1654, § 6 and a somewhat different formulation of the idea in No. 578 below. Cheremis: Sebeok, 3. 6. 6 (Soulless one chases one with a soul). Mehri and Soqotri: Müller, p. 360, No. 1 (It hurries from valley to valley). Lithuanian: Mickevicius, p. 581, No. 45 (If you flee from it, then it flees. If you flee, it will not catch you. If you chase it, you will not seize it). German: Wossidlo, 390 (One can see it with one's eyes, [but] cannot seize it with one's hands). French: Mensignac, p. 300, No. 15 (The more one runs, the less one can catch it); Bastien, *Hayti*, 136 (Here I am, you cannot catch me).

445. For parallels see Nos. 304, 451; the headnote to Taylor, *English*, 946–950; the Japanese "What thing in the mountain is beckoning?—Fern" (Starr, p. 45); the Russian "A peasant stands over the water; he shakes his beard" (Sadovnikov, 1508); the Kamba "The dancer danced without moving the chains ornamenting the ankles.—Tree" (Lindblom, 21); and the Tonga-Shangan "I have entered the field and found young men standing.—I have entered the field and have found only reeds" (Junod and Jaques, p. 246, No. 104). The Kamba use a similar comparison in another connection: "Tell me a girl: she does not get tired dancing and wherever she is she only dances.—Tail of cattle" (Lindblom, 82).

446. For a similar comparison in which the actor is a worm see No. 64 above. For discussion of the comparisons or a candle or lamp to a person, animal, or thing that consumes itself see Taylor, *English*, 774 and the note. See also Yakut: Ionova, 83 (Who consumes his own body?—Candle). An Annamese riddle for incense, "White feet and black body, wearing a cap of lotus flowers, he is in the emperor's presence" (Dumoutier, p. 201) involves the comparison of a flame to a flower; for this see the note to No. 667 below.

447. Shor: Dyrenkova, 2 (A sobbing girl cuts wood). See also the parallel in No. 326 above, in which the riddler mentions a piebald horse. Compare Taylor, *English*, 788.

448–450. For a survey of similar riddles see the note to No. 109. The solution is usually an onion, a lily bulb, or a cabbage, all of which have many layers.

449b. For other references to a cap of fox fur or a yellow cap see No. 451, 455 (coat), and 516. The most important lamaist sect wears yellow caps.

451. For another reference to a cap of fox fur see No. 449b and the note. For parallels to the comparison of a reed bending or bowing to a person see No. 445 and the note.

452. For parallels see the headnote to Taylor, *English*, 531–534, § 2.

453. Compare the Serbian "The whole world died, but a little old man with a blue whistle began to whistle and the whole world came back to life" (Novaković, p. xx, No. 11) and some of the riddles collected in the note to No. 286. See also the comparison of a rooster to a lama in No. 349 above and other comparisons to dignitaries in the headnote to Taylor, *English*, 539–543, § 2. See also the Santal "He has a crown but is not a king; he wakes men but is not a sepoy" (Elwin and Archer, p. 306, No. 30).

454. The meaning of the word translated "plate" is uncertain. For other Mongolian riddles having the answer "woodpecker" see the Index of Solutions. Riddlers often use a comparison to a person wearing a red cap. See the Bengali "Many constables with red turbans are dancing on a shrub.—Red peppers" (Elwin and Archer, p. 313, No. 10 [chili]. See also p. 314, No. 4). See the discussion of this means of comparison in the headnote to Taylor, *English*, 632–644.

455. For references to yellow fur or fox's fur see the note to No. 449b. For other descriptions of a fox see the Index of Solutions.

456. The rope or lasso (*uraya*) is a loop attached to a pole; it is used for catching horses. For a less elaborate version of this riddle see No. 25.

457. Yakut: Piekarski, 69 (There is a field mouse that clings to an icicle.—Cow's kidney). The icicle is the suet next to the kidneys. Arabic: Giacobetti, 295 (Some bustard eggs in a pile of sand in the middle of hillocks [and] dunes and in a difficult country.—Kidneys).

458. The riddler has chosen the name Byrgyt to alliterate with *byse* (belt). For another name chosen for the sake of alliteration see Galba in No. 497. The theme of this riddle is used to describe horse's excrement in No. 482 below. For other examples of the use of the same comparison to describe two different objects see the note to No. 476.

459. The belts are bands of metal encircling the kettle. See a description of a gun encircled by metal bands in the headnote to Taylor, *English*, 678, § 6 and of a barrel encircled by hoops (Cheremis: Sebeok, 3. 8. 4. 1).

461, 462. A gentleman is unthinkable without these utensils. See a similar Yakut description of a horse, which lacks gall and bile: "Important people lack a leather sack for kumiss for their travels. To whom does that happen?" (Ionova, 19) and "A man without traveling equipment" (Iastremskii, 60). For other references to the horse's lack of a gall bladder see No. 1009 below. There is also a reference to this lack in the mention of the horse among the twelve cyclical animals; see Paul Serruys, "Folklore Contributions in *Sino-Mongolica*. Proverbs," *Folklore Studies* (Peiping) 6: 65, No. 284, 1947. European riddlers often refer to the fact that the dove has no gall; see German: Wossidlo, 170 and note; E. Schneeweis, "Taube," *Handwörterbuch des deutschen Aberglaubens* 8: cols. 693–694, Berlin, Walter de Gruyter, 1936–1937.

464. The fatty skin is the membrane enveloping the intestine. See the Yakut "Underground there are eight bear's toes.—Stomach into which the cud passes when chewed a second time" (Iastremskii, 86) and "In a stable there is a fur cap with ornaments" (Iastremskii, 87). For riddles on this theme see No. 713 and the note.

465. Compare the note to No. 410. The first clause seems to refer to weighing under the king's supervision or by his authority. Riddlers often refer to the authority of the scales or the respect accorded to them. See the Abchaz "On its back it has its tongue. Whatever it says people believe" (Guliia, 5). The marker on the top or back of the scales is here called a tongue. The Hausa say, "If thou goest to the market, buy for me the market judge.—Measuring cup" (Fletcher, 9). Compare the Lappish "Who is the wisest of all in the world?" and "Without speech or sense, the wisest in the world" (Qvigstad, 25, 27).

466. Swedish: Wessman, 400 (black dwarf).

468. Compare Taylor, *Ainu*, 24. For discussion of the form of this riddle my article "Riddles in Dialogue," *Proceedings of the American Philosophical Society* 97(1): 61–68, 1953.

469. Compare a Ten'a riddle for roosting grouse, when they eat: "Riddle me: it scatters little crumbs from the trees" (Jetté, 18).

470. For comparisons to a person, an animal, or a thing creeping into a hole see the note to No. 49. These comparisons are used to describe stockings, shoes, or trousers; see the headnote to Taylor, *English,* 1416–1419, §§ 1–3.

472. For a comparison of a jerboa's tail to a calf's tail see No. 48 above. Several entirely different riddles for an animal consist of enumerations of details belonging to several animals; see the riddles for a wolf (No. 143), a hare (Nos. 315, 316), a camel (No. 752), a pig (No. 755), and a grasshopper (No. 765). A gun (No. 755) is also made up of the members of several animals. A donkey (No. 764) and a cow (No. 929) are said to be composed of various kinds of materials. For additional examples see Russian: Sadovnikov, 1641 (mosquito). Mandingo: Monteil, *Contes soudanaises,* pp. 182–183 (such an animal is an omen of the end of the world). Compare also a Bihari lizard riddle (Mitra, *Bihar,* 8); a Chinese description of a dragon cited in Serruys, *Folklore Studies* 6: 19–20, 1947; and the discussion in the headnote to Taylor, *English,* 1405–1408, and Archer Taylor, "A Riddle for a Locust," *Univ. of Calif. Publ. in Semitic Philology* 11: 429–432, 1951.

476–478. For other comparisons to a dog that runs about see the headnote to Taylor, *English,* 445–458. In these riddles the same comparison is used in riddles having different answers. Such a use of a comparison is frequent in riddling. See Nos. 15 and 16; 77 and 78; 86, 91, and 92; 125 and 126–129; 130 and 131; 144 and 145; 159, 160, 161, 162, and 163; 199 and 200; 308 and 309; 347 and 349; 359 and 360; 386 and 387; 417 and 418; 458 and 482; 477 and 478; 505 and 506; 568 and 569; 576 and 577; 579 and 580; 608 and 609; 621 and 622; 689 and 690; 698 and 699; 710 and 711; 761 and 762; 809 and 810; 822 and 823; 857 and 858; 911 and 912; 939 and 940.

479. This may be an adaptation of the spark riddle, No. 442. See a more definite suggestion of an animal in No. 30. For parallels to the formula "in the steppe" see the note to No. 253.

479a. By inverting the usual order of words in Mongolian the riddler has caused them to fall in the ordinary English order. He has probably made this inversion for the sake of emphasis.

480. Samoyede: Lehtisalo, 211 (In summer weather she is dressed in the beaver garment), 212 (A soldier in armor). Abyssinian: Littmann, *Tigriña,* 23 (A little boy with his pelt.—Fly).

482. See the note to No. 458.

486. See also No. 964, which uses a similar comparison but does not clearly suggest a person.

487. Yakut: Iastremskii, 230 (Whenever I should rise, I would reach the sky, so something says), 231 (An old man is lying down, seizing the earth with his hands. "If I could rise, I should reach the sky," he says,—so they say). Samoyede: Lehtisalo, 147 (If I raise myself, I would reach to heaven). Russian: Sadovnikov, 1322, 1323. For additional parallels see the headnote to Taylor, *English,* 575.

488. The serpent may be the constellation Draco between Ursa Major and Ursa Minor and the spile may be the North Pole.

489. Yakut: Iastremskii, 196 (Neither on a horse nor on a bull, without wings, without legs, it reaches everywhere.—Human thought). Samoyede: Lehtisalo, 200 (There is a distant land, without reindeer, he goes [thither] invisible.—Thought). Mordvin: Paasonen and Ravila, p. 612, No. 4 (I am not alive, I am not dead, in an hour I traverse the whole country.—Sleep and dream). See also such riddles describing the eyes as the Gondi "It is here now, in a moment it is miles away, as suddenly it returns" (Elwin and Archer, p. 276, No. 12) with parallels in the headnote to Taylor, *English,* 1471.

491. Turkish: Hamamizade, 386 (A black boy [i.e., a soldier] guards the door), 387 (A black lackey at the door). Russian: Sadovnikov, 97 (A little one with a little belly guards the entire house.—Doorcatch and lock). In the Low German "As small as a mouse, it watches the whole house" (Wossidlo, 225), the actor is not identified. Quite different from any of these versions is the ingenious Parsee "Brother stays at home and sister goes for a walk.—Lock and key" (Munshi, p. 414, No. 17).

492. Votyak: Wichmann, 350 (He does not see himself, but he guides others.—Road). The Votyak use the same riddle to describe the posts marking the versts (Wichmann, 225). For other versions of the riddle for mileposts see Zyrian: Wichmann, 258. Russian: Sadovnikov, 1335.

493. Riddles on this theme are widely known in European and Asiatic Russia and are somewhat less abundant in adjoining countries to the west. The very definite personification of this Mongolian version is unusual. See Siberian Turkish: Katanov, p. 240, No. 63 (It is as tall as a tree but is invisible to both the sun and the moon.—Heartwood). Mordvin: Ahlqvist, 17 (What is invisible in the forest?—Pith of a tree); Paasonen, 18; Paasonen and Ravila, p. 612, Nos. 2, 3. Cheremis: Beke, 16 = Sebeok, 7. 20. 12 (The sun cannot see it, the dog cannot lick it). Votyak: Buch, 38 (It is as high as the trees and yet one does not see it). Zyrian: Wichmann, 169, 179 (Sits without ceasing, never sees the light of day). Lappish: Qvigstad, 1; Koskimies and Itkonen, 61 (Hardly thicker than the band of a salmon net, but never does the sun see it). Finnish: Koskimies, 238, as cited in the note to Qvigstad, 1. Russian: Sadovnikov, 1396. Polish: Saloni, *Rzeshów,* 148 (It is as big as a tree but it never sees the sun). Lithuanian: Basanavicius, p. 196, No. 152 (As high as a tree, yet it never sees the sun). The Lithuanian "Born in the forest, grown up in the forest, the sun has never seen it" (Volteris, p. 450, No. 13; Mickevicius, p. 572, No. 36) has been adapted to fit a formula that I have discussed in "An Allusion to a Riddle in Suetonius," *American Journal of Philology* 66: 408–410, 1945. Swedish: Noreen, 13; Dybeck, *Runa,* 1848, p. 47, No. 61; Ström, p. 123, "Trädet," 4; Olsson, *Bohuslän,* 309; Wessman, 529. Norwegian: Aasen, 9. For additional parallels see the headnote to Taylor, *English,* 1058–1062.

The Mordvins use this comparison to describe a beam under a bench: "A long, long boy, but he never sees the sun" (Wichmann, 134). It is rarely, but correctly enough, used to describe a shadow: "As high as a tree, yet it never sees the sun" (Lithuanian: Mickevicius, p. 482, No. 15).

494. The solution is, more exactly, the crossed ribbons attached to the felt over the smoke opening. When they are pulled, the felt closes the opening.

495. Bulgarian: Ikonomov, 29 (A tail-less bear has its ribs burned). I do not understand the allusion to kittens in the Lithuanian "A lord is black like a Gypsy, and the red kittens whip him" (Balys, *Fifty riddles,* p. 326, No. 7). Similar riddles are very numerous and exhibit ingenious modifications of the fundamental idea; see the headnote to Taylor, *English,* 871–877. In this Mongolian version the riddler has introduced the fire, which belongs to the solution, into the text in place of the red actor.

496. Yakut: Iastremskii, 69 (A divine child is chewing black pitch), 411 (A good lad chews tar). Probably the "divine child" in the first of these riddles is a "child from Heaven" and involves the formula discussed in the note to No. 337 above. The precise meaning of "iron sulphur" is obscure. For parallels see Cheremis: Genetz, 7 = Sebeok, 5. 12. 7 (Iron is cooking in a pot of flesh). Turkish: Hamamizade, 190 (In a bony clay pot iron plays); Kowalski, *North Bulgaria,* 19. Hungarian: Kriza, p. 347, No. 67 (I climbed an iron ladder, I sat on my leather chair, I made the bone chew iron), which contains some elements belonging to No. 714 below. Lithuanian: Balys, p. 157, No. 546 (In a pot iron boils with flesh); Basanavicius, 20; Mickevicius, p. 574, No. 98 and p. 586, No. 195; Schleicher, p. 211; Jurgelionis, 737. Compare the Yakut "A hundred horses cannot eat up one wisp of hay" (Priklonskii, 21).

497. The riddler chooses the proper name, Galba, to alliterate with *gadzar* (earth, soil). For another name chosen for its alliterative value see No. 458 above. For a parallel in which no actor is named see No. 729 below and compare a different description of walking in No. 325.

499. The riddler suggests a comparison to a divinity or an idol. See another reference to eight cups in No. 269 above.

500. The name, Adian, may be related to Sanskrit *adiyā* (sun, day) and may suggest the marmot coming out into the light of day.

501–504. Compare the Kolarian "A man is strutting about with a crooked stock" (Wagner, 45) and the Uraon "The man who always carries a bent stick" (Elwin and Archer, p. 294, No. 37), "The boy with a sickle" (Archer, 84), and "The boy with a hockey stick" (Archer, 85). This conception is somewhat enlarged upon by adding a reference to the motion of the stick in the Muria "Whistle and the pole waves to and fro" (Elwin and Archer, p. 269, No. 31), the Munda "The fishing rod that waves when you whistle" (Elwin and Archer, p. 291, No. 36), and the Uraon "The sal tree that shakes without a wind" (Archer, 119). See also the Shilluk riddle for a cow's tail: "Which sorcerer spends the whole night in swinging?" (Westermann, p. 241).

503, 504. The knife in No. 503 seems more appropriate to the riddle than the plume in No. 504. Perhaps the plume (*otogo*) is a mistake for the knife (*xotogo*).

505. This is an adaptation of a riddle for a frog (No. 506) to a new answer. For other examples of such adaptations see the note to Nos. 476–478. This riddle contains some elements found in No. 408.

506. This frog riddle employs the comparison used in the riddle of an eagle owl (No. 505). For other examples of a comparison used to describe entirely different objects see the note to Nos. 476–478. For discussion of the many widely differing riddles for a frog see the notes to Nos. 40–42 and 797.

507. Apparently the name, Engkhe, has been chosen for the sake of a play on the vowels *e* and *i*. A similar name is found in No. 563. The Mongolian *phod phool* (heap) with an aspirate *p* is an onomatopoetic formation like the German *Klacks.* For parallels to the riddle see Turcoman: Samojlovich, 107. Siberian Turkish: Katanov, p. 286, No. 221 (It falls here, it falls there, it falls like a frying pan). Turkish: Kowalski, *Zagadki,* 117 (The box is open, the nuts have spread about). Hungarian: *Magyar Nyelvör* 5: 89, No. 22, 1876 (They are dropping pewter in the woods.—Cow dung). Bakongo: Denis, 48 (Papa's wife counts her money while walking, while walking.—Goat dropping excrements).

508. Munda: Elwin and Archer, p. 289, No. 15 (The hole of the coppersmith says *keon cheon*.—Hub of a country cart). Kabardin: Talpa and Sokolov, 12 (It never enters the house, it moves with lamentation.—Bullock cart). Turkish: Boratav, 4 (Comes from the mountain, grumbling, at its feet [are] great irons). Swedish: Ström, p. 142, "Skottkärran" (What is it that goes around the corners and says, *"Järrk, järrk?"*). A similar Swedish riddle has the answer "broom"; see Olsson, *Bohuslän,* 115.

509. The sound made by the bird resembles the reading of a holy book in a ritual. For similar conceptions see the note to No. 343.

510. Compare the hollow curved tree in No. 642 and see the note to Nos. 308b, 308c.

513. For parallels see the note to Nos. 158, 159.

516. Bazarov also gives the answer "saxicola" with a question mark. For references to a yellow cap or a cap of fox fur see the note to No. 449b.

519. The three crows are the supports of the gun; see the note to Nos. 11, 12.

520. Ariabalo (Sanskrit Aryabalo, Noble Strength), who is addressed in hymns and prayers as a spiritual teacher, is the Boddhisattva Avalokiteśvara, the protector of Tibet and lamaism. His face is represented in the handball used in lamaist rites. Here the riddler seems to conceive the sides of the bell as Ariabalo's thighs. The handle of the bell has the shape of a lama's sceptre (*ochir,* Sanskrit *vajra*) with the head of a divinity.

Compare the Greek bell riddle, "A pillar here, a pillar there, and a maiden in the middle" (Stathes, p. 335, No. 18).

521. For another description of chinaware or porcelain see No. 284. Compare also Taylor, *English,* 666 for a different riddle that mentions dying on uttering a sound.

522. Compare No. 192 and Cheremis: Sebeok-Beke, 2. 9. 6.

523–525. Riddlers have often compared the eyelids or the eyelashes to men swinging sticks or striking at each other; see the Yakut "Two men from two sides of a lake beat with poles.—Eyelashes" and "Ten children beat with poles on a small lake" (Iastremskii, 178, 179) and the parallels in the headnotes to Taylor, *English,* 1044, n. 8 and 1003–1004, n. 10. The reference to the ten children, who here represent the hairs of the eyelashes, has been suggested by riddles for the ten fingers. See further the Birhor "A boy that strikes itself [*sic*] against some hard substance in the morning" (Roy, pp. 539–540) and "The boy who strikes himself in the morning" (Elwin and Archer, p. 284, No. 3). The Serbians say, "A hundred blacksmiths are forging on one log and one does not hear the other" (Novaković, p. 225, No. 1). For other variations of this theme see the headnotes to Taylor, *English,* 788–789, § 2 (chop and leave no chips), 968, n. 7 (embrace at night), and 1665–1666, § 3 (chop and leave no mark).

Riddlers have expressed similar comparisons in terms of animals. See the Ainu "What animals fight, although they are on different sides of the river?" (Taylor, *Ainu,* 19) and the Turcoman "At the opening of the well there are forty mares, and they quarrel among themselves and kick one another" (Samojlovich, 3). Comparisons to things striking together are rare, but see the Low German "Two rough rags that clap together" (Gilhoff, 5).

526. See Nos. 419, 420 and the note.

528. The thong through the lattice wall has a knot at each end and can be compared to a man's clenched fist. For other references to this thong see the note to No. 192.

529. Kashmiri: Knowles, 114 (From that side an old woman, speaking through her nose, ran at me like a tigress and jumped on me and held me to her breast). Mordvin: Ahlqvist, 15 = Ahlqvist, *Moksha Mordvin,* 52 (A black cow, it conquered all men.—Night). Turcoman: Samojlovich, 16 (*Beede-beede,* it knocked me over and went off by itself). Russian: Sadovnikov, 2049 (My dear one came and threw me over by force), 2052. Arabic: Giacobetti, 309 (It comes from behind and knocks you to the ground). Spanish, Argentinian: Lehmann-Nitsche, 110 (A thing that comes to you and falls upon you without touching). Chilean: Laval, p. 93, No. 10 (It overcame the lion, it overcomes the tiger, it overcomes the enraged bull, it overcomes gentlemen and kings, who fall defeated at its feet). Ila: Smith and Dale, 2: 328, No. 27 (It is a small thing that choked my father). A different conception is seen in the Ila "I give your father a small cupful of porridge and it does not end" (Smith and Dale, 2: 328, No. 5).

530, 531. See the note to Nos. 599, 600.

532. Compare the Wamajame "Many warriors have clubs.—Grain"; "Warriors have come this year.—Shoots of bananas"; and "The father is in the plantation with his magic thong on his arm.—*Drazäne* [a plant]" (Ovir, 26, 27, 32). The first of these has a parallel in the Taveta "I have blown the horn and they came with nothing but clubs. —Grain of Eleusine corcana" (Hollis, 35). For additional parallels see the headnote to Taylor, *English*, 946-949, § 2 and the note to No. 946 in that collection.

533. The Mongolian *tangreen cyadel* (seam of Heaven) signifies the Milky Way. The notion of a seam naturally suggests measuring.

534. The riddler refers to an old fashioned gun with a stand such as the Calmucks use in hunting. The legs are the legs that support the gun. For other references to a gun on a stand see the note to Nos. 11, 12.

535. Votyak: Wichmann, 209 (Having shot downwards, the nose is hit). Turcoman: Samojlovich, 14. Russian: Sadovnikov, 2065, 2066. Estonian: Wiedemann, p. 275. Lappish: Turi, p. 223; Koskimies and Itkonen, 58 (It aims at the heel but hits on the head). Modern Greek: Polites, 130, 291. Danish: Kristensen, 82*b*. Swedish: Wessman, 103*b*. The Muria use a similar comparison to describe urination: "You fire the arrow with all your might, but it falls below your feet" (Elwin and Archer, p. 268, No. 20). Compare Makua: Harries, *Riddles*, pp. 285–286, No. 15.

536. The word here translated *high* may be a proper name. The Russian translator translates it as *short* and gives *high* in parentheses with a question mark. For parallels to the last descriptive detail see the Yakut "There is a Russian girl with girdles in three places.—Larva of a dragonfly" (Iastremskii, 146. See also his ant riddle, No. 142); the Indian Moslem "Black it is but not a crow. It crawls on trees but it is not a snake. Slender is its waist but [it is] not a panther" (Elwin and Archer, p. 311, No. 32), the Kurd "My uncle Qucûr, his head is larger than his belly" (Lescot, p. 348, No. 299), the Turkish "Below the earth there are horses, there are winding and twisting roads, there are thin waists" (Hamamizade, 337). The Turkish "*Hatatay, matatay,* a thin-waisted black colt" (Hamamizade, 339) has parallels in Siberia and Bulgaria; see Moshkov, p. 267, No. 34; Kowalski, *North Bulgaria,* 7. See further the French "Big behind, big in front, thin in the middle" (Marchessou, p. 167, No. 11); the Kamba "Tight-laced in its side.—Waist of a biting ant" (Lindblom, 55); and a West Indian story that explains why the jackspaniard (a kind of wasp) has a constricted waist (G. W. Basent, *Popular Tales from the Norse,* 2d ed., London, n. d., p. 389).

537. The Mongolians have many riddles for a spindle, distaff, or bobbin on which thread is reeled up. Comparisons to a thing are rare. For comparisons to an animal see the note to No. 260. Comparisons to a person are cited in this note. See the Cheremis "A pregnant woman dances. —Distaff and spindle" (Beke, 26 = Sebeok, 3. 8. 8. 2. 3; 8. 9.1.1.–8.9.1.2.3; and 8. 9. 3) and the parallels collected in the headnote to Taylor, *English,* 1455–1457, § 2. The Hungarian "The little one is just running along. How does he run? The little one keeps on running because he wants to fill his belly.—Spindle" (*Magyar Nyelvör* 4: 282, No. 47, [1875]), which may perhaps imply an animal rather than a person, represents a curious adaptation to narrative style. The comparison to a dancing woman resembles the riddles for a churnstaff; see the note to No. 393. See also a very different personification of a spindle in the Abyssinian "A woman who veils herself before her master" (Littmann, 57).

538. Riddlers usually compare the white page to a field and the writing to the seeds and equate the act of reading to plowing. For parallels see the headnote and note to Taylor, *English,* 1063. See also Chuvash: Mészáros, 154 (He sows black grain on a white field. He who sows knows), 157 (They are sowing black seeds on a white field). Cheremis: Sebeok, 4. 16 (On my white field I sow buckwheat); Sebeok-Beke, 4. 16. 1. Swedish: Wessman, 124. The Mongols prefer to write in Tibetan, but there is now a renaissance of Mongolian literature.

539. A pole is often used to lift or close the flap that covers the smokehole. A similar Surinam riddle describes a mortar and pestle: "A small boy shows God a fist" and "A tall man shows God his finger" (Herskovits, 49, 49*a*). This has, curiously enough, a Korean parallel with the same answer: "What is it that shakes its fist at the sky?" (Bernheisel, p. 82). A Makua riddle for wild millet with its head pointing upwards is "Let's sharpen an arrow and pierce God" (Harries, *Riddles,* p. 278, No. 16). In Surinam a similar riddle is used for a cabbage (Penard and Penard, 32). Compare also the description of the young banana, which is said to shoot the earth and not God (Taylor, *English,* 800). The underlying notion in these riddles is perhaps allied to the mythological theme of the shot at the sun-stag; see the headnote to Taylor, *English,* 391, n. 1.

540. The meaning of the riddle is obscure.

541. According to Golstunskii, Mongolian *cerge* means the pole to which horses are tethered.

542. Compare the Turkish "*Sak, sak,* it chatters, all the tree shakes, the root is in my hands.—Loom" (Moshkov, p. 271, No. 88). For comparisons to a solitary tree see Nos. 641, 679, 684, 687, 688 below.

543. For comparisons to a person having a defect see the note to No. 363.

544. In riddle contests, according to Gomboyev, this riddle is proposed first. It is therefore called "the mother and father of riddles" (*oniskhon ekhe echige*) or "the head of riddles" (*oniskhon t'yry*).

547. Tatar: Kalashev and Ioakimov, p. 66, No. 2 (In our house there are two daughters-in-law, both of an equal height). Such riddles for a door may contain the additional detail that these persons are in motion as in the Chinese "Two brothers equally tall; when they go out, they start wrestling" (Serruys, 12). Compare a reference to making sounds in No. 634 below. In those riddles which contain personifications of the door and the doorpost the latter is described as a subordinate or as standing still; see the Turcoman "One slave is ill, the second goes to inquire" (Samojlovich, 73) and the Cheremis "Aktolla the slave, Jañgojža the master" (Genetz, 88 = Sebeok, 3. 8. 1. 1). Some similar riddles for a door make comparisons to animals rather than persons. See the Armenian "I have a two-winged bird. It keeps flying, but does not move from its place" (Zelinski, p. 59, No. 33) and the SeSuto "The ribs of a dog firmly joined" (Norton and Velaphe, 54). The notion that a door moves but does not leave its place appears again in the Chinese "An old man, ninety-nine years old, who is swaying day and night" (Serruys, 47) and Taylor, *English,* 127.

Riddlers use the notion of persons of equal size to describe various things. See the Caucasian riddles for the corners of the room: "We are four brides. All of equal size" (Armenian: Zelinski, p. 57, No. 14) and "There are four men in our house, all are of the same height" (Tatar:

Kalashev and Ioakimov, p. 66, No. 5) with a Turkish parallel, "I have four daughters of the same stature" (Hamamizade, 539). Compare also the Hausa granary riddle, "The maidens of our house are very stout" (Fletcher, p. 52, No. 7); the Wanamwezi knee riddle, "Nubile maidens completely alike" (Dahl, 8. See also his No. 78); the Kamba riddles for women's breasts, "Two bullocks of equal size" (Lindblom, 63) and for piles of firewood, "Your mother and father are of equal size" (Lindblom, 50).

548. The faces are the fingernails. For comparisons of the fingernails to aprons see Taylor, *English*, 588 with the headnote and note. For comparisons to caps worn on the back see the headnote to Taylor, *English*, 989. The fundamental idea of the Mongolian riddle is analogous to the comparison of the calf of the leg to a man with his belly at the back; see No. 435 and the note. Compare also Nos. 594, 595.

549. Since Mongolian has no plural sign, No. 398 above can be regarded as a variant of this riddle.

550. Compare Siberian Turkish "Girls with mother of pearl buttons are walking on the mountain.—Wild goats" (Katanov, p. 240, No. 66).

551, 552. For parallels see the headnote to Taylor, *English*, 908–916. Mordvin: Ahlqvist, *Moksha Mordvin*, 49 (It has no windows, no doors, its interior is filled with men.—Cucumber); Passonen and Ravila, p. 615, No. 3 (It has neither door nor window. Its interior is full of people.—Cucumber) and p. 615, No. 8.

553. The meaning of the italicized words is obscure. For similar riddles see No. 89 above and the note. Compare the Marshallese "Riddle, riddle, take from the bush, throw to the white stones, what?" (Davenport, p. 265, No. 1). In the Marshall Islands men and women crack lice with their fingernails and women do so also with their teeth.

554. One end of the pillow is embroidered and one end is plain. For comparisons of a pillow to a torn ram's belly see No. 116 above and to torn trousers see No. 867 below.

555. Yakut: Iastremskii, 370 (For three lads there is one cap.—Tripod). Kanawari: Joshi, 3 (Three friends with one turban.—Cooking tripod). Cheremis: Sebeok, 3. 8. 3. 1. 1; 3. 8. 1. 2; 3. 8. 3. 4. 1–7; 3. 8. 14. 7 (Four Tatar women sit in one place); Sebeok-Beke, 3. 8. 14. 7. 1. Mordvin: Ahlqvist, *Moksha Mordvin*, 6 (Four priests have a single cap), 7 (Four priest's daughters under a single cap). Votyak: Fuchs, p. 242, No. 12 (Under a bridal veil four young women weep), p. 244, No. 34, and p. 245, No. 44. Chuvash: Mészáros, 110 = Karahka and Räsänen, p. 98, No. 63 (Four girls cry under one bridal veil). Kurd: Lescot, 295 (Three brothers with the black belly.—Tripod), 296 (Three legs under something that makes the sound *ting!*—Tripod and pot). Lithuanian: Basanavicius, 136; Mickevicius, p. 572, No. 8, p. 578, No. 58, and p. 586, Nos. 179, 183. Note a novel variation in the Cheremis "I carry four Tatar women, making the dance.—I pull the table" (Sebeok, 3. 8. 8. 4). For additional parallels see Taylor, *English*, 993 and the note.

556. The ten people are the ten fingers. For comparisons of the fingers to people see Nos. 352 and the note and 583–585 and the note.

557. The Mongolian *daku*, which is here translated "in furs," means a pelt with the fur outside. In No. 557d, the riddler mentions the color of the skins. For a parallel see the Turkish "I have four donkeys; two with blankets and two without blankets. Cow's horns and ears" (Boratav, 206a).

Riddlers describe a cow's horns in various ways. They notice that snow does not cling to a horn. See the Altai Turkish "On a slanting birch no snow remains" (Menges, p. 86, No. 9; Radlov, 1: 261, No. 6; Katanov, p. 239, No. 57 [crooked tree]); the Cheremis "The snow does not cling to a crooked linden" (Sebeok, 4. 14); the Zyrian "A fence corner, where snow does not gather" (Wichmann, 84); and the Votyak "Snow does not stay on the smooth maple" (Wichmann, 215). The notion that a horn does not freeze is less popular and less widely known; see the Yakut "Half a tree freezes, the other half doesn't.—Horns on a cow in winter" (Ionova, 55) and "A crooked tree does not freeze through" (Priklonskii, 95 = Piekarski, 72. Compare also Piekarski, 71). In both India and Africa riddlers contrast wet and dry or living and dry things in riddles for horns. See the Santal "Two dry poles on a live body" (Elwin and Archer, p. 303, No. 7), the Kamba "Tell me a tree, it dries up among the branches at the top, at the base it is fresh" (Lindblom, 66), the Makua "There is a tree, it has four fresh branches [legs], two leaves [ears], and two dry branches [horns].—Goat" (Harries, *Riddles*, p. 280, No. 6), and the Lamba "Part raw, part dried.—Elephant's tusk" (Doke, 101). The last of these is perhaps suggested by the contrast of raw and dried food rather than of fresh and dry parts of a plant. See also Tabaru: Fortgens, p. 530, No. 26. The Muria contrast the horns and the teats: "Two are dry and four are slimy" (Elwin and Archer, p. 268, No. 21). Compare also Yakut: Iastremskii, 79.

For a comparison to a person in a fur coat see the Nandi caterpillar riddle: "I have met your father wearing his fur coat" (Hollis, p. 140, No. 33).

559. Yakut: Piekarski, 170–172. Turkish: Boratav, 138 ([In] its yellow [color] it resembles saffron, [in] its black [color] it resembles tar, its throat is like a fife, we almost swallowed it.—Lamb's liver), Orhan, 2: 7 (Below, black; above, red. We ate it.—Liver); Hamamizade, 103, 104. The black object is the lungs and the red one the liver. The Turks always eat the lungs and liver together. See also the Turkish "One side spotted, one side black, in the center a pipe [or: flute], we ate it" (Orhan, 2: 19). The Samoyede conception of the lungs of a reindeer is very different from these riddles. It is: "It drags two swans at the end of a knotted (?) cord" (Lehtisalo, 201). Compare also the Turcoman gall riddle: "On the top of Mt. Yalam there sits a maiden in a green gown. She eats the flesh of a young lamb dripping in fat" (Samojlovich, 11).

560. A more exact identification of the plant intended by the riddler would have greatly aided us in the interpretation of the riddle. According to the dictionaries, *temsym* signifies "field crops, potatoes," but the Russian translator renders it "lily." The adjectives "bony" (the text is literally "bone") and "empty" seem to refer to a hard hollow stalk. For parallels to the formula "in the steppe" see the note to No. 253.

561. For parallels see Nos. 604–607 below with the note and the headnote to Taylor, *English*, 1017 *bis*.

561a. The branchy, tufted mother is wood; the son of the king of hell is fire; the black seed of the lonton, which is used as a bead in a chaplet, is the pot. For similar descriptions of fire, wood, and smoke or a pot see the headnotes to Taylor, *English*, 941–942 and 1017, § 3 and the Samoyede "One of them is the son of the masters of stones, one of them is the son of the masters of dense forests, one of them is the son of the masters of iron. Among them they beget a child.—Steel, flint, tinder" (Lehtisalo, 247).

561b, 561c. For a description of Yama see Getty, pp. 134–137.

562b. The black son-in-law is the kettle, and the white daughter is a dishclout or brush.

565. The place-name Bilÿty seems to be derived from *bilÿ* (whetstone). It may involve an allusion to the stone or stones occasionally found at the entrance to a felt tent.

566. Compare the Tungus "[Go] to this side, you to that" (Poppe, 3). Samoyede: Lehtisalo, 223 (Just go farther on, I shall find you later). Zyrian: Wichmann, 117. Cheremis: Wichmann, 30 = Sebeok, 3. 8. 10. 2 (You thither, I hither, at Terentius' mill we shall meet.—Tying the laces of a bast shoe). Serbian: Novaković, p. xviii, No. 8; p. 82, No. 5 (You come from yonder, I come from here. When we meet, we fight); and p. 160, No. 1 (One went there, the other came here, and they met in the middle of the field.—Woman's girdle). Lithuanian: Sabaliauskas, p. 320, No. 165. Chinyanja: Rattray, p. 155 (You go in this direction, I go in that, we must meet). Makua: Harries, *Riddles*, p. 289, No. 3 (You pass there, I will pass here, let us meet). Dschagga: Stamberg, 214 (Stand on this side, I shall go and stand on that side, and let us put some cloth around the young woman.—Tying a pot with a green banana leaf). Tlokoa: Krüger, 8 (Goes around the mountain.—Pearl ornament for the hips). Lamba: Doke, 79 (That which encircles us.—String tying a loincloth or a belt). Note also the SeSuto "You go that side, I go this side, let us catch a chicken.—Reed fence with two corners meeting in the middle" (Norton and Velaphe, 42).

567. Compare Mordvin: Paasonen and Ravila, p. 615, No. 9 (It sits and makes butter, [it has] two, a horned one [fem.] has four, and one with a snout has twelve.—Sheep, cow, pig), p. 620, No. 2, and compare p. 660, No. 4 and p. 661, No. 7. Siberian Turkish: Katanov, p. 286, No. 213 (I have two that shake and eight that walk.—Teats of mare and dog). Chuvash: Karahka and Räsänen, p. 101, No. 97. See also Yakut: Iastremskii, 70, 71. Arabic: Giacobetti, 143. Russian: Sadovnikov, 893, 894; Preobrazhenskii, p. 170. Polish: Saloni, *Rzeshów*, 66; Gustawicz, 180, 1811. Sukuma: Augustiny, 32 (I cut eight pieces of wood.—Teats of a dog).

568. This comparison to a person moving among warriors is also used to describe a dipper; see No. 569. For other examples of a comparison used to describe entirely different things see the note to Nos. 476–478.

569. Siberian Turkish: Katenov, p. 286, No. 210 (Among my ten thousand sheep runs a shaggy ram.—Mixer that stirs toasting barley). Cherekessian: Tambiev, p. 59, No. 67 (The horseman dashes out against a hundred horseman.—Small mortar [with a pestle] and grains in it). A similar theme is expressed in somewhat different terms in Mordvin: Paasonen and Ravila, p. 616, No. 7 (On the hearth a hand sled, one keeps sheep in it.—The dish and noodles on the table). Kharia: Elwin and Archer, p. 286, No. 26 (The old woman who dives into boiling water.—Country spoon).

570. The conception is not entirely clear but resembles somewhat other Mongolian button riddles.

571. Turkish: Kúnos, 1: 155, No. 103. The comparisons in the very curious Modern Greek "Five soft pies, a crooked bow, a bag of cheese" (Ligyros, p. 300) are limited to familiar domestic objects. For more remote parallels see Nos. 616 and 617 below with the note.

572. Yakut: Piekarski, 135; Iastremskii, 412 (I would retire into a beautiful spot, but this encumbrance hinders me). Siberian Turkish: Katanov, p. 160, No. 1329 (If I did not have three fellow travelers, I should have gone away long ago); Katanov, *Urianchai*, 42. See other riddles for a hobble or a hobbled horse in No. 44 above and the note.

573. The meaning of Mongolian *mad* is obscure.

574. Tushiyetu Khan is the ruler of a region of Outer Mongolia that has its center at Urga, now Ulan Bator. Dzasaktu Khan's principality lies east of this region.

576. For parallels see the headnote to Taylor, *English*, 379–380. See a description of a needle and thread in similar terms in No. 577. For other pairs of riddles using the same comparison to describe entirely different objects see the note to Nos. 476–478.

577. The horseshoe is the thimble. See the note to No. 577 for further comment.

578. Compare the theme of a shadow that cannot be caught; it is discussed in the note to No. 443 above. To the texts there cited add Japanese: Moore and Preston, 4. 43 (What is it: chasing and chasing but not catching?). Cheremis: Sebeok, 3. 6. 6 (Soulless chases one with a soul). Togo: Schönhärl, 108 (A man walks with you and you cannot seize him). Makua: Harries, *Riddles*, 2 (Even though you chase him, you do not catch him), 2 var. For the comparison of a mirage to a gazelle that cannot be caught see No. 280 above.

579. The meaning of *dobrotor*, which is perhaps a place name, is obscure. The riddler has given the widely known riddle for wagon wheels (Nos. 580, 582) a new answer. For other examples of a comparison used to describe entirely different objects see the note to Nos. 476–478.

580. For parallels see Taylor, *English*, 1014, 1015, and the headnote to the texts. Cheremis: Sebeok, 3. 8. 7. 2. 1 and 3. 8. 7. 2. 2. Nagaibak: Vitevskii, p. 276, No. 11 (Four Tatars leap, they do not reach one another). Swedish: Wessman, 286.

581. For parallels see the headnote to Taylor, *English*, 952–957, § 10.

583. Polish: Saloni, *Rzeshów*, 129 (Ten brothers pull a skin on a bare mountain). Swedish: Wessman, 148. See a Breton description of pulling on trousers, "Five push and ten pull," quoted in the headnote to Taylor, *English*, 970–982, n. 3.

584. Although explanations of Khorkudai in No. 583 and Arzadai in No. 585 are offered, a native speaker can make no suggestion to explain Aksadai. Siberian Turkish: Katanov, p. 241, No. 78 (Five men are putting old man Orenday on a horse) and p. 286, No. 219. See also No. 352 above and the note.

585. Arzadai signifies "one who grins, one who opens his mouth" and is therefore an appropriate name for a shirt.

586. The nomad horde is to be understood in the light of No. 620 below.

587. Riddlers often compare the eyelashes or eyebrows to trees standing around a lake and also to persons who carry sticks or strike with sticks; see the note to Nos. 523–525 above.

588. Compare the Bakongo "These go, those return" (Bufe, p. 59, No. 8; Denis, *Bakongo*, 57) and the Irish beehive riddle, "There is a wee little hut in the garden that hundreds would go into. I would not find room in it nor half my clothes" (Delargy, 53 = Hull and Taylor, *Irish*, 329a). The Irish describe an ant hill with the same riddle (Ó Dálaigh, 43 = Hull and Taylor, *Irish*, 330a).

588b. Compare No. 611 below.

589. The meaning of *gurbuts*, which appears in the Russian translation, is obscure.

591. Compare the African "I saw a chief walking along the road with flour on his head.—Gray hair" (Werner, p. 213). See also the texts collected in the headnote to Taylor, *English*, 46, nn. 4–12.

592. For the Sanskrit prayer "Ōm, maṇi padme, hūṃ!" see Getty, p. 172. It is here cited in the Mongolian form.

593. Korean: Bernheisel, p. 59 (What is it that on going beats a new tomtom and coming in beats a drum?). Cheremis: Sebeok, 3. 8. 13. 6. 1 (It descends crying; it rises laughing), 3. 8. 13. 6. 2–3. Turkish: Bahaeddin, 79. Walloon: Colson, *Wallonia* 5: 57, No. 226 (Who sings while going down and weeps on rising?). For additional parallels see the headnote and note to Taylor, *English*, 768 and compare No. 176 above.

594, 595. Yakut: Ionova, 3 (Children are carrying windows of ice on their backs and they scatter in every direction); Iastremskii, 168, 169. Turkish: Hamamizade, 115–119; Katanov, *Urianchai*, 45 (The kinsfolk have loaded themselves with ice). Bulgarian: Stoilov, § 30, No. 3 (Ten priests all wear caps). Lithuanian: Schleicher, p. 198 (Five Cossacks with iron napes of necks); Mickevicius, p. 578, No. 78 (Five Cossacks have helmets of pebble-skin). Tlokoa: Krüger, 7 (Our young lads go about with little caps). For a comparison of a fingernail to a rock that cannot be opened see No. 724 below. See also No. 548 above with the note.

596. The meaning of the riddle is obscure.

597. The scolding and cursing are the squeaking of the saddle under the rider. According to Rudnyev, neither the collector, who was himself a Buriat, nor any of the Aga Buriats whom he consulted could explain all the words. Although some of the words are not in the dictionaries, the riddle offers no difficulty, if the Russian translation is correct. The two saddlebows, one in front and one behind, are imagined to be sulking and turning their faces in opposite directions. For the Mongolian *tarixu* (to scold or curse) we might perhaps read *tarnixu* from the Sanskrit *dhāraṇi* (to mutter incantations or curses).

599, 600. The phrase "to warm one's liver" may be a Mongolian colloquialism for "to warm oneself." For parallels see No. 530 above. Ainu: Taylor, *Ainu*, 14 with the note. Icelandic: Arnason, 1035 (A black rump sits by the fire and warms itself). See also the headnote to Taylor, *English*, 871–877 and especially the note to No. 873.

603. The felt is made of cow's hair and the drum is made of leather. Compare Tibetan: Tafel, p. 492 (Two sons beat their father. The feather cries so loudly that the whole village must hear it. However, no one has compassion on the father, but many rejoice. What is it?). Yakut: Piekarski, 20 = Priklonskii, 4 (Not having a head, it bellows, and having a head, it cries out.—Drum and shaman). Arabic: Ruoff, p. 25, No. 28 (There is one whose son strikes him, thereupon he raises his voice to heaven, yet no one comes to aid.—Bell). Russian: Bardin, p. 244, No. 16 (The living beats the dead one, and the dead one yells for all he's worth.—Bell). Rumanian: Papahagi, 53 (The son kisses his father.—Bell clapper). See also the somewhat similar comparison of a lama and a lapwing in Nos. 347, 348 above. For other comparisons in animal terms see the Yakut "The colt of the grey mare is kicking" (Iastremskii, 228) and "The grey colt kicks the lord's liver, all its sides, they say" (Iastremskii, 229). See finally the Albanian riddle for a church bell and clapper: "The son strikes the father, the father overturns the world" (Hahn, p. 160, No. 19).

A widely known sieve riddle shows some similarity to this conception of a drum. See the Hungarian "I have a girl. Wherever she was taken, she was spanked" (*Magyar Nyelvör* 3: 329, No. 64, [1874]). See also *ibid.* 5: 127, No. 35, [1876]; 18: 376, No. 13, [1889]; 21: 527, No. 17, [1892]). In "Whenever I take it, I slap it. Whenever I put it back, I also slap it" (*Magyar Nyelvör*, 7: 476, [1878]), the riddler makes a comparison to a thing rather than a person.

For other comparisons of a drum to a man see the note to No. 351.

604–607. See also No. 561 above. Yakut: Ionova, 99 (When Kilyabyagya hit Chukuruya's teeth, sparks appeared.—Steel for striking fire, flint). The proper names may suggest common nouns pertinent to the theme to speakers of Yakut. Agaria: Elwin, p. 119 = Elwin and Archer, p. 270, No. 8 (Father beats mother and the child springs out). Although Elwin finds a sexual connotation in this riddle, it does not seem particularly important. Riddlers often compare flint, tinder, and a spark to a father, a mother, and a child; see No. 606 and an Indonesian parallel in the headnote to Taylor, *English*, 966–968, § 5. Compare also Mordvin: Paasonen and Ravila, p. 689, No. 5 (Five rule and compel, two fight and quarrel, they shed drops of blood as big as a flea.—Flint and the stone with which it is struck); Ahlqvist, *Moksha Mordvin*, p. 144, No. 72. Russian: Sadovnikov, 184 (I will strike with the sword across the stone chambers. A princess will come out and will sit down on a downy feather bed). Bulgarian: Gubov, 183 (Two dragons are fighting, bright sparks are flying), 260 (Two dead [men] got into a fight and produced a third [man], a living one). Serbian: Novaković, p. 151, No. 2 (I took an iron mallet and hit an iron fortress with it; out jumped the king, everybody chased him but could not catch him; only the soft crab caught him). See also Novaković, p. 151, Nos. 1, 3–6.

607. A burning candle is said to have a red nose; see No. 730.

608. Ōkhön, an endearing term used by parents in addressing children, signifies here the fingers. The meaning of Chökhön, if it is more than merely a rhyming word, is obscure. For the comparison of a button and buttonhole to a creature that spreads its legs see Nos. 11, 12 above and the note, and also No. 959. For comparisons to a person or an animal being choked see Nos. 164, 165 and the note. For comparisons to struggling animals see No. 318. Still other themes occur in riddles describing buttons. See the Yakut "They say that Ykyłyky and Čykyłyky call upon (or: visit) each other" (Piekarski, 283), the Tibetan "Mornings and the whole day it looks out a window, in the evening it goes back through the window" (Tafel, p. 493). A somewhat unusual comparison to things is found in the Yakut "They say that a large bowl has a crevice" (Piekarski, 287).

609. Compare the riddles for churning, Nos. 393 and 817.

610–612. Riddlers often describe the objects used in chess, backgammon, and various card games as persons. See the Yakut "They say: during their life time four districts have lived in one place as co-lodgers.—Markings on playing cards" (Piekarski, 445) and "They say that, in one town, four foreign kings and their entire retinues weigh an important matter.—Playing cards" (Piekarski, 447); the Hindi "There are eight kings in one town and each has a separate estate. They consult and come to an agreement, and all have their accounts in one book.—The game of Gangifa, in which there are eight kings of different colors on the same board" (W. J. D'Gruyther, *Panjab Notes and Queries* 3: 15, § 64, No. 6, [1885]); the Persian "Two bodies in two caravans I saw, their heads bared, their bodies blistered, the caravans do not move without the permission of these two, nor do these two move without the permission of the caravan.—Dice in backgammon" (Phillott, 25) and "What is that city that is populated by lifeless men? It is sometimes flourishing and sometimes desolate. You will see it prosperous in the time of war and desolate in the time of peace.—Chess" (Kuka, 1); the Arabic "Two tribes have met; the powder spoke a great deal and no one was injured.—Chess" (Giacobetti, 435); and the Icelandic backgammon riddle, "I saw two islands with two slaves running around, thirty maidens fought there bitterly" (Arnason, 138. See also his Nos. 596 and 1132). Riddles describing chess naturally stress the comparison to a battle. They are very similar to the Mongolian texts under discussion, but are not clearly connected with them in origin. Typical examples are the Icelandic "Two kings possess a kingdom. They contend against all the subjects, prelates, and earls, but the women are the best fighters"; "What is this battlefield where men contend? There are sixteen soldiers on each side. They use as a front sixteen children, who are usually killed before the others"; "The people of a certain country defend themselves without arms, while all the men are struggling over the realm. Clerics, women, and the common people fight alongside the heroes"; and "I know a kingdom where every subject goes to war. If they are all killed, they rise up quickly and resume the fight" (Arnason, 338, 573, 829, and 1112 respectively). See also the Icelandic riddles for playing cards (Arnason, 667, 861). Perhaps the most interesting problem in riddles of this sort is a description of tarot given by Larivey in his French translation of Straparola, *Piacevoli notte* 13 : 7. It is not in the Italian text; see M. De Filippis, *The literary riddle in Italy*, p. 37. Larivey gives many details and leaves us the task of interpretation.

611. Compare No. 588b.

613. Yakut: Ionova, 1 (Two brothers are sitting side by side without seeing each other). Uraon: Archer, 98 (The two brothers who sit together but never look at each other). Cheremis: Sebeok, 3. 8. 12. 3. 1 (The older and the younger brother cannot see each other), 3. 8. 12. 3. 2. Mordvin: Paasonen and Ravila, p. 611, No. 1 ("Come, friend, to us!" "How can I come to you, a tree trunk has fallen between us?") and p. 627, No. 4 (Beside an overthrown tree the two daughters of a *pope* [Russian priest] are living. They live all their lives and do not see each other). Samoyede: Lehtisalo, 274 (Two men look at each other behind a fallen tree). Lithuanian: Basanavicius, p. 189, No. 8 (Two brothers beside the road, yet they can never see each other); Sabaliauskas, p. 317, No. 30 (sisters). Swedish: Olsson, *Bohuslän*, 13. Compare the Fijian "Two men fight every day and all the day. Their fighting ceases at night and begins afresh in the morning" (Fison, 16). For additional parallels see the headnote to Taylor, *English*, 1003–1004 (comparisons to birds, animals, brothers, or objects). Note the ingenious Togo "Two pots on a narrow hearth, but they never come together" (Schönhärl, 95). Compare also the riddles for eyelashes or eyelids cited in the note to Nos. 523–525 above.

615. Yakut: Piekarski, 142, 143, 144 (dogs), 146, 147; Iastremskii, 72; Priklonskii, 8; Ionova, 18 (the riddler gives the answer "cow," but describes a mare); Poppe, p. 289 (Four Russian children urinate in the same place, they say). Votyak: Wichmann, 31; Fuchs, p. 245, no. 69. Zyrian: Wichmann, 277. Cheremis: Sebeok, 3. 8. 16. 4. 1–3. 8. 16. 4. 4; Sebeok-Beke, 3. 8. 16. 4. 6. Mordvin: Ahlqvist, p. 39, No. 3; Ahlqvist, *Moksha Mordvin*, 8; Paasonen and Ravila, p. 654, No. 5. Lappish: Qvigstad, 95. Chuvash: Mészáros, 118, 183. Siberian Turkish and Turkish: Katanov, p. 91, No. 766, p. 108, No. 936, and p. 241, No. 83; Katanov, *Urianchai*, 2; Hamamizade, 275. Bulgarian: Gubov, 385. Russian: Sadoynikov, 868b. Lithuanian: Jurgelionis, 754–757; Sabaliauskas, 59; Mickevicius, p. 587, No. 239; Schleicher, p. 211. Polish: Gustawicz, 47.

For a survey of the comparisons used to describe milking a cow see the note to No. 889 below.

616, 617. Similar riddles are widely known in both Asia and Europe, but not (I believe) in Africa, where only a few Arabic examples might be cited. In such riddles the riddler enumerates and characterizes the members of an animal or the parts of a thing; he does not ordinarily combine them into a description of an object that is not the answer to the riddle. For discussion of such riddles see the headnote to Taylor, *English*, 1476–1494, and for parallels to this particular riddle see § 6 in that headnote. Note also the similarly conceived description of a camel in No. 571 above. Riddlers do not confuse riddles of this sort with the description of an animal as being composed of the members of various other animals; for this conception see the note to No. 472 above.

Perhaps the most ingenious variation of this manner of riddling is a description of an elephant current among the Moslems in India: "Four pillars are standing,/ Two fans are moving,/ Two lamps are lighted,/ And a cobra plays within" (Elwin and Archer, p. 310, No. 17). This is an exception to the usual form of these riddles, for the riddler expects us to see these details as a picture of an Indian temple. The same theme is less skillfully used in the Rajput-Kayesth "Lamps she burns,/ Four posts she moves,/ And she dangles a cobra" (Elwin and Archer, p. 299, No. 288).

616. The word here translated "Russian" may mean any white man.

619. Kashmiri: Koul, 31 (Five Pândavas lifted up a rock [and] hurled it to Lukshari Yâr; the weak mother gave it a push; it reached Khâdan Yâr suddenly). Uraon: Elwin and Archer, p. 295, No. 47 (The girl with the round little body works the pounder, while the red girls give the grain). Moslems in India: Elwin and Archer, p. 309, No. 12 (Pick me up, take me up, five brothers turn back, I am going away). I have emended the punctuation of this text. Munda: Elwin and Archer, p. 290, No. 27 (The five brothers who go into a narrow hole together.—Five fingers go into the mouth). Juang: Elwin and Archer, p. 278, No. 11 (In the corner of the house there is a rice husker. It husks the grain *lusur lasar* and someone pushes the rice into the hole). Asur: Elwin and Archer, p. 282, No. 32 (The five brothers that cross the white stone.—Eating rice). In this Asur riddle the "white stone" is the tooth; it is elsewhere often the rice that is being eaten. Mordvin: Ahlqvist, *Moksha Mordvin*, 33 (Thirty thrashers, one who turns.—Teeth and tongue). Turkish: Boratav, 176 (Five Negroes [or: servants] throw stones into a well.—Fingers and the mouth). The comparison to throwing stones into a well is also used to describe milking a cow; see the note to No. 889 below. Modern Greek: Polites, 66 (Thirty-two hammer, Maria sweeps up, and Poor Fellow pours out), 67 (The five gather up, the hammers beat up, Chaoush [the sergeant] picks up, and the Agha [ruler] unloads), 178 (Five, ten carry, eighteen hammer, Madame Maria sweeps up and down, round and round); Stathes, p. 344, No. 78 (Five by five do the carrying, the white flies mangle them, the dust-cloth cleans, the canary pushes it down and stores it in the hold, and the "poor thing" puts it out.—Fingers, teeth, tongue, larynx, stomach, and arse); Stathes, p. 346, No. 87 (The hammer hammers, the five transport, Theodora calls down the long passage.—Teeth, fingers, tongue, and stomach). Lithuanian: Volteris, p. 451, No. 29 (A mare sank in the black swamp, five wolves pushed, two wolves wailed.—Bowl, fingers, eyes). For additional parallels see the headnotes to Taylor, *English*, 841, §§ 4–7 and 980–982. Compare also the ingenious Javanese riddle for chewing betel, which turns red in the mouth: "Five thieves are mentioned who want to go a-thieving. Four have already entered the opening; they are aiming at the house within the hedge (i.e., the teeth). The one who remained behind follows the others and closes the opening. Those who are in the house (i.e., the betel and the materials chewed with it) are all caught and put to death; blood streams out of the opening" (Rannefft, *Poëzie*, pp. 9–10, No. 18. See also Rannefft, *Proza*, pp. 38–39, No. 170).

Similar comparisons are occasionally used to describe other things than eating or the fingers and the mouth. See a Chinese riddle for a cotton gin: "The feet trample on it, the hands take it up, it eats white flour and spouts little balls" (Serruys, 1) and a Berber riddle for the heart, the eyes, and the four limbs: "A single person who commands a whole group and has in his service six persons of the tent. See what is the key [to that]," as cited by Loubignac, p. 421, No. 3.

620. Cheremis: Porkka, 124 = Sebeok, 3. 8. 10. 3. 3 (I lifted a piece of linden bark and forty-one soldiers fell out); Beke, 12 = Sebeok, 3. 8. 10. 3. 4 (I lift one of my fingers. Forty-one soldiers leap); Wichmann, 4 = Sebeok, 3. 8. 10. 3. 2; Sebeok, 3. 8. 10. 3. 1; Sebeok-Beke, 3. 8. 7. 4. Haytian: Bastien, 24. See Nos. 458, 482, and 507 above.

The Muria conceive excretion in terms of animals: "The basket broke and out came the tiger.—A pig excretes" (Elwin and Archer, p. 267, No. 9). For a comparison in terms of things see the Votyak "The young woman strewed her arm-band of pearls, as she went to fetch water" (Wichmann, 312), which has a Cheremis parallel, "Jəldərssika goes to fetch water, her bracelet pearls roll down" (Sebeok, 3. 8. 11. 5). Note also the Votyak "The tip of the pole projects, thirty [a noun is lacking] fell down drop by drop" (Wichmann, 341). See also the comparison of excrements to a sandalwood bowl in No. below.

621. The riddler has adapted the riddle for the hairs in a horse's tail (see No. 622) to a new answer. The many entering are the fagots, and the one coming out is the ashes. For other examples of a comparison serving two purposes see the note to No. 476–478.

622. Tatar: Kalashev and Ioachimov, p. 60, No. 6 (If it enters the water, it goes apart. When it comes out, it comes together.—Horse's tail and women's hair). For additional parallels see the headnote to Taylor, *English*, 1448–1453, nn. 2–6.

623. There are usually three actors. For similar riddles but no close parallel see the headnote to Taylor, *English*, 138–140.

624, 625. See the comparison of leaves to children who leave their mother as cited in the headnote to Taylor, *English*, 1021, nn. 12–14. Siberian Turkish: Katanov, p. 158, No. 934 (The scabby stallion has left, but the fallow-bay horses scattered).

626. The hind feet step into the imprints of the forefeet. The conversational form of this Mongolian riddle has a parallel in the Baiga "'You stay behind, I am going away'" (Elwin, p. 464, No. 3 = Elwin and Archer, p. 323, n. 1) and an Asur (a tribe in Chota Nagpur) riddle, "'You are always going and leaving me behind'" (Elwin and Archer, p. 283, No. 43). Compare also the Ila riddle for feet, "'My dear, you leave me! My dear, you leave me!'" (Smith and Dale, 2: 328, No. 331). See further the Uraon "A man who goes out to see the world and a dwarf stays behind" (Archer, 184), the Tabaru "Something of yours that you leave behind" (Fortgens, 47), the Tatar "'I shall go, it will remain.'—Tracks" (Kalashev and Ioakimov, p. 49, No. 13. See also the shadow riddle, No. 12), the Siberian Turkish "'Stand farther off and I will step in your tracks'" (Katanov, p. 239, No. 59), and the Turkish "'I go, she remains'" (Kowalski, *Zagadki*, 34). The last of these has been altered to make a riddle for the voice: "'I remain, she goes'" (Kowalski, *Zagadki*, 33). Compare the Lamba "Mr. Beard has crossed the river and left his sister on the other side.—Foot and footprint" (Doke, 118). The beard is the fetlocks. See also the Chuvash "A white kerchief lies in the field.—Snowshoe track" and "A tall Russian lies in the field.—Furrow" (Mészáros, 98, 99). The description of an animal's footprint in No. 871 below concerns only its shape.

A similar comparison describes the dying banana leaf that a new one replaces: "'Get out of the way, so that I may occupy the place'" (Dschagga: Raum, 2).

628. The third query should probably refer to alcohol, which the snake may represent. For a survey of the Mongolian riddles for distilling and related themes see the note to No. 337. For parallels to the notion that smoke goes without feet see the headnote to Taylor, *English*, 265, § 6.

629. Japanese: Moore and Preston, 4. 3 (What is it: it meets with grandmother [*baba*], but it does not meet with grandfather [*zizi*]?). Dr. Roy A. Miller of the Institute of East Asiatic Studies has kindly sent me the following very curious quotation from S. Yoshitake, *The phonetic system of ancient Japanese*, Royal Asiatic Society, James G. Furlong Fund, 12, London, 1934:

"An interesting example may here be cited of the sound of modern [*h*] as pronounced in Kyōto about 400 years ago. It occurs in a riddle, *Nazo* 'What is it?' proposed by the Emperor Gonara (before his accession) in A.D. 1516: *Haha ni wa nido aitaredo mo chichi ni wa ichido mo awazu* —*Kuchibiru* 'lips.' When translated in an ordinary way the riddle can only mean '(I) met (my) mother twice, but have not met (my) father even once,' which does not fit in with the answer. If, on the other hand, we follow Professor Simmura's phonetic interpretation and translate it 'In (pronouncing) *fafa* (the lips) met twice, but in (saying) *chichi* (they) do not meet even once,' then the riddle is solved. This means that the word [*haha*] 'mother' must have been pronounced [*fafa*] or [*FaFa*] at that time in Kyōto."

For other parallels see Turcoman: Samojlovich, 4, citing several examples. Tatar: Filonenko, 88. Turkish: Hamamizade, 161, 162; Bahaeddin, 2. See the texts collected in the headnote to Taylor, *English*, 944–945, n. 2. Compare the Bihari "They say 'unite,' but they do not unite; they say 'separate' but unite with each other. I propound a riddle. O ye clever people, find it out" (Mitra, *Bihar*, 65).

Riddlers describe the lips as persons kissing; see the headnote to Taylor, *English*, 1016, n. 4. Flemish: Joos, 67. A Santal riddle for the lips, "The two men who are always beating each other" (Elwin and Archer, p. 305, No. 20), resembles the riddles for the eyelids or eyelashes discussed in the note to No. 523 above. The eyes are said to be persons, who are often called sisters, who do not kiss; see the headnote to Taylor, *English*, 1016, nn. 2, 3.

630. Muria: Elwin, p. 595, No. 86 (There's white water in the black pot. Queen Thanka is dancing there). Korean: Bernheisel, p. 82 (What is it that bows to the mountain opposite?—Mill pestle). Yakut: Ionova, 67 (A hasty man enters the house of white milk, jumps around, divides the milk into two different kinds.—Bucket, twirling stick, butter, and whey). Mordvin: Paasonen, 351 (A child hops in a bowl). Lappish: Qvigstad, 115 (A pig goes about under a bridge and Sara stabs with her stick.—Churning).

In No. 393 above, which is also a riddle for a churnstaff, there is no mention of an act. Some riddles cited in the note to No. 363 describe a churnstaff or pestle as a person performing ritualistic acts. Compare also the riddles for a pestle cited in the note to No. 539.

632. Turkish: Kúnos, I, 153, No. 94 = Hamamizade, 364 (It comes from the mountain, it comes from the rocks, it looks like your brother-in-law with an open rump.— Goat) and p. 154, No. 96 (The mammy is coming down from the hill, she has no tail, her rump is bare, presently you will see her, and you will die laughing.—She-goat); Boratav, 117; Hamamizade, 363; Yanikoglu, 33 (It comes from the mountain, it comes from the stone, my brother-in-law with open arse); Moshkov, p. 266, No. 19 (Into the field there goes a little kid; into the village it goes, its arse uncovered.—She-goat). Tatar: Filonenko, 76 (In the morning it goes with an open arse, and it returns at night with a closed arse.—Goat). Arabic: Giacobetti, 142. For a riddle about the bare rump of a hen see the headnote to Taylor, *English*, 1437, § 10.

633. The word *mangut*, which signifies "ogre," has been added by Bazarov. Its pertinence to the riddle is obscure.

634. Although the import of the riddle is clear, the implications of the references to the emperor and the queen are obscure. See also the comparisons of doors or a gate to the daughters of Peaceful in No. 563 and to persons of equal stature or rank in No. 547. These riddles do not refer to the sound made by the doors. For mention of this sound see the Shor "In the clear frosty air my grandfather's voice is heard" (Dyrenkova, 30) and the Turkish "A black chicken is nailed up, its wings creak" (Hamamizade, 322).

635. Moksha Mordvin: Ahlqvist, 67 (Three brothers together, one loves summer, one winter, but the third loves both.—Wagon, sled, horse). This Mordvin riddle and the Polish "One looks for summer and one looks for winter.—Wagon and sledge" (Saloni, *Rzeshów*, 196) imply a desire to work. See further Lithuanian: Jurgelionis, 677 and the parallels collected in the headnote to Taylor, *English*, 138–140, nn. 38, 39, 42. In most of the parallels the actors look forward to a time when they can rest.

637. Yakut: Iastremskii, 92 (Between Khamystakh and Khamagaččaia there grow reeds, they say.—Spinal column of cattle). Uraon: Archer, 13 (There is only grass on the top of the mountain). Icelandic: Arnason, 26 (On the heaths of gray rock the gray cattle roam. Green roots and yellow oaks grow there.—Scaldhead). African, Wanamwezi: Dahl, 23 (A big field that has an abundant crop this year). Compare No. 663 below.

639. Compare the description of a pine in No. 921. Juniper is burned at the ceremony called *sang talbixu*, which is performed in conjunction with the daily offering to the windhorse (*kei morin*). By performing this ceremony religious merit is acquired.

640. See also the curious Lamba and Ten'a parallels quoted in the note to No. 681 below.

641. In No. 190 an ax is compared to a bull with a nosepeg. For a parallel to the cord that hangs down or draws a mountain see No. 709. For parallels to the comparison to a lonely tree see No. 542.

642. For comparisons to a hollow tree see the note to Nos. 308*b*, 308*c*.

643. Note a remote similarity to an English riddle that compares a ship spreading sail to a tree putting forth leaves as cited in Taylor, *English*, 1036.

644–646. For parallels to the comparison of the year to a tree and its branches see the head note to Taylor, *English*, 1037–1038. See further Yakut: Iastremskii, 20 (There is a divine oak, on it are seven partridges, twelve branches with thirty cones), 21, 25, 26; Ionova, 45 (A solid tree has twelve branches, each branch has thirty cones and fifty-two leaves, each leaf has seven berries). Siberian Turkish: Katanov, *Urianchai*, 46 (The golden poplar tree has twelve twigs, three hundred and sixty branches). Gilbertese: Hughes, 2 (A tree with twelve branches and three hundred and sixty-five and a quarter leaves). Lithuanian: Basanavicius, 93; Mickevicius, p. 580, No. 133, p. 583, No. 70, and p. 584, No. 154. Swedish: Wessman, 532–534. Portuguese: Pires de Lima, 14*b*. See also a curious Mordvin version that adds the solution "sky" to the usual solution: "In the middle of the sea an oak, in the top of the oak a nest, in it twelve eggs, in each egg four young.—Sky, [year], months, weeks" (Paasonen and Ravila, p. 652, No. 7). Chuvash: Karahka and Räsänen, 107.

644. For parallels to the formula "at the source of the river" see the note to No. 38 above.

645. The Altai and Khangai mountains are in northwestern Mongolia. For parallels to the formula "on the top of the Altai and Khangai mountains" see the note to No. 90. Agra sandal is a Sanskrit name of a tree.

647–653. The Mongolians describe several plants in this way and still other plants appear in the parallels. See, as examples, the Cheremis pea riddle, "Twigs upon twigs, nest upon nest, egg lies by egg" (Sebeok, 5. 2. 1. 1. See also his 5. 2. 1. 2), the Lithuanian flax riddle, "At the end of the field there grows a litle oak, a God's tree with a hundred branches, on each little branch is a little nest, in each little nest is a little child" (Mickevicius, p. 575, No. 151); and a Lithuanian riddle for a cabbage that has gone to seed, "There is only one root, but there are hundreds of branches, on each branch are a hundred apples, each apple has a hundred seeds" (Mickevicius, p. 585, No. 170). For additional parallels see the headnote to Taylor, *English*, 1161–1164 and the important remarks of Erich Seemann, *Jahrbuch für Volksliedforschung* 8: 162, No. 44, 1951.

647, 648. For parallels to the conventional use of the number eighty thousand see the note to No. 146 above.

651. Agrophyllum bears edible seeds that are eaten in times of drought.

654. The act of pacing, which is not appropriate to a tree (the clapper of the bell), forms an enigmatic contradiction. The abyss is the interior of the bell. For comment on Tchjintchji see note to No. 40.

655. The Mongolian *burkhan* signifies the image of a divinity. Such images are made of metals, wood, stone, leather, and cloth; they are occasionally painted. For another reference to a *burkhan* see No. 694.

656. Note the Votyak variations of this theme in "A two-tined fork behind the mill," "Rizai's switch is behind the house," and "A hop-pole behind the house" (Wichmann, 220, 253, 256). The Palestinian Arabs say "Two Negroes ride on your mother's back" (Ruoff, p. 19, No. 23).

657. According to Bazarov, *bambakhi* is a grass with which mice line their holes for winter. They discard it in the spring. The word is applicable to fluffy and friable objects. See another version of this riddle in No. 683, in which grass is not mentioned. The note to No. 337 surveys riddles for distilling alcoholic liquors. For comment on Denji see the note to No. 40.

658. The conception resembles that of No. 882.

659. The food is the windpipe and the epiglottis is the reed. Compare the Yakut "At the house door there is, they say, a multicolored hairy string stretched out.—Cow's throat" (Iastremskii, 76) and the Lamba "The chief's principal wife [being] about to come out, the thorn trees obstructed the doorway.—Tongue in mouth" (Doke, 108). See a similar comparison in No. 673 below and compare the Marshallese "Foot of a tree.—Tongue" (Davenport, p. 266, No. 12).

660. Kashmiri: Koul, 35 (There is a fence around a small lake). Dusun: Evans, 31 (Small ponds surrounded by tabu fences). Marshallese: Davenport, p. 265, No. 9 (Coconut trees which are above a pond). For additional parallels see the headnotes to Taylor, *English*, 544, § 12 and 1044. Note a somewhat different conception in the Abyssinian "The door of her house consists of small bits of wood" (Mittwoch, 9).

661. The two meanings of north and south confuse the hearer. For a similar use of right and left see No. 248 above. For other puns in Mongolian riddles see Nos. 22, 24*b*, 695, 708, and the note to No. 22.

662. By mentioning the felts, the riddler admits the solution into the riddle.

663. Compare No. 637 above, the Serbian "A bunch of reed grows on top of an oak" (Novaković, p. 164, No. 2), the Kamba "A beautiful little hill on which one cannot plant beans.—Hump of cattle" (Lindblom, 11), and the Kanuri "The place of a court of young people, in which water does not stand.—Back of a cow" (Lukas, 39).

664–666. The Mongols ascribe the winter cold to the Pleiades. For riddles about the Pleiades see No. 675 below and the note to Taylor, *English*, 988. Yakut: Iastremskii, 6 (On the bottom of the sea lie seven pennies). The

Mongolian riddler does not mention the seventh star in the constellation. According to Mongolian tradition, Merope or, in Mongolian, Mellut (ape) hides out of shame for having yielded to a mortal. This story explains the feeble light of the star. For parallels to the formula "on the summit of the western mountain" see the note to No. 90 above.

665. The Mongolian *t'awak* means the sole of the foot, a paw, a saucer. In conjunction with *săwak* (Artemisia campestris), it seems to mean a particular kind of artemisia.

667. For comment on the lamp (*bumba*) see Getty, p. xxxix. Compare the Persian "In the depths of this sea there dwells a shark that holds in its mouth a single pearl; strange that though it has no belly, it drinks the sea to the last drop.—Wick" (Phillott, 20) and the Turkish "A deep well, in it water, in it a snake, in its mouth corals.—Lamp" (Yanikoglu, p. 222, No. 38). Another Turkish version adds "A watermelon on the corals" (Yanikoglu, p. 226, No. 62). See also the headnote to Taylor, *English*, 1440–1441, n. 22.

Note also the comparison of a lamp, light, or flame to a flower. See a riddle for incense cited in the note to No. 466, the note to No. 776, the Korean "What is a flower blossoming on dead wood?—Lamp stand" (Bernheisel, p. 60), the Tibetan "Flaming flower of gold. Flame of fire" (Mitra, 4), the Uraon "The champa blossoms in a small tank" and "Little the garden, beautiful the flower.—Candle" (Archer, 53, 155), the Muria "On the dry tree blossoms a flower" (Elwin and Archer, p. 267, No. 10), the Persian "I saw a rose without a thorn. It had no perfume, nor was it culled from a garden. No one buys it, and no one sells it, but notwithstanding that, it is to be seen in every shop in the bazar" (Kuka, 9), the Armenian "A long tube (gut) with a flower on the end" (Seidlitz, p. 70, No. 5), the Turkish "Above, a rose; below, a lake" (Boratav, 143), the Modern Greek "I planted the speck of a speck, the speck of a speck came up, and upon the speck of a speck a golden button blossomed.—Night lamp" (Stathes, p. 351, No. 115), and the Rumanian "A well with a flower" (Papahagi, 43). Note also an analogous comparison to a bird in the Uraon "In a small pond is a flashing stork" (Archer, 4). The conception is reversed and describes a flower in the Kashmiri "A little plate of fire in the lake.—Lotus" (Knowles, 40). For comparisons of a flame to a flower that cannot be plucked see the note to No. 50 above. Compare the note to No. 702 below.

669. Mongolian *dumba* is perhaps an abbreviation of Sanskrit *udumbara* (*Ficus religiosa*). In Mongolia the lamp is chiefly a religious object.

670. The meaning of the riddle is obscure. The yellow poppy may be fire.

671. The translations are those given by Potanin. The meaning of the riddle is obscure.

673. See a similar conception in the larynx riddle, No. 659.

674. Since Mongolian has no plural sign, this riddle may also be understood in the plural. For discussion of riddles for the ears see the note to Nos. 872, 873 below.

675. For riddles describing the Pleiades see Nos. 664–666 and the note.

676, 677. Chinese: Serruys, 46 (A red jujube, which the whole room cannot contain). In the parallels the *tertium quid comparationis* varies greatly. See the oral Chinese "Pu ta, i-ko wu-tzu chuang-pui-hsia (Not big, not big, it cannot be packed into one room)". Baiga: Elwin, 148 (From one grain of rice there is a houseful of husks). Uraon: Archer, 200 = Elwin and Archer, p. 293, No. 22 (With one ear of corn the house is full). Moslems in India: Elwin and Archer, p. 302, No. 2. Telugu: Taylor, 9. Atjeh: Kreemer, 7. Javanese: Ranneft, *Proza*, p. 11, No. 52. Arabic: Littmann, 87 (As small as a barley stalk, it fills the city with bright light). Mehri and Hadrami: Hein, p. 184, No. 3 (Guess, guess: with the old man's beard he has filled the house). Turkish: Boratav, 144 (Ammoniak fills [all the] four walls); Kowalski, *North Bulgaria*, 35. Surinam: Herskovits, 78 (One grain of corn whitens the whole room). Tlokoa: Nakene, p. 7, No. 7 (It is only one, but it fills the whole house.—Candle). Songaï: Ben Hamouda, p. 278, No. 3. Comparisons to a bird are unusual but see "A little sparrow scattered its feathers about the whole house" (Muria: Elwin and Archer, p. 268, No. 23) and "A little minivet lightens the whole house" (Munda: Elwin and Archer, p. 288, No. 5). For additional parallels see the headnote and note to Taylor, *English*, 1473.

679. For parallels to the single tree see No. 542 and the note. For the comparison of hair to a tree without joints see No. 299.

681. For another reference to the Tunka country see No. 839. Compare the Ten'a "Riddle me: it is like a spruce tree lying on the ground.—The upper side of the bear's forepaw" (Jetté, 1). Jetté comments: "When a spruce-tree is felled down, its branches stick up, all bristling with needles. The upper side of the bear's forepaw has coarse, thick hair, standing up not quite vertically, but on a slant, just as the spruce branches. The simile is remarkably accurate for details of position." Compare also the Lamba "A little patch of long grass with mice tracks innumerable.—Palm of the hand" (Doke, 50). The allusion to long grass, which seems to represent hair, suggests that the riddler has in mind the back rather than the palm of the hand. The mice tracks might be the veins. See also the Omaha "There is a place cut up by gullies. What is it?—Old woman's face" (Dorsey, p. 344) and my comment in "American Indian Riddles," *Journal of American Folklore* 57: 6, 1944 and the headnote to Taylor, *English*, 1100–1108. See further the Nandi "I have a large plantation, but it went out of cultivation in the middle.—A goat's leg, the knee of which had worn bare" (Hollis, p. 141, No. 35) and the Dschagga "The meadow up there above from outside.—Human face" (Stamberg, 159). For another comparison of a part of the human body to a scene in nature see Nos. 705, 887, 892 and compare Nos. 339 and 640.

682. See No. 579 above.

683. See No. 657 and the survey of Mongolian riddles describing distillation in the note to No. 337. For comment on Dendein see the note to No. 40.

684. For parallels to the lonely tree see the note to No. 542.

685. The tip of the bellows is made of bone. The air is compressed in the "stone well" by squeezing the leather bag. The saddle riddle (No. 407) similarly describes an object composed of various materials. See also Nos. 761–767 and compare Taylor, *English*, 553.

687, 688. For parallels to the lonely tree see the note to No. 542.

689. Chinese: Serruys, 10 (Above, a line of heaven; beneath it is white snow. You strike it with the hand [the palm] and it flings up the [i.e., its] behind.—The flour sieve: one knocks it with the hand to make the flour fall down). Yakut: Piekarski, 373, 376. Tibetan: Tafel, p. 492 (In the upper story snow falls, in the lower story rain falls, and no one gets wet.—Watermill). Ossete: Schiefner, 36 (Our little sky rains snow). Tatar: Filonenko, 14; Kalashev and Ioakimov, p. 49, No. 10 (Snow falls from a low hill). Turcoman: Samojlovich, 82 (Snow comes from a low mountain) with several parallels. Siberian Turkish: Katanov, p. 242, No. 108 (In one spot a snowstorm is rising). Turkish: Zavarin, *Brusa*, 31; Kowalski, *North Bulgaria*, 31; Kowalski, *Zagadki*, 45 (The old ox looks at the sky, from his rump falls boiled milk),

55; Kúnos, p. 142, Nos. 15, 16; Hamamizade, 173 (From a low roof snow falls), 331. Chuvash: Mészáros, 168 (A snowdrift rises across the hedge), 174 (Snow falls among the lindens). Mordvin: Paasonen, 313. Votyak: Fuchs, p. 245, No. 40; Wichmann, 36, 81 (Snow is driving around a stone house), 176, 177, 326, 366. Cheremis: Genetz, 48 = Sebeok, 5. 1. 10. 1 (Fog goes through the linen forest), Genetz, 94 = Sebeok, 5. 1. 10. 2 (Around a small island snowflakes fall); Wichmann, 39 = Sebeok, 5. 1. 10. 5; Sebeok, 5. 1. 10. 3 and 5. 1. 10. 4. Zyrian: Wichmann, 271. Armenian: Grigorov, p. 123, No. 5 (Snow falls from a small sky). Modern Greek: Polites, 249 (A low sky and low falling snow). Lithuanian: Mickevicius, p. 580, No. 12 (A boar runs, grumbling [and] heaping up white snow flakes). Swedish: Olsson, *Bohuslän*, 92. Bolivian: Costas Arguedas, p. 339.

The same comparison to falling snow also serves to describe carding cotton. When the contrast of rain and snow in such riddles occurs, it refers to the separation of cotton fibres from the seeds. For examples see Chinese: Serruys, 48 (One half is wood, one half is iron, there falls a part of hail and another part of snow). Korean: Bernheisel, p. 82 (What is that on one side of which it snows and on the other side it hails?—A cotton-jinny). Kashmiri: Knowles, 137 (On that side of the hill hailstones are falling; on this side of the hill rain is falling.—Cotton carder); Koul, 48. Georgian: Glushakov, p. 22, No. 2 (Over there it snows, over here it rains.—Spinning wheel). Turkish: Kowalski, *Zagadki*, 40, 60 (I have a mountain. On turning it one way snow falls, on turning it the other way hail falls). As the parallels show, the Kashmiri and the Georgian riddlers have given inexact answers or were not understood correctly by the collector.

In some riddles the notion is confused and falling meal serves to describe grinding flour. See the Votyak "Meal falls from a little cloud" (Wichmann, 37) and the Siberian Turkish "I sow meal" (Katanov, p. 238, No. 41). In the Turkish "From a low roof snow is poured" (Hamamizade, 331), which has the answer "snow," the riddler has admitted the answer into the riddle or has confused the conception.

A Telugu riddle for flour ground from *ragi*, a grain, as it lies around the stone grinder, employs an entirely different scene from nature: "Around a bush is bird manure" (Taylor, 11).

689b. For a parallel to the scene "at the higher end of the tsaidam" see No. 696. The Mongolian *tsaidam*, which often appears as a place name, is a swampy area with an efflorescence of soda. It is often covered with feather grass (Lasiagrosis splendens, Mongolian *deres* or *dayres*). In Ordos the higher end of a tsaidam is usually toward the west. For a parallel to the drizzling rain see No. 692.

690, 691. For parallels to the scene "at the top of the mountain" see the note to No. 90.

692. This is an adaptation of the riddle for bolting flour, No. 689. For other examples of a comparison used to describe two different things see the note to No. 476. For parallels to the grassless cavity see No. 249 and compare No. 610 and the notes to Nos. 61 and 306.

694, 695. These are variations of a comparison of smoking tobacco to mist or smoke rising. In No. 694 the riddler suggests a comparison to the burning of incense. Perhaps the riddler has in mind the genius protector (*itegel burkhan*) as the object of sacrifice. For comment on this figure see the note to No. 655. In No. 695 the Mongolian *urida* signifies both "in front" and "in the south" and *toluɣai* signifies both "head" and "hill." For other Mongolian words used in two senses see the note to No. 661. For parallels to the theme of the riddle see a Fijian riddle for a fire-rubber, "A little child runs to and fro. As it runs, a mist arises and then the sun appears" (Fison, 10), the Armenian "Today is Wednesday. What is in my mind? Smoke arises from the sea [water-pipe]. What is cooking inside?" (Zielinski, p. 55, No. 2), and the SeSuto "Smoke rising from a round well.—Smoking pipe" (Norton and Velaphe, 16). Compare the Siberian Turkish "In the upper course of the Chingé River smoke is visible.—Smoking tobacco in a pipe" (Katanov, *Urianchai*, 10).

696. A windhorse (Mongolian *kei morin*, Tibetan *rlung rta*) is a small flag on which a horse, a sun, and other auspicious emblems are printed. See L. A. Waddell, *The Buddhism of Tibet*, pp. 408–419. See another reference to a windhorse in No. 240 above. For a parallel to the formula "at the upper end of the tsaidam" see No. 689b with the note.

697. The meaning of the riddle is not clear.

698. Zhamtsaranov cites a few parallels. See also Taylor, *English*, 268–269, § 11. Baiga: Elwin, p. 469, No. 47 = Elwin and Archer, p. 272, No. 17 (No leaves, no branches, the tree stands solitary.—Column of smoke). Samoan: Pratt, p. 131, No. 26 (A man who has a white head stands above the wall and reaches to the heavens.—Smoke rising from oven). Siberian Turkish: Katanov, p. 240, No. 67 (An arrow shot from earth rises as far as the sky). Turkish: Bahaeddin, 42 (*Fildirin firek*, a mast to heaven.—Smoke from tobacco or a chimney). The untranslatable words are an introductory formula. Irish: Ó Dálaigh, 112 = Hull and Taylor, *Irish*, 312 (I set a stick last night and it is higher than the air today). Wanamwezi: Dahl, 63 (A thin long stalk of grass approaches the cloud like a bridegroom). Mahua: Harries, *Riddles*, 9 (A straight bamboo). Note also the comparisons of smoke to a tall person. See Tlokoa: Nakene, p. 129, No. 10 (A tall man). Kxatla: Schapera, 101 (Tell me: the tall man he-haw). Modern Greek: Polites, p. 247, No. 309 (I have a sister, she was so tall she reached the sky). Compare the Ten'a pillar riddle: "Riddle me: I am a round stiff thing, stretched toward the sky" (Jetté, 88).

698b. For parallels to the phrase "came down from Heaven," which seems to mean "is of natural origin," see the note to No. 337.

699. Compare the Siberian Turkish "A needle rocks in the sky.—Camel's tail" (Radlov, 1: 262, No. 15), which seems to be incorrectly translated. The phrase "in the sky"—Radlov says "Am Himmel"—should be rather "from Heaven," which has both its literal meaning and the meaning "made by God"; see the note to No. 337 above.

701. Lithuanian: Basanavicius, p. 190, No. 23 (A very small little room, full of white clubs). For additional parallels see the headnote to Taylor, *English*, 1150.

702. Parsee: Munshi, 1 (What is that thing which is buried in [the] ground [at night] and turned into bars of gold the next morning?). Serbian: Novaković, p. 16, No. 5 (I folded the gold, I unfolded the gold, but the gold was not asleep). Kamba: Lindblom, 13 (I plant in the ground a digging stick which will be visible.—Smoke of a fire in Yata). See also the comparisons of a fire to a person who is dressed in the evening and undressed in the morning (Taylor, *English*, headnote to 587, n. 11) and to the dead burying or covering the living (Taylor, *English*, 835, 836 with the headnotes and notes). For the comparison of fire to a flower see the note to No. 667 above.

Comparisons to a golden or silver object serve also to describe a carrot in the Parsee "In a jungle there is a golden nail" and a radish, "A silver nail in a jungle or a forest" (Munshi, 12, 13).

705. The word "mountain" hints at the solution because the Mongolian *shili* signifies both a flat elevation and the jugular vein. For other uses of a word in two senses in Mongolian riddling see the note to No. 661.

707. See a similar comparison to a stone in Nos. 719, 720 below. For parallels and discussion see the note to Taylor, *English*, 1101; W. A. Kozumplik, Seven and Nine Holes in Man, *Southern Folklore Quarterly* 5: 1–24, 1941; Howard Meroney, *Lecc Thollcind* and the Twelve Doors of the Soul, *ibid.* 11: 257–259, 1947. Reinhold Köhler cites parallels and includes among them references to the rare version discussed by Howard Meroney; see *Kleinere Schriften* 3: 368, n. 1, Berlin, Verlag von Emil Felber, 1900. For additional parallels see the Kharia "The clod of earth with seven holes" (Elwin and Archer, p. 285, No. 6); the Kashmiri "A new pot with seven holes in it" (Knowles, 124), which involves an allusion to the fact that a new pot has been washed; the Samoyede "In a grassy hill there are seven holes" (Lehtisalo, 177); the Crimean Tatar "A hammer with seven holes" (Filonenko, 95), which is virtually identical with the Turkish "A beetle [for beating clothes] with seven holes. Who does not know this is stupid" (Bahaeddin, 10). See similar versions in Boratav, 94 and Orhan, 55. Note a reference to six holes (the two nostrils are counted as one opening) in Diamantaras, p. 233, No. 4. Chuvash: Karahka and Räsänen, 62 (A block of wood has nine holes). Cheremis: Sebeok, 5. 8. 4. 1, 5. 8. 4. 2. Mordvin: Paasonen and Ravila, p. 618, No. 2; Ahlqvist, *Moksha Mordvin*, 71. Lithuanian: Jurgelionis, 158 (A ball with holes). Parallels to the second clause of the Cheremis "There are seven holes in a ball of yarn; two holes gleam" (Beke, 11 = Sebeok, 5. 8. 5) are rare. Swedish: Wessman, 79 (ball of yarn); Ström, p. 76, No. 1; Olsson, *Halland*, 46. The Zyrian "On a pitchfork a baker's trough, on the baker's trough a cross, on the cross a porridge pot with seven holes" and "In the top of an oak a porridge pot with seven holes, on the porridge pot there is green grass, in the green grass Polish pigs graze" (Wichmann, 219, 56, respectively) are curious and unusual combinations with a widely known riddle describing a man. For this latter riddle see the headnote to Taylor, *English*, 1100–1108.

708. The aptness of the comparison is not obvious. For parallels to the notion that a name is firmly attached to a person see the headnote to Taylor, *English*, 1573–1575, nn. 7–16. Compare also the Yakut "It is an immovable black tag, it is said" (Popov, p. 286) or "The trace of a seal applied by a white priest is never lost" (Iastremskii, 219) and the Irish "You have it inside on you, and you have it outside on you, and [yet] you do not deem it heavy" (Ó Máile, 1 = Hull and Taylor, *Irish*, 412). A similar notion appears in the Kharia "The dry gourd cracks, but the stalk stays" (Elwin and Archer, p. 287, No. 39), but the appropriateness of a comparison to a gourd is not entirely clear. Compare this Kharia riddle with the Yakut "The kettle is drowned, its handle remains" (Iastremskii, 220). See also Swedish: Wessman, 600. For parallels to the formula "on a solid hillock" see the note to No. 90.

709. For another riddle on the theme of leading a camel see No. 641 above. The scene used in this riddle describes a woman's hair in the Armenian "A black cord extended down the mountain slope" (Seidlitz, *Ausland* 57: 71, No. 21).

710, 711. For riddles using the same means of comparison but having different answers see the note to Nos. 476–478. For parallels to the formula "on a solitary mountain" see the note to No. 90.

711. For a description of this spire see Getty, p. xlvii.

712. In the circular Mongolian house the bed or the hill of sleeping is at the back, the hearth or the hill of fire is in the center, and the entrance or the hill of the pass is in front.

713. Compare the Ten'a rennet riddle, "Riddle me: there are lumplike clouds around the horizon" (Jetté, 92). See also such Ten'a riddles on related themes as "Riddle me: its inside is folded up with balls.—The manyplies of the caribou" (Jetté, 91); "Riddle me: light clouds on the sky. —Caul of a ruminant; or, the skinning of an otter, i.e., the flesh side of an otter's skin freshly removed" (Jetté, 90); "Riddle me: it looks like a place where ptarmigans have hidden themselves under the snow.—The bighorn's belly" (Jetté, 25); and "I store sundry things in a house of small sticks.—Eating" (Jetté, 100) with the variant "I dump things into a house of small hills." The Bulgarians have a somewhat different conception of a stomach: "All the children have caps, the father has none" (Chacharov, 30). For other descriptions of an animal's stomach see No. 464 and the note.

714. Yakut: Iastremskii, 68 (A mountain of flesh, an ascent of iron); Piekarski, 87 (They say that there is a hill of flesh and some iron stairs). Russian: Sadovnikov, 981. White Russian: Wasilewski, 68 (I climb, I climb on iron, when I ascend a fleshy mountain). For additional parallels see the headnote to Taylor, *English*, 1436–1447 and a Hungarian text cited in the note to No. 496 above.

715. The sinews are mentioned in a more appropriate context in No. 56 above.

716, 717. Yakut: Iastremskii, 30 (A white mare went out, a roan one galloped away at a gentle trot, a light bay one remained.—Snow thawed, spring came and went, summer reigned supreme), 31 (A white mare went out, a roan mare arrived galloping.—Melting of snow [the roan mare is not explained]), 37 (A roan mare gallops gently, a black mare goes at a walk.—Snow, rain); Popov, p. 283. For other comparisons to horses of various colors (not, however, for the seasons) see the note to No. 262 above. Mordvin: Paasonen and Ravila, p. 654, No. 4. Bihari: Mitra, 72 (It has four parts cold, four hot, and four full of storms and high winds. It is a deer with twelve hoofs. It browses on different kinds of fodder). Kharia: Elwan and Archer, p. 287, No. 33 (The twelve deer with the three legs who graze apart.—Months and seasons). Baiga: Elwin, p. 479, No. 149 = Elwin and Archer, p. 274, No. 49 (In four it boils, in four it cooks, and in four it sinks into the water). Arabic: Giacobetti, 48 (Three of cold and ice, three of moistened plants, three load and carry away.—Winter, spring, summer), 49 (Three: squat; three: warm yourself; three: flower of broom; three: quill of porcupine), 51 (Three yield flowers, three yield fruits, three yield dust, three are red), in which the last is explained as a reference to the red color of plowed earth, 52 (Ninety-six days bring a lively cold, ninety-six days have greens and dew, ninety-six days have a lit fire, ninety-six days follow those that precede). Turkish: Bahaeddin, 29. Russian: Sadovnikov, 1497 (with the answer "ice"). Scotch Gaelic: Nic Iain, 16 (a man came bitter [*sic*] over the crests of the waves; a pale yellow man, a wand-slender brown man, a man threshing with a flail, a man stripping the trees). See other descriptions of the seasons in the headnote to Taylor, *English*, 984.

717a. Crackling refers to burning fuel. The pass of desolation refers to the snowbound steppe and frozen soil characteristic of spring, which according to the Chinese calendar may begin in late January.

717a. The *yidam* is the personal genius chosen by the lama. The *obō* is a pile of stones erected by the roadside or on mountain tops. It is supposed to be the seat of the *genius loci*. See another reference to such a cairn in No. 725 and compare Eugen Kagarow, "Mongolische Obo, griechische Hermaia und deren ethnographische Parallelen," *Zeitschrift für Volkskunde*, n.F. 1: 58–64, 1930 (with two illustrations).

The three months of spring are compared to three mountain passes that one must cross under the protection of one's personal deity. Spring is a hard time for the cattle-breeding nomads, a time of death, epidemics, and epizootics. The three *obō* are the three autumn months, which are marked by special activities and festivals, among them perhaps a sacrifice to the *obō*. The icy depressions of the three winter months, which are differentiated by three degrees of cold, are contrasted with the three blossoming summer fields, each of which has different flowers.

719, 720. The word *shin* is not in the dictionaries. The answer to the riddle should be "body." See No. 707 and the note.

721. The flask often has a long spout and a bunch of flowers projecting from the stopper. The implications of the place names are obscure.

722, 723. Compare the headnote to Taylor, *English*, 801, § 1.

724. In other languages this comparison serves to describe entirely different objects. See a Batak riddle for the knee cap: "The box of Our Lord cannot be opened" (Ophuijsen, p. 466, No. 77), a Bankon riddle for the stomach: "My father bequeathed me a chest that no one can open. What is it?" (Ittmann, p. 106, No. 7) with a Kundu parallel (Ittmann, 62), a Yakut riddle for the second stomach of cattle (quoted in the note to No. 870 below), and a Dschagga riddle for a cow's hoof (Raum, 11). Note also a Hausa riddle for a stone: "God's ball that cannot be flattened" (Fletcher, 3). For riddles describing a nut, an egg, or a watermelon in a similar fashion see the headnote to Taylor, *English*, 1187, where an incorrect solution of this Mongolian riddle is given.

725. For comment on the cairn see the note to No. 717a. For a survey of Mongolian riddles for the distillation of alcohol see the note to No. 337.

726. See the headnote to Taylor, *English*, 1605, § 3. Yakut: Iastremskii, 232, 233; Ionova, 22. Mordvin: Ahlqvist, *Moksha Mordvin*, 29. Turkish: Bahaeddin, 68 (In Stambul he cooked milk, its smell came to us). Russian: Sadovnikov, 2153. Swedish: Wessman, 347. This comparison also describes the sound of a bell; see "They hack in Spass, but the splinters come flying here" (Russian: Sadovnikov, 1023). The Dschagga use it for a plague of locusts (Stamberg, 107, 132).

727. Bulgarian: Gubov, 338. Polish: Gustawicz, 336. Lithuanian: Daukantas, 5. Swedish: Wessman, 149.

728. For a comparison of coals of fire to ankle bones or dice see Nos. 740–742. Note a Frisian comparison to a button (Dykstra, p. 101).

729. See No. 497 above, in which a person is named.

730. See No. 607 above and compare the headnote to Taylor, *English*, 607–631.

732. For parallels to the notion that a shadow cannot be cut see No. 16 above and the note.

733, 734. For comparisons to a defective member of an animal see the note to No. 113 above.

735. The tail is conceived as having been split open after slaughtering.

737. Muria: Elwin, p. 594, No. 64 (The vulture eats the bullock, but can never finish it). Yakut: Piekarski, 344 (They say that one hundred people cannot eat one weight of butter). Taveta: Hollis, 1, 1a (My meat was small. People came and cut it, but they were unable to finish it). Dschagga: Stamberg, 10 (The chief thrust out a tiny bit of flesh, the men eat it but cannot consume it.—The chief is the earth), 113, 216 (I begin eating in the morning and cannot finish). For another description of a whetstone see No. 237 above. For a similar comparison referring to the impossibility of erasing a camel's tracks see No. 172, in which the answer is the spot where a fire has burned.

738. The same symbolism of concave and convex occurs in No. 391.

740–742. Votyak: Wichmann, 304. Zyrian: Wichmann, 10 (red spoons in a red basket), 128. Compare Nos. 800 and Taylor, *English*, 375.

Loaves of bread in an oven are similarly described in riddles. See the Turkish "A yellow chest (or: trough), a red nut" (Moshkov, p. 269, No. 60). Arabic: Giacobetti, 18. Zyrian: Wichmann, 69. Russian: Sadovnikov, 162, 164–166.

742. Mongolian children like the ankle bones of a sheep as much as our children like marbles. In fact, they collect and prize them more because these bones symbolize the good luck of a family and are regarded as a source of wealth. Old and young play with them and use them as dice in some games.

743, 744. Zyrian: Wichmann, 129 (A basket full of bones, but two in it are too many). For additional parallels see the headnote to Taylor, *English*, 1227, § 1.

745. Yakut: Iastremskii, 85 (In ice there is a red *pol'evka*.—Kidneys of cattle). The ice is the fat surrounding the kidneys; the meaning of *pol'evka* is obscure. Samoyede: Lehtisalo, 152 (Two little sacks of the door-corner of the tent).

746. I have found no description of a dog eating, but this riddle has a slight similarity to descriptions of a man eating; see No. 8 above with the note. Compare a Ten'a riddle for the wood left by a beaver after eating: "Riddle me: it looks like a heap of bones on the bottom of a shallow river" (Jetté, 5).

747. These idols represent the souls of dead shamans. They are usually erected on mountains. For parallels to the formula "on the mountain" see the note to No. 90.

748. The Mongols call all bones found in the earth the "bones of whales." For parallels to the formula "on the top of a mountain range" see the note to No. 90.

751. Mostaert translates *shara shiwoo* as screech owl and Golstunski as eagle owl. Compare the Turkish "With small little eyes, with small little feet, with *militan* eyes, with falcon claws" (Boratav, 119). The meaning of *militan* is obscure.

752. These animals appear in the Mongolian zodiac and belong to the cycle of the twelve animals, on which see Edouard Chavannes, "Le Cycle turc des douze animaux," *T'oung pao*, 2d Ser., 7: 51–122, 1906; Paul Pelliot, "Le plus ancien exemple du cycle des douze animaux chez les Turcs," *ibid.* 26: 204–212, 1929. For examples of the twelve animals used as chronograms see Peter Boodberg, "Marginalia to the Histories of the Northern Dynasties," *Harvard Jour. of Asiatic Studies* 3: 223–253, 1938, and "Chinese Zoographic Names as Chronograms," *ibid.* 5: 128–136, 1940. The camel was not admitted to the zodiac and was recompensed by receiving a member from each of the twelve animals. For riddles of similar construction that describe an animal as being composed of the members of several animals see the note to No. 472 above. For an altogether different camel riddle see Kanuri: Lukas, 43.

753. The meaning of the dog's cap is obscure.

754. The peacock's tail is called wise because it can write.

755. Compare the note to No. 472 for other examples of riddles describing an animal as being composed of the members of several animals.

757. For another description of scissors see Nos. 1, 2 above.

758. Compare the note to No. 472 for other examples of riddles describing an animal as being composed of the members of several animals.

759. Yakut: Pierkarski, 132 (With six legs, horns, and wings, it resembles neither a horse nor a cow nor even a bag). Shor: Dyrenkova, 24 (A six-legged particolored ox). Russian: Sadovnikov, 1656, 1671; Arkhangel'skii, p. 76; Bardin, 11. See also the riddles cited in the headnote to Taylor, *English,* 46–87, and an Uraon ant riddle cited in the note to No. 219.

760. The bottle is the comb and the brandy is honey. The droning of the bee suggests the comparison to a lama. For other examples of this comparison see the note to No. 343.

761, 762. Compare the Bulgarian frying pan riddle, "A magpie's tail, a camel's leg" (Gubov, 361). For other examples of two different objects described by the same comparison see the note to Nos. 476–478.

763. The riddler does not clearly suggest the object to which the canopy is compared.

764. The adjective *muriu* alludes to the donkey's peculiar gait. What the hoofs of Manjushrī, a Boddhisattva representing wisdom, may be is obscure. He ordinarily rides a lion. The thunderbolt, a utensil used in ritual, is Indra's weapon and is a symbol of indestructibility. For another reference to Manjushrī see No. 124 and compare the discussion in Getty, pp. 95–99. The pattern of this riddle is discussed in the note to No. 472.

765. Compare the note to No. 472.

766, 767. See the headnote to Taylor, *English,* 1435, n. 16.

770. The crutch stick, which here represents the head and horns, is used as a rake. The tents are the ears. A somewhat similar conception is seen in the Cheremis "I sweep two ovens with one broom.—Cow's tongue [when licking its nose]" (Sebeok, 5. 11. 8; Sebeok-Beke, 7. 20. 15), which has a parallel in Votyak (Wichmann, 90). See also Votyak: Wichmann, 343 (One poker cares for two stoves). Kashmiri: Koul, 17 (A mosque with two doors. "Come, sir, let off a cracker"). Turcoman: Samojlovich, 112 (Two carts have one poker). Here "carts" is probably a misunderstanding of some sort. Lithuanian: Mickevicius: p. 580, No. 3 (Two stoves are heated with one piece of wood) and p. 589, No. 327.

771. See the Samoyede "The dens of two polar foxes are beside each other" (Lehtisalo, 217), the Zyrian "Nikolai [sits] between two corncribs" (Wichmann, 112), the Uraon "A hut on the slope of a hill" (Archer, 62), the Asur (a tribe in Chota Nagpur) "The sloping hut with two doors" (Elwin and Archer, p. 281, No. 13); the Mehri and Soqotri "My two little houses are upside down" (Müller, 17), which is analogous to a description current in the same tribes of the eyes as springs upside down (Müller, 27). A Filipino riddle communicated to me in manuscript is "Two holes in a rice mortar." Much the same conception is expressed in a different way in the Samoan "A long house with only one post" (Pratt, p. 129, No. 3). For additional parallels see the note to Taylor, *English,* 1143.

The comparison of the head to a hill or mountain is rather rarely mentioned in riddles for the nose. It occurs in the Uraon riddle quoted above and in the Javanese "A bundle leans against the mountain" (Ranneft, *Proza,* p. 42, No. 159). It is often found in riddles describing braids, earrings, or the ears.

772. The white felt is the pericardium, but the Mongolian word for it and the Russian translation are not entirely intelligible. For parallels to this riddle see the Ossete "It is one but [is also] manifold.—Heart" (Schiefner, 28). Compare the Yakut brain riddle, "A birchbark basket is filled with white thread, so they say" (Piekarski, 167), with the parallel, "They say that there is enough thread to make a birchbark basket, not too high but wide enough and enough horsehair packthread for a full (or: complete) leather vat.—Thought, brain" (Piekarski, 224). See also the note to No. 779 below.

773. For parallels see the headnote to Taylor, *English,* 909–915. For a similar comparison in which the seeds are compared to persons in a house see the note to Nos. 551, 552 above.

774. Compare the headnote to Taylor, *English,* 1150.

775. For parallels see the headnote to Taylor, *English,* 1037–1038, § 6.

776. Murray B. Emeneau gives me an unpublished Toda parallel: "There is a flat stone, on the flat stone is water, on the water is a creeper, on the creeper is a flower. What is it?—A lamp." Compare the Uraon "The garden is lovely as a blossom" (Elwin and Archer, p. 295, No. 40). For the comparison to a flower see the note to No. 667.

777. The phrase "given by nature" seems to be an equivalent of the formula "descended from heaven"; see the note to No. 337. The phrase "given by us" signifies a manufactured object.

778. The untranslated words seem to have an onomatopoetic sense.

779. For a similar reference to white felt see No. 772. The notion of a yurt lacking an essential part resembles the notion of an animal lacking an essential member, for which see the note to No. 113. For references to a thing lacking an essential part see Nos. 543 (tree without color), 643 (tree without leaves), 679 (tree without branches), 681 (steppe without vegetation), 686 (country without characteristics, building without architecture), 734 (torn eagle's hide), 771 (two houses with one pillar), 773 (house without door or smokehole), 788 (one-wheeled cart), 824 (dipper with broken edge), 838 (half a saucer).

780. The riddler compares a kettle to a yurt. The rising steam, if it were mentioned, would be the smoke.

781. For comment on Barguzin see the note to No. 8.

782. Compare the Cheremis "Under the fence pole there lies a black snake" (Wichmann, 20 = Sebeok, 2. 3) and the Serbian "I carry it with me, yet I have no need for it" (Novaković, p. 142, No. 7. See also his No. 2 on p. 7 and No. 6 on p. 235).

783. For parallels to the formula "in a puddle" see the comment on the formula "in a well" in the note to No. 61.

784. For other riddles describing distillation see the note to No. 337. The meaning of *solovko* is obscure.

786. The riddler suggests a comparison to a gaily decked cart. For other riddles describing distillation see the note to No. 337.

787. For the comparison of the finger to a tree see the Turkish "On a dry stem (tree trunk) sits a *kukhüvallahi*-bird.—Ring" (Boratav, 248). The word kukhüvallahi refers to a sura in the Koran and an inscription on a ring. For comparisons to an object on a tree see the note to Nos. 846 and 892 below.

788. *Khur khur* is the sound of grinding buckwheat; *jee jee* is the sound of grinding flour. These sounds are here intended to suggest driving a horse and a squeaking cart.

789. The cart is the shaman's drum. The significance of the boots is obscure. The Tungus are noted for their good shamans. For similar riddles see the Yakut "The jingling of scissors owned by the girl in Vierkhoyansk is heard by the girl in Vilyusk, and the jingling of scissors owned by the girl in Vilyusk is heard in Vierkhoyansk.—Female and male shamans" (Piekarski, 19), the Shor "The back of the rock trembles and shakes; the leather bridle shines and sparkles.—Shaman's tambourine" (Dyrenkova, 4); the Siberian Turkish "The creator of the forest mounted on a horse and the top of the willow shook" (Katanov, p. 100, No. 866) and "It walks rumbling and thundering; it shouts, imitating a stag and a *maral*" (Katanov, p. 303, No. 274 and p. 339, No. 343). A *maral* is a kind of stag. See also the Kxatla "Tell me: the white chief of Ramanyobo, where he rises the horns cry out.—Magician" (Schapera, 95).

791. For parallels to the formula "behind the mountain" see the note to No. 112 above.

795. Gondi: Hivale and Elwin, p. 150, No. 21 (A half-eaten *chappāti*). Kashmiri: Koul, 16 (A cake of chaff is on the wall; neither thy mother can reach it nor my mother can reach it). Thai: Haas MS (Half a coconut, it can cross the sea). Cheremis: Sebeok, 5. 13. 5 (On the house roof half a loaf); Sebeok-Beke, 5. 13. 5. 1. Votyak: Fuchs, p. 242, No. 16. Chuvash: Mészáros, 145 (Half a loaf of bread lies atop the house); Karahka and Räsänen, p. 100, No. 89. Turkish: Boratav, 16, 18, 19. Lithuanian: Mickevicius, p. 574, No. 113 (A pancake is lying in the well), p. 580, No. 132 (A pancake lies in the middle of the courtyard); Basanavicius, 210 (A pancake on the chimney). Compare Nos. 835, 836 below, and the note to Taylor, *English*, 1231.

796. During the day only part of the opening is covered; at night the opening is closed. For another description of this flap see Nos. 938, 939 below.

797. Compare the Yakut "In the meadow there is a purse with lard fat, they say" (Iastremskii, 123). See also the Yakut "In the meadow there is a small boy with lard" (Popov, p. 284). These references to fat imply that the frog is eaten as a delicacy. Compare the Mordvin riddle for a rabbit cited in the note to No. 824 below. For a different comparison of a frog to a thing see the Munda "The little pot of the witch floats in the river" (Elwin and Archer, p. 289, No. 16). For discussion of riddles for a frog see the note to Nos. 40–42 above. Compare also a Shor riddle for a hare: "Falling from heaven, snow hanging on the tree, all four paws crooked" (Dyrenkova, 21).

798, 799. Although riddles for mucus in the nose are rather numerous, comparisons to a scene in nature are unusual. I can cite only the Ossete "Avalanches go out of two ice-cellars" (Schiefner, 21) and the Makua "Something descending from the hill" (Harries, *Riddles*, p. 284, No. 13 var.). Note the comparison to curds in No. 324 above. See also the Makua "The cooking pot of the chief never finishes being scooped out of" (Harries, *Riddles*, p. 284, No. 13).

800. Compare No. 740 above, where bones rather than flesh are mentioned.

801. Compare Nos. 60 (worm), 200 (calf), 338 (horse), and 828 (things), and the versions collected in the headnote to Taylor, *English*, 1140, nn. 17–19. Berber: Basset, 10 (Negresses among the whites).

802. Zyrian: Wichmann, 199 (At the end of the shoot a dough-trough.—Ear of wheat). Compare a curious Lithuanian riddle for dew, "This morning's daughter-in-law with a litle cap of velvet" (Jurgelionis, 111) and an Irish riddle on the same subject, "I went up the little road and down the little road, and I brought the jugs and glasses with me on the tips of my fingers" (Ó Máile, 30 = Hull and Taylor, *Irish*, 351). Makua: Harries, *Riddles*, 5 (The chief sits on a chair), 5 var. (The children of Mwalia all on chairs). Tlokoa: Nakene, p. 129, No. 33 (Wizards are dancing on the thorn.—Drops of rain).

804. Such a word as *jok* (nourishment), a very elegant synonym of food, enhances the humor of the riddle. The Mongolian *tatakhu* (to draw, to suck) is the usual word for smoking. The word used in the solution is *uuku* (to drink).

805. For parallels see the note to No. 807.

806. According to Mostaert, *khuloo* means tongue. This is true as far as the solution of the riddle is concerned, but in the comparison it should mean a stick with which one stirs. Dictionaries define *khuloo* as wax in the ear. It seems to mean here a stick for scraping wax from the ear. For the comparison of eating to grinding see the headnote to Taylor, *English*, 841, § 5. For the Mongolian riddles for eating see the note to No. 89 above.

807. Kanawari: Joshi, 16 (Sweet food in a tiny vessel. —Walnut). Cheremis: Sebeok, 5. 12. 8. Mordvin: Paasonen and Ravila, p. 622, No. 5 (A little pot, sweet soup); Ahlqvist, *Moksha Mordvin*, p. 141, No. 16. Chuvash: Mészáros, 103 (Sweet is the pulp of the tiny boiler, i.e., pot.—Hazelnut), 129; Karahka and Räsänen, 77, 82. Russian: Sadovnikov, 1372. Lithuanian: Mickevicius, p. 574, Nos. 100 (A very small pot, but the mush is tasty), 106; p. 578, No. 67; p. 581. Nos. 51 (A little neat pot contains tasty porridge, although it is not cooked over a fire), 68; and p. 583, No. 38. For additional parallels see No. 805 above and the texts collected in the headnote to Taylor, *English*, 1187, § 1.

808. Riddles describing a part of the body that one cannot reach or see are numerous and varied. See Yakut: Iastremskii, 198 (On that spot where your friend sat you cannot sit.—Man sits on another's knees). Cuman: Németh, 12 (The goat's horn stabs, how does it stab without stabbing?—Put the object on the two points of the horns), which seems to need a slight emendation to read "between the horns." Soqotri: Müller, p. 36, No. 10 (It is on you, almost invisible to you.—Back of the head). Balochi: Dames, 5 (You see the palm wine that papa brought, you do not see that which you yourself carry.—Nape of the neck). Fijian: Fison, 25 (A child who reaches up to the shelf. He can reach the big upper shelf, but he cannot reach the little lower shelf. He is too short for it.—The hand can touch the shoulder, but cannot touch the bend of the arm). Bakongo: Denis, 6 (They did not take each other.—Elbow and mouth). The Nandi "Thy sister's house is near, yet thou canst not reach it. What is thy sister's house?—Backbone" (Hollis, 60) with a SeSuto parallel, "I tried in vain to see my mother-in-law's sister, that is, fellow wife.—The back of my head" (Norton and Velaphe, 20), involves the untouchability of one's sister or mother-in-law. For discussion of such untouchability or riddles about it see Taylor, *English*, 1070; R. M. Dawkins, *Forty-five tales from the Dodekanese*, 198, Cambridge, Eng., Univ. Press, 1950; Nakene, p. 134, Nos. 17, 18. For further parallels to the Mongolian riddle see Kxatla: Schapera, 78 (Tell me: I tried to look behind for Manakane but I could not see her.—Nape of the neck). Kundu: Itmann, 273 (You live without seeing him.—Occiput). Pangwe: Tessmann, 2 (You see everything except this.—Occiput). Yoruba: Bascom, 35 (I kneel, I hang a bag; I stand up, my hand cannot reach it any more.—Knee). Irish: Delargy, 34 = Ó Dálaigh, 1 = Hull and Taylor, *Irish*, 464 (I see it and you don't see it, and yet it is nearer to you than to me.—Poll of the head); Ó Máile, 31 = Hull and Taylor, *Irish*, 466b (What part of your body can't you see?—The back of your head and your backbone). Compare the Welsh game: "How can a candle be placed on a spot in a chamber so that everyone can see it at one time except one [person]?—Put it on the head of that one" (Hull and Taylor, *Welsh*, 485). These riddles usually refer to the back of the head, but a manuuscript Filipino riddle in my possession makes a reference to the front of the head: "The house of your brother, but you can't see him.—Forehead." See also the English heart riddle, "You feel it; you never saw it and never will" (Taylor, *English*, 1579). Compare No. 951 below.

809. Siberian Turkish: Katanov, p. 143, No. 1162 (He took out the gold and threw away the box.—Marrow in a bone). A comparison to a precious object is unusual. Riddlers often use similar comparison to describe a fruit or a bottle of wine; see the headnote to Taylor, *English*, 805–818.

810. The curious Yakut "A snipe has laid her eggs in a copper kettle.—Human brain" (Popov, p. 286) implies familiarity with anatomy and especially the colors of membranes within the head. Compare a Turkish brain riddle, "Think, think, making think, inside the box a sheepfold" (Hamamizade, 66), in which the white sheep in the sheepfold are analogous to the white eggs of the Yakut riddle and the white felt of the heart riddles, Nos. 772 and 779 above. See also the Modern Greek "I have a box that has something inside. If that something should be lost, what use would I have for the box?" (Stathes, p. 339, No. 45 and compare also p. 350, No. 112). For the comparison used in this Mongolian riddle see also No. 809 above and the note.

811. Siberian Turkish: Katanov, p. 258, No. 154 (I could not empty a certain purse.—Thoughts) and p. 367, No. 319 (I cannot throw out all the stones that are in my purse). Fijian: Fison, 29 (A box into which goods are continually poured but which is never full.—Souls or minds, desires). For other inexhaustible containers that cannot be filled see the note to Nos. 820, 821 below and a Yakut riddle for water: "They say, however much they dip out, they cannot dip out all of it" (Piekarski, 89).

812, 813. See the headnote to Taylor, *English*, 1193, § 1. See further Yakut: Iastremskii, 141 (Under the earth glue is boiling). Chuvash: Karahka and Räsänen, 135. Cheremis: Sebeok, 5. 12. 6. 1–5. 12. 6. 3 and 5. 13. 1. Turkish: Yanikoglu, 96 (Under the earth a pot is boiling). Lithuanian: Mickevicius, p. 583, No. 20 (In the midst of the field a pot boils) and p. 585, No. 162. The Kabardin use the same comparison to describe a mole: "A little kettle boils at the wall of the house" (Talpa and Sokolov, 20). A Lithuanian comparison of a cow's udder to a pot boiling in a field is unusual; see Mickevicius, p. 483, No. 68. So, also, is the Chuvash riddle for boiling wort for beer: "In a large pit boils *sim* [the upper and best part of beer]"; but in this riddle the correct solution seems to have been lost. See Karahka and Räsänen, 8. See finally a Mordvin riddle for an anthill: "A basket of millet has fallen in the middle of the field" (Paasonen and Ravila, p. 657, No. 8).

813, 814. For parallels to the formula "on the steppe" see the note to No. 253.

814. Compare the Turcoman "On the road is a yellow silk fabric.—Camel's urine" (Samojlovich, 109) and the analogous "On the road are greasy loaves.—Camel's dung" (Samojlovich, 110). I do not fully understand the Ten'a "Riddle me: the trail on the hilltop lies close by me.—A thing on which the wolf has urinated" (Jetté, 39). Compare the Irish "Smoke in the glen and not a single spark there.—Horse dung" (De Bhaldraithe, 34 = Hull and Taylor, *Irish*, 300b), which has a general resemblance to the Ainu "Who is sleeping in the mountain wearing bearskin? —Black dung" (Taylor, *Ainu*, 24, with a Ten'a parallel). The bearskin is probably mould or dew. Note the personification in the Kanuri riddle for urination, "A cripple digs a pit" (Lukas, 33. Compare his No. 34) and its Turkish parallel, "A man without hand or foot digs (lit.: opens) a well.—Drops" (Kowalski, *North Bulgaria*, 43). A spring is often compared to a boiling pot; see Taylor, *English*, 1193, § 2. In this Mongolian riddle urine is compared to tea. In the Marshallese "If it is a heron or an eel, put sand [inside], red urine [comes out]," as cited in Davenport, p. 266, No. 14, the theme is reversed. The sand is the tea, the heron or eel is the spout of the teapot, and the infusion of tea is compared to urine.

815. Like butter or fat, the marmot is edible. I have not found a parallel with the answer "marmot," but see such comparisons as the Altai Turkish bear riddle, "Under the earth lies a fat log" (Menges, 44), and the widely known snake riddle, "Under the earth lies a fat thong" (Turkish: Kowalski, *Zagadki*, 17, 99; Kowalski, *North Bulgaria*, 50. For additional parallels see the note to Taylor, *English*, 1466). The theme is old, for it occurs in the fourteenth-century Cuman hedgehog riddle, "On the plain lies a fat hammer" (Németh, 27).

816. For parallels to the formula "from above" see the note to No. 337.

817. For comparisons of churning to a person bowing or praying see No. 393 above and the note.

820. The word "caressing" in No. 820a is to be understood as "suckling." For parallels see Nos. 313 and 341 above. Yakut: Iastremskii, 379 (A hundred men cannot eat up a bit of flesh without a bone, they say), 380 (Ten children cannot eat up a fibrous bit of meat of a two-year old calf), 381. Tabaru: Fortgens, 80 (A ball of rice has been eaten by hundreds and thousands, but one cannot eat it up. Children and grandchildren abandon it.—Woman's breast). The interpretation of the last sentence is somewhat uncertain. It may mean "They outgrow it." Serbian: Novaković, p. 41, No. 3 (Ten bear cubs were eating one pear, yet they could not eat it up). See further No. 429 above and the note. The comparison used here occurs again in a Kxatla riddler for a trader's store: "Tell me: an animal which when eaten by the vultures cannot be finished" (Schapera, 123), to which he cites a South Sotho parallel: "The vultures tear at the skull of a horse, but cannot finish it." See also SeSuto: Norton and Velaphe, 44. It is curious to note that the Muria in India use this same riddle to describe the mind; see the note to No. 737 above. The Kxatla use it to describe sleep: "Tell me: the small pot which cannot be exhausted" (Schapera, 86).

821. This resembles the concluding formula in Russian folktales; see Robert Petsch, *Formelhafte Schlüsse im Volksmärchen*, 72–76, Berlin, Weidmannsche Buchhandlung, 1900; J. Bolte and G. Polívka, *Anmerkungen zu den Kinder- und Hausmärchen* 4: 29–30, Leipzig, Dieterich'sche Verlagsbuchhandlung, 1930. For parallels to the conventional "on a mountain" see the note to No. 90 above.

Since a riddle is an apparently inexplicable statement, riddlers have often described paradoxical scenes that actually have no explanation. In this Mongolian riddle the answer "dream" is equivalent to "lie." Compare the Cheremis "On a bare linden I climb up backwards.—A lie" (Sebeok, 3. 8. 10. 7). A widely current riddle of this sort is the Rumanian "What went out, a blind man saw it, a dumb man called it out, and a deaf man was frightened at its voice?—A lie" (Papahagi, 62). This is probably connected with the German "A millstone floated there on the water, three men sat on it. The blind man saw a hare, the lame man wanted to seize it, the naked man wanted to put it in his pocket. What is it?—A lie" (Wossidlo, 467). To a similar riddle the Estonians give the answers "Setting sun, night, dawn, moon." It is: "A fiery coach came down from the mountain, in it sit a man without a foot, a blind man, a naked man. A hare meets them. The blind man sees it, the footless man catches it, and the naked man puts it in his bosom" (Wiedemann, p. 290). The Russians say: "A wonder brewed beer, a blind man saw, a legless man ran after a ladle, an armless man poured, you drank it but did not interpret it" (Sadovnikov, 2067). See also a Trinidad version of this lying tale given to me by Dr. Elsie Clews Parsons: "A man without an arm shot a bud [i.e., bird], a man without a leg ran and take the bud and put it in a naked man pawket." For additional references see J. Bolte and G. Polívka, *Anmerkungen zu den Kinder- und Hausmärchen* 3: 116–118, Leipzig, Dieterich'sche Verlagsbuchhandlung, 1918. Armenian: Glushakov, 39. Irish: Hull and Taylor, *Irish*, 696, 697.

823. The hay bunch is the rumen or second stomach.

824. Mordvin: Paasonen, 67 (Next to a tree blown down by the wind [is] a bowl of cottage cheese.—Rabbit). This reference to cottage cheese means only that something edible is intended. See similar comparisons for a frog cited in the note to No. 797 above. The Yakut use a comparison similar to this Mongolian riddle to describe the ear;

see the text quoted in the note to No. 827 below. Compare also the Yakut dipper riddle: "They say that old Pelagia lacks half a head" (Piekarski, 363).

825. The following parallels refer to various kinds of grass and reeds, which I have not attempted to identify precisely. Cuman: Németh, 25 (On the little tub a tub). Arabic: Ruoff, p. 54, No. 40 (One house on another, it holds a half-pound of oil). Cheremis: Sebeok, 5. 12. 10 (Milk pail on milk pail, on it [i.e., on top] there's a heckle. —Angelica); Genetz, 37 = Sebeok, 5. 12. 2 (Barrel on barrel, brush on brush). Hungarian: Kálmány, p. 169, No. 19 (Tussock, tussock, more tussocks, above the tussock is a tail.—Cattail). Lithuanian: Mickevicius, p. 581, No. 19 (On a butter vat stands a little vat; on this a smaller one; etc. [sic]; at the top [stands] a wolf cub). Surinam: Penard and Penard, 28 (sugar cane). For additional parallels see the headnote to Taylor, *English*, 1105–1106.

826. The cup, which is ordinarily made of wood, is supported by the fingers. Siberian Turkish: Katanov, *Urianchai*, 30 (A tripod of flesh, a head of wood).

827. Comparisons of ears to household objects are cited here; comparisons to objects found in nature are cited in the note to No. 872. See the comparison to a saucer in No. 838 and the Yakut "On the slope of a valley turned to the south a broken birch vessel" (Iastremskii, 180. See also his No. 181 and the note to No. 824 above); the Samoyede "Two sledges, they do not know how to set themselves, they lie on their sides" (Lehtisalo, 218), the Cherekessian "Under the prince's head there lies a piece of pastry in the shape of a shell" (Tambiev, p. 55, No. 10), the Siberian Turkish "Half a spoon is stuck to the wall" (Moshkov, p. 265, No. 10), the Turkish "A ladle without a handle is attached to the wall" (Bahaeddin, 93), "I hang a sieve on the rock, I put fat in it.—Earring" (Boratav, 139), and "On the cliff a sieve is hung" (Kowalski, *Asia Minor*, 83), and the Abyssinian "A little loaf that hangs on the flank" (Littmann, *Tigriña*, 75), the Bulgarian "Two saucers hanging on a wall" (Bozhov, 3), "Half a plate is hanging on the wall" (Bozhov, 23), "Half a bowl is hanging on the wall and it knows what is happening" (Chacharov, 133), "A crooked mortar in the attic" (Gubov, 377), "A notched bowl stands on the hill" (Gubov, 376), and the versions collected in Stoilov, § 10, Nos. 1–6. The Serbian texts resemble the Bulgarian; see Novaković, pp. 229–230. Note also the Hawaiian "My lopsided gourd hanging on a shelf" (Judd, 180). The Turkish "Half a spoon, there is gum on the sides" adds an unusual detail; see Hamamizade, 429; Kowalski, *North Bulgaria*, 5; Katanov, p. 367, No. 322. The spoon referred to in these riddles is made by splitting a cow's horn and is, therefore, quite similar to an ear. See further the Togo "A crooked iron hangs on the wall" (Schönhärl, p. 107, No. 50) and the Ewe "A bent iron on the wall. What is that?" (Spieth, p. 598, No. 12).

The Hungarian "In the cave there is half a pancake" (Kriza, p. 342, No. 23) is an unusual use of the familiar comparison for the moon (see the note to No. 795 above). See also the Munda riddle for a bullock's ears, "A pair of fans on the side of a hill" (Elwin and Archer, p. 292, No. 49).

828. Parallels to the comparison of the eyes to particolored things are cited here. See Uraon: Archer, 208 (Water of two colors in a single pot). Moslems in India: Elwin and Archer, p. 308, No. 1 (Water of two colors in a single china pot) and p. 311, No. 26 (Two gems, queer they are, half black and half white). Turkish: Hamamizade, 212 = Kúnos, p. 164, No. 163 (I have a bowl of yogurt, half white and half black). A parallel in Kowalski, *Asia Minor*, 74 is not entirely clear. For discussion of the comparison of the eyes to something particolored see the note to No. 801 above.

828b. The Mongolian *alak bulak* means either multicolored or a multicolored fountain.

829. For parallels to the formula "from above," which is here used in a literal sense, see the note to No. 337.

830. A daw has a red beak. The collectors query the solution "gnat."

831. Compare the Uraon "A dish sinks in a tank" (Archer, 49); the Lithuanian "A plate lies in the well" (Sabaliauskas, 23. See also Jurgelionis, 79); the Kosi "My flat round stone is far behind at the springs" (Ittmann, 6); the Letsoalo "Father's wooden plate has been carved by the gods" (Krüger, 43), which contains a comparison to a plate and an unusual reference to the appearance of the moon; and the Yucatecan "Over the flat rock is inverted a flat gourd" (Redfield, 3, 12 [on a rock pool]). See also Nos. 835, 836 below with the note.

832. The Mongolian *kyng* signified originally a birchbark pail and later a pail in general. Because a birchbark pail is white, it is an appropriate comparison for the moon. For parallels to the formula "in the steppe" see the note to No. 253.

833. The dictionaries translate *subayāsun* as plaster or stucco rather than droppings (*argal*). See also No. 850. This rather rare comparison for the sun seems to have been suggested by a similar comparison for the moon. Although the Yakut "In the midst of the sea there floats a silver bowl" (Popov, p. 283; Iastremskii, 4, 5) and "A silver cup floats along the water, it cannot be caught by hands" (Ionova, 32) as well as the Lithuanian "A white plate is lying in the well" (Mickevicius, p. 574, No. 116) have the answer "sun," they seem to be properly riddles for the silvery moon. For other sun riddles see the Moksha Mordvin "A butter tub over a plowed field" (Ahlqvist, *Moksha Mordvin*, 1. See also his No. 2), the Bengali "From this place I cast a bell-metal platter. The bell-metal platter went to the other side of the ocean" (Mitra, *Pābna*, p. 332, No. 4), the Bihari "In the whole lake there is one brickbat" (Mitra, *Bihar*, 1), and the Arabic "A china plate goes to the west and returns toward me" (Giacobetti, 25).

835, 836. The Yakut "Over the yurt there lies a wooden spoon" (Popov, p. 283; Ionova, 25; Iastremskii, 10, 11) or "On the top of the yurt lies a crooked spoon" (Priklonskii, 88) refers to the similarity of the moon, especially the crescent moon, to a spoon carved from a cow's horn. For versions that resemble the Mongolian riddle more closely see Votyak, 384, 385, 429, 445 (In the middle of the floor an ice trough). Turkish: Boratav, 15 (On the roof a bowl is buried). Lithuanian: Mickevicius, p. 582, No. 10 and p. 586, No. 200 (In the middle of the pond lies the half of a dish). For other comparisons of the same sort see the notes to Nos. 795, 831, and 832 in this collection and the headnote to Taylor, *English*, 1189–1191. The conception of the moon is quite different in the Lamba "A great expansive pond, one samba fish" (Doke, 49. See also his No. 91).

838. See the note to No. 827.

839. The comparison resembles that used for leaves in Nos. 624, 625. The Tunka country, which is also mentioned in No. 681, is south of Lake Baikal.

840. The phrase "going to Pekin" refers to the pot (made in China) in which the silversmith boils the ornament to give it a white color. The pasture is the woman's head; the ornament is tawny with enameled spots.

842. I have found no good parallel to this riddle, although the Lithuanian "A little round hole, a little hairy thief" (Schleicher, p. 203) might be called analogous. The Estonian "A black hole, a red plug.—Beet" (Wiedemann, p. 280) has a superficial similarity to the Mongolian riddle, but both it and the Lithuanian riddle involve an entirely different *tertium quid comparationis*.

843. Compare Samoyede: Lehtisalo, 224 (The one is in a dress of otter fur, the other is in a dress of beaver fur, their books are equally large.—Heaven, earth), in which the allusions to the furs and books are not altogether clear. See another Samoyede allusion to otter and beaver furs in a riddle cited in the note to Nos. 874, 875. Compare the Asur "The piece of sal wood that is cut in two and never comes together" (Elwin and Archer, p. 282, No. 34), the Makua "My father plaited for me two reed baskets, one for playing with, one for not playing with" (Harries, *Riddles*, p. 275, No. 1), and the Kuanyama Ambo "The baskets of Nangobe are equal in size" (Loeb, 32). See also No. 874 below with the note.

846. For parallels to the formula "on a tree" see Nos. 787, 847, and 892 in this collection. It may be used in a literal sense or it may refer metaphorically to a man's body or finger. For discussion of the latter use see the note to No. 892. The formula is an old one, for it appears in the fourteenth-century Cuman riddles; see Németh, 13, 14. It is very frequent in Turkish riddles; see Hamamizade, 98, 101, 264, 390, 412, 507, 521, 769; Dyrenkova, 20, 21; Katanov, p. 243, No. 120 and p. 369, No. 336. It occurs in Turkish riddles for fruit on a tree as cited by Kowalski, *Asia Minor*, 5, 6, 21. Note a parallel to this use in Yakut (Iastremskii, 197). Compare further the Cheremis "From the tip of the spruce the woodcock makes dirt.—Pine torch" (Genetz, 21 = Sebeok, 2. 2. 11. 1).

847. Use makes the thick leather tops of thimbles black and greasy. They resemble the black ears of a hare. It is not clear why the collector Zhamtsaranov uses the Russian provincialism *ushkan* (hare) in his translation. For comment on the formula "on a birch tree" see the note to No. 846.

850. Compare No. 833. The Sukuma say "I go round about a copse and see a spread-out pelt.—Cattledung" (Augustiny, 19). An early allusion is seen in the medieval Latin "Nunc ex urbe meat—post se tortas quoque iactat:/ Vacca iacit stercus faciens ex urbe meatus" (Claretus, p. 71, No. 67).

851. See the note to No. 433.

852. The calendar promulgated by the emperor as his prerogative was printed or written on coarse cloth for the Mongols.

853. The significance of the colors is obscure.

854. Silken cloth of five colors, which represent the five types of wisdom, plays a great part in Lamaist symbolism; see F. D. Lessing, *Yung-ho-kung, an Iconography of the Lamaist Cathedral in Peking*. Report from the Scientific Expedition to the North-western Provinces of China under the Leadership of Dr. Sven Hedin. The Sino-Swedish Expedition 18. Part 8. Ethnography. Vol. 1, Stockholm (publ. Göteborg, Elanders boktryckeri), 1942. For other comparisons of a rainbow to a cloth see the Yakut "On the sky there hangs a kerchief of red cloth, it is said" (Popov, p. 283), the Estonian "Motley striped, striped with beautiful bands" (Wiedemann, p. 279), and the Icelandic "What is this wide and high wall, nobly adorned with stripes? It is yellow, red, green, and blue; made by a master's hand" and "What fringe is finely woven across the brain of Ymir? When men see it, they thank God for his gentle covenant" (Arnason, 571, 598). Ymir is a figure in Old Norse myth; God's covenant will be found in Gen. 9:12 and Ezech. 1:28. The Icelandic reference to a striped wall may be compared to the Turkish "I saw a bridge on heaven, its color was of three [kinds]" (Yanikoglu, p. 225, No. 55). See also Taylor, *English*, 654, 655, and the references to a rainbow as something that cannot be grasped in the note to No. 952 below. For parallels to the formula "in the field" see the note to No. 253 above.

855, 856. Compare Arabic: Littmann, 1 (A coat with countless buttons on it which one can neither fold nor wear.—Sky). Riddlers often say that a road cannot be rolled up (see No. 885 below), but they do not often say it of the sky.

860. See No. 929 below and the headnote to Taylor, *English*, 1437, § 11. Cheremis: Sebeok, 5. 6. 3 (Sewn, [and yet] provided with patches).

861. The meaning of the word which is here translated "small" is uncertain. For parallels see the headnotes to Taylor, *English*, 1213, § 4 and 1437, § 9. Turkish: Katanov, *Urianchai*, 8 (My silk is without a seam, my pearls are without a string); Boratav, 69 (Blue atlas, no needle pierces it, no scissors cut it, no tailor makes it up); Orhan, 2: 48 (Blue satin, the needle does not stick into it, persons do not cut it, yarn does not sew it.—Air or sea); Kúnos, p. 169, No. 178.

863. Lithuanian: Sabaliauskas, p. 321, No. 147 (A Russian butterbox has nine skins). Riddlers usually make a comparison to a person wearing many layers of clothing; see the note to Nos. 448–450 above. For the less frequent comparisons to an animal with many skins see Nos. 109, 226, 227 above. Comparisons to a thing, as in this Mongolian version, are unusual.

864. A tube shaped like an arm or sleeve projects from the vessel. See another reference to it in No. 337b. The black sable is probably the soot on the tube. Compare the Cheremis "He put on a green coat, he put on a red belt, he tied on a white apron, he tied on a red shawl" (Sebeok, 3. 8. 5. 1. 1. See also his No. 3. 8. 5. 1. 2). Although the interpretation of the details of this Cheremis riddle is obscure, it may be compared to an Arabic riddle for brandy: "Orange trousers, a Syrian apple [is] the belt, and I,—what have I done, when I felt love for the Christian, i.e., when I drank brandy?" (Littmann, p. 59, No. 63). For other descriptions of distillation or alcoholic liquors see the note to No. 337 above.

865. A *dartsok* is a cloth inscribed with sacred sayings and conjurations. It is hung up to flutter in the wind like a flag.

866. This involves an allusion to appropriating the edible roots laid up by mice. See also No. 330 above.

867. A *dyre* is an oblong bag used as a pillow. At one end it has an oblong opening through which straw or hay is stuffed. The end facing the fire is embroidered with silk and is adorned with silver disks. For another description of such a pillow see No. 116.

868. The meaning of *alchik* is obscure.

870. Yakut: Piekarski, 104 = Priklonskii, 49 (They say that in a cow's peritoneum there is a pile of money.—Hay eaten by a cow). The folds of the intestine suggest leaves, especially the leaves of a book, and this resemblance has given rise to such names for the intestine as *manyplies*, *psalterium*, and the Russian *knizhka*, a diminutive of *kniga* (book). This idea is utilized in such riddles as the Yakut "Ivan has a book not sewn by hands, he never opened it nor will he ever open it.—Second stomach of cattle" (Ionova, 8), which also contained the theme of the box that is never opened (for this theme see the note to No. 724). See further the Yakut "There is a person who has placed a book within his bosom [and] who stands there and does not return it, so they say.—The book is the stomach of a ruminant" (Piekarski, 67), "Under a bridge there is a layer of books, so they say.—Stomach of a cow" (Piekarski, 68), "A fellow has not read through his letter, he could not [do so]" (Iastremskii, 75). Samoyede: Lehtisalo, 264 (They are like the layers of tinder.—Omasum of the reindeer).

871. A camel's footprint has the shape of a small pouch, but the usual comparison for it is a plate or bowl. See the

Munda "In the middle of the jungle a cup has been put upside down.—A tiger's pug marks" (Elwin and Archer, p. 289, No. 13), the Uraon "The old woman who makes a leaf cup as she comes and goes.—Foot print" (Elwin and Archer, p. 294, No. 27), the Arabic "Plates, plates from here to Constantinople" (Bauer, p. 44, No. 20), which is the same as the Rumanian "A little plate as far as Stambul" (Weigand, 27) and differs only insignificantly from the Bulgarian "There are little bowls from here to Constantinople.—Horse tracks" (Gubov, 349), the Serbian "Plate after plate as far as Varadin.—Horseshoe, also road" (Novaković, p. 170, No. 3. See also his p. 181, Nos. 7, 8 and p. 224, Nos. 5–9), or the Russian "All the road is full of trays.—Tracks" (Sadovnikov, 1333). Similar comparisons appear in such related riddles as the Vogul "A man walks, he leaves wheels behind him.—Tracks of the cane" (Ahlqvist, 31), which has a parallel (since I suspect the translation is not exactly correct) in the Mordvin "An old man goes along the road, he makes kopeks.——Tracks of bast shoe" (Paasonen and Ravila, p. 630, No. 9 and compare p. 631, No. 4) and in the Turkish "I go, he goes, he leaves traces like money.—Cane" (Boratav, 52). Note also the Malayalam "A rice measure on the road.—Elephant's footprints" (Schmolck, p. 243, No. 18), the Uraon "The banyan leaf that stops where it fell" (Archer, 137), and the Hawaiian "My adzes that hew little canoes and long-masted canoes" (Judd, 241). See also Mordvin: Paasonen, 406. Lappish: Qvigstad, 109.

The Kxatla "Tell me: little girl, why do you lie on your back so that young men should see you?—Footprint" (Schapera, 83), which refers to a cow's footprint, involves the comparison found in the second Cheremis riddle cited in the note to No. 892 below.

For parallels to the formula "in the steppe" see the note to No. 253 above.

872. Comparisons of the ears to objects found in nature are cited here. Comparisons of the ears to household objects are cited in the note to No. 827. See the Uraon "A stone in the middle of a hill" (Archer, 70), the Tabaru "Two ships that sail to the other side of the mountain" (Fortgens, 33), the Mehri and Soqotri "At my side two fences" (Müller, p. 363, No. 28). The Muria "The tree has only two leaves" (Elwin and Archer, p. 268, No. 16) contains also the comparison of a man to a tree that is discussed in the note to No. 892 below. See also the Lithuanian "Two trees stand at the edge of the forest" (Mickevicius, p. 572, No. 20). The Lithuanian "At the edge of the forest two wheels are standing" (Mickevicius, p. 573, No. 35 and p. 589, No. 331; Schleicher, p. 206; Jurgelionis, 167) are variations of the riddle for earrings discussed in the note to Nos. 233, 234 above. Compare further the Ila "The fish-eagles that sit on one tree" (Smith and Dale, 2: 329, No. 34).

Other comparisons for the ears range more widely than those that have been cited. See the Mordvin "Mushrooms are fastened to the end of a stake" (Paasonen and Ravila, p. 656, No. 3), the Tschuana "Cow posts under a small hill" (Kuhn 8), the Tlokoa "Villages on the side of the mountain" and "Two young men are standing, one on each side of a mountain" (Nakene, p. 134, Nos. 3, 4), and the Lamba "That which builds a house in the spinney" (Doke, 82). Note also three Lamba comparisons of the head to an anthill that also mention the ears: "A mushroom on an anthill"; "Two burrows beneath an anthill," which seems to be an adaptation of a riddle for the nostrils discussed in the note to No. 771 above; and "A lean-to on an anthill" (Doke, 138, 86, and 90).

873. Summer boots are made of soft, shapeless cloth. Ammianus Marcellinus (16: 2. 12) describes the summer shoes of the Huns as "calcei formis nullis aptati."

874, 875. The wool represents the clouds. For parallels see the headnote to Taylor, *English,* 1230–1234. Samoyede: Lehtisalo, 182 (Two striped squirrel pelts, they are equal in size, neither is larger [than the other]), 232 (One is a beaver, the other a fish otter, they are of equal size). For the contrast of beaver and otter fur see the note to No. 843 above. Nuer: Huffman, p. 105, No. 14 (Guess what are two big rugs.—They are the sky and the earth).

878. For a description of Mongolian monks see Getty, p. xxxv.

879. The term "honey ridge" may be a proper name or intended to suggest one. For parallels to the formula "on the honey ridge" see the note to No. 90.

880, 881. Compare Nos. 857, 870, and the note to No. 870. Yakut: Iastremskii, 80 (There is a quarrel between what is twisted and what is twirled, a heavy [weapon] is the judge.—Disemboweling cattle). Arabic: Ruoff, p. 16, No. 5 (Rods are in a deep valley; they see neither the sun nor lightning flashes); Löhr, 15. Russian: Sadovnikov, 1791 (Hooks and crooks lie behind a bench.—Bowels), 1792 (Under a bridge, under a necklace, there lies a folded kaftan). Compare the Altai Turkish description of the ribs: "In a valley the trees are bent to one side" (Menges, p. 86, No. 10). For parallels to the formula "in a deep well" see the note to No. 61 above.

882, 883. For parallels to the notion that a road has no end see Taylor, *English,* 575 with the headnote.

884–886. For parallels to the notion that a road cannot be rolled up see the headnote to Taylor, *English,* 575, nn. 22–29. Tabaru: Fortgens, 88. Turkish: Yanikoglu, p. 218, No. 16 (I have a clue, I roll it up, roll it up, but it never ends). Russian: Sadovnikov, 1328, 1329.

884. Compare "A loincloth of our ancestors that is not broken.—Path" (Dusun: Evans, 12).

887. Santal: Elwin and Archer, p. 306, No. 27 (The woman who always ties her black goat at the back of the house.—A way of dressing the hair) with a Kharia parallel, "The goat is tied to the back.—A lock of hair" (Elwin and Archer, p. 286, No. 29) and Uraon parallels: "The bashful girl who stays behind" and "A girl tidies a room and goes to the back of the house" (Elwin and Archer, p. 293, Nos. 16, 21). Cheremis: Porkka, 117 = Sebeok, 5. 14. 6 (Behind the stable there hangs a hide.—The lower, hanging part of a Cheremis woman's cap); Wichmann, 74 (Behind the cow stable hangs the hide of the evil one.—Woman's head ornament). The queue is a peculiarity of northern Asiatic headdress; see O. J. Maenchen-Helfen, *Byzantion* 18: 236–237, 1946, citing Kurakichi Siratori, "The Queue among the Peoples of Northern Asia," *Memoirs of the Research Department of the Toyo Bunko,* No. 4: 1–69, Tokyo, 1929.

887b. Bazarov says that *gedeng yodong* means "horizontal undulating motion"; Golstunskii, 3: 406 says that it means "in a frightened manner, looking around timidly"; G. I. Ramstedt informs F. D. Lessing orally that it refers to the dangling of an object; and Mostaert translates it "se mouvoir, se balancer [épis des céréales, extremités des herbes]."

888. Compare the Makua "I went to my friend and a piece of sugarcane was broken for me without notches" (Harries, *Riddles,* p. 279, No. 1) and the Nandi "Which would you rather bind around your waist, a dry stick or a short cord?—A dry stick, because a soft cord is a snake" (Hollis, p. 138, No. 25).

889. Riddlers describe milking a cow as

1. beating or striking. Polish: Kopernicki, 37 and 37, var. 3; Saloni, *Łańcut,* 5 (Four lads beat on one log). See also Saloni, *Rzeshów,* 25–27.

2. throwing stones. Turkish: Kowalski, *Zagadki,* 95; Bahaeddin, 72 (Four brothers throw stones into a well);

Orhan, 33; Yanikoglu, 44a; Kúnos, p. 155, No. 104. A similar comparison describes eating; see a Turkish riddle cited in the note to No. 619 above. A Turkish riddler's application of this comparison to bees in "Tiny little birds throw stones at the mosque" (Boratav, 12) does not seem appropriate.

3. shooting. The oldest version of this comparison that I have noted is "Quatuor in solum dant tela rubum simul unum/ Fratres: ubera sunt, que [quae] lac in vana remittunt" (Claret, p. 68, No. 15). See also Ossete: Schiefner, 17 (Four guns aimed at the earth). Votyak: Wichmann, 141, 142. Abchaz: Guliia, 16. Hungarian: Arany and Gyulai, 2: 370, No. 107 (Four *jager* pinetrees are shooting one log. What is it?); *Magyar Nyelvör* 2: 559, 1873 (Four *csive* shoot into the same target). The meaning of the italicized words is obscure. Polish: Kopernicki, 37, vars. 1, 2; Gustawicz, 46, 48. Faeroic: Hammershaimb, *Anthologi*, p. 324, No. 33. In this Mongolian riddle the bow is the teat and the white arrows are the milk.

4. singing (a reference to the milk falling into the pail). Svanian: J. Nizheradze, pp. 66–67, No. 8 (Four sisters sing through one throat.—Udder). Georgian: Glushakov, p. 26, No. 29 (There are two of them, both are of the same age. When they enter a dwelling, they begin to sing); Kapanadze, p. 144, No. 5 (Two people of the same age walk to town and sing.—Cow's udder). These riddles refer to a mare rather than a cow. Lithuanian: Jurgelionis, 753 (Four brothers blow in one horn).

5. weeping. Lappish: Qvigstad, 64 (Four sisters weep in the same vessel).

6. spitting. Russian: Sadovnikov, 868a.

7. urinating. See the note to No. 615 above.

8. catching geese. See Nos. 83, 84 above.

I can cite no parallel to the Santal "The water of four rice lands in a single field.—Udder of a cow" (Elwin and Archer, p. 307, No. 36).

890. The meaning of the word translated as "taut" is uncertain.

891a. *Yag* is a very hard wood that burns with a bright flame. The ulna is called the "guest's bone" in Mongolian. It may not be eaten by a stranger of low social standing. When filled with gilagana burs, it is suspended against the yurt as a protection against wolves. See also No. 344 above.

892. For comparisons of the human face or a member of the human body to a scene in nature see No. 681 above and the note. This comparison of the face to Russian characters resembles Nos. 897, 898 below, which have the answer "brain."

Mongolian riddlers often use the formula "at the top of a tree"; see the note to No. 846 above. The formula often occurs in descriptions of the human body and examples of that use are collected in this note. The Cheremis say for the membrum virile, "On a little spruce tree there is the handle of a frying pan" (Beke, 14 = Sebeok, 4. 6) and for the pudendum muliebre, "On a little spruce tree there is a cow track" (Beke, 15 = Sebeok, 4.7). The second of these riddles has a Kxatla parallel which is cited in the note to No. 871 above. See further the Chinese "One tree with two pears. When the child sees them, it is impatient" (Serruys, 41) with a Bulgarian parallel, "In the middle of a birch tree two apples" (Stoilov, § 2; Ikonomov, 71), the Cheremis "On a linden tree there hangs a pair of woodcocks.—Breasts" (Porkka, 111 = Sebeok, 2. 2. 8. 4. 2), the Bulgarian "Two fans on top of a birch.—Ears" (Stoilov, § 10, No. 6), "There is a thicket on top of a birch tree.—Hair" (Ikonomov, 69), "There is a cover (i.e., lid) on top of the birch tree.—Cap" (Ikonomov, 75), and "On the top of a birch two wells.—Eyes" (Stoilov, § 11, No. 10). A related but quite different conception is seen in a riddle of the Indian Moslems for a man: "Two trunks to a tree, two branches, and ten fruits. Such a tree I never saw, though I searched all the lanes" (Elwin and Archer, p. 310, No. 21). Compare also an Ila riddle cited in the note to No. 872 above.

897, 898. The word *akhä* is not in the dictionaries. This riddle may be connected with the Cuman "I have knotted a knot and have laid it on the chimney" (Németh, 35), which some have supposed to have the answer "mind." Németh, whose translation is quoted here, suggests the answer "smoke." Since the translation "have laid it on the chimney" is very uncertain, Németh's suggestion is equally uncertain. His predecessors translated this clause as "that which was knotted," which fits better the answer "mind," i.e., brain. For other comparisons of parts of the body to physical objects see No. 892 above and the note.

900. The patch is probably a cloud and the sheepskin the sky.

908. The forked wood is the frame, the sable cap the felt cover, and the cross the wooden lattice wall.

909. Siberian Turkish: Katanov, *Urianchai*, 27 (Whiter than sugar, blacker than soot; lower than a dog, taller than a camel). Mordvin: Paasonen and Ravila, p. 613, No. 5 (White as snow, black as soot, walks in hops, a bone in its mouth) and p. 642, No. 7. The Mordvin phrase "a bone in its mouth" may be understood literally or it may mean "its mouth is bone." For additional parallels see Taylor, *English*, 1379–1382, with the headnote and notes.

910. In this riddle and its parallels *long* (*high*) and *low* are contrasted and the word translated *long* means also *high* or *tall*. The English use of long in the sense of high or tall is not familiar enough to be material for a good riddle. It is found in the name Long John Silver in *Treasure Island*. See the Mordvin "Higher than trees, lower than grass" (Paasonen and Ravila, p. 679, No. 3; Ahlqvist, *Moksha Mordvin*, p. 144, No. 73); the Turcoman "Higher than the mountain, lower than the grass" (Samojlovich, 155); the Chuvash "Lower than the grass, longer [taller] than the forest" (Karahka and Räsänen, 46). Russian: Sadovnikov, 1231. Estonian: Wiedemann, p. 284. Lappish: Qvigstad, 70; Koskimies and Itkonen, 3 (Higher than the mountains, lower than all twigs). The Lappish "Higher than all the mountains and lower than all the heather" (Qvigstad, 5; Poestion, p. 267) has the alternative solution "fog." For additional parallels see the note to No. 399 above and the headnote to Taylor, *English*, 1281.

Riddlers often use this contrast of higher and lower to describe a saddle, but employ somewhat different comparisons. See the Tatar "Higher than a horse, lower than a dog" (Kalashev and Ioakimov, p. 49, No. 14; Filonenko, 31). Turkish: Jarring, 1, 2. Turcoman: Samojlovich, 114, with additional parallels in the note. Armenian: Grigorov, p. 123, No. 16. Chuvash: Mészáros, 1 (Lower than the rooster, higher than the horse), 86 (Higher than the horse, lower than the road). Votyak: Wichmann, 324, 327. Hungarian: *Magyar Nyelvör* 4: 424, No. 57, 1875; 5: 460, No. 89, 1876. Russian: Sadovnikov, 982. Polish: Saloni, *Rzeshów*, 168. Lithuanian: Basanavicius, p. 190, No. 13 (Bigger than a horse, smaller than a dog); Sabaliauskas, p. 319, No. 768; Mickevicius, p. 574, No. 85, p. 578, No. 52, and p. 582, No. 17; Schleicher, p. 208; Jurgelionis 678–680. See additional parallels in the headnote to Taylor, *English*, 1281, n. 7. The Russians use a similar comparison to describe a bow over the shafts of a cart (Sadovnikov, 971). The Arabs say of sparrows and doves: "Higher than a minaret and lower than a stiltshoe" (Littmann, 14, 15).

911, 912. The adjective translated "feathery, dented" refers to the notches made for the spokes of the smokehole.

913. The Siberian Turkish "It came down as if from the sky and it is trimmed as if by iron" (Katanov, p. 241, No. 80) contains two elements of the Mongolian riddle. For parallels to the formula "fallen from above" see the note to No. 337.

915. This is an adaptation of the egg riddle, No. 913. The flower is the copper base of the button. For other examples of a comparison used in two different riddles see the note to Nos. 476–478. For another description of a rank button see No. 90.

916. The cake (Mongolian *baling;* Sanskrit *bali;* Tibetan *gtor ma*) is an offering made of dough. It is used in Buddhist ceremonies.

917. The halter is the oesophagus and the lama's cloak is the peritoneum. For another description of a stuffed stomach see No. 45. The stomach is stuffed with buckwheat flour mixed with blood. Before cooking it, the opening is closed with a bit of intestine and a small transverse peg. The riddler compares this peg to the nose-peg of a camel. The priest's cloak (*jantsa*) has many creases; these symbolize the complexity of his vows. The creases resemble the folds in the stomach. The conception is akin to the Scotch Gaelic "Which cowl was never made by human hands?—Omasum or manyplies" (Nicolson, p. 39). See also the comparison of the stomach to a book with many leaves in No. 870 above.

919. Yakut: Iastremskii, 200. Kashmiri: Knowles, 131 (I came and I went, I sat on many branches, I was sweet—and where did I go?). See also the Tatar "It is not found in the market, it cannot be weighed, it is sweeter than honey, yet it cannot be eaten" (Kalashev and Ioakimov, p. 51, No. 34; Filonenko, 112); the Turkish "It cannot be found in the market, it cannot be put in a handkerchief, one cannot find anything sweeter" (Kúnos, p. 175, No. 238) with parallels in Zavarin, *Brusa,* 4 and Hamamizade, 691; and the Turkish "Cannot be bought in the market, cannot be wrapped in a piece of cloth, one never gets too much of it" (Bahaeddin, 14). The Kabardin "Sweeter than honey, heavier than lead, if you put it on your back, you can't carry it away, if you take it to market, some will buy.—Sleep" (Talpa and Sokolov, 15) is corrected by the Cherekessian version which ends: "If you should take it to market, no one would buy it" (Tambiev, p. 54, No. 16).

Parallels to the first clause in the Mongolian riddle are found in the Armenian "Sweeter than honey, but it cannot be eaten" (Zelinski, p. 58, No. 21), the Yakut "It is sweeter than sweet.—Sleep" (Popov, p. 286; Piekarski, 196); the Cheremis "It is on earth, sweeter than everything" (Beke, 7 = Sebeok, 10. 4. 1). Turkish: Kowalski, *Zagadki,* 105. See further the Bulgarian "The sweetest, mildest thing, it is not placed on the table" (Ikonomov, 45), which contains an element characteristic of a riddle for the mother's breast (see the note to No. 429 above), and the Lithuanian "It is sweet and tasty, but it is not put on a plate" (Mickevicius, p. 576, No. 189). The Lithuanians also have the usual form of the riddle: "What is sweeter than honey?" (Schleicher, p. 208). The Serbian "Darker than coal, and sweeter than honey.—Sleep" (Novaković, p. 198, No. 2) contains a theme not represented in the previously cited versions. The comparison to something sweet also occurs in a Yakut triad: "From the full to the fullest, from the sweet to the sweetest, from the fat to the fattest.—World, dream, earth" (Piekarski, 1).

For a discussion of the superlative question, "What is the sweetest thing?," which has such various answers as "sleep, honey, sugar, or other food; love or a wife" and random answers see Jan de Vries, *Die Märchen von den klugen Rätsellösern,* FF Communications, **73**: 79–84, Helsinki, 1928. Swedish: Olsson, *Bohuslän,* 372.

921. Compare Nos. 147 and 639 above.

924. A Chinese cash (a coin) is round with a square hole in the center. It is inscribed with legends in Chinese (four characters) and Manchu (two characters).

925–927. The stand has three hoops, which are called "wheels" in No. 926, and several hooks.

929. For parallels to the cloak without seams see Nos. 860a–860c.

930. The Mongolian *minggaldak* alliterates with *minggan* (thousand) and rhymes with *janggildak,* which is used in place of the ordinary word *janggā* (knot). Similarily, *xonggildak,* which is also in rhyme, is used instead of the usual *bödö* (peg, stick). For a parallel to this riddle see Hungarian: Arany and Gyulai, **2**: 366, No. 82 (Holes, holes all over, knots, knots all over—Net).

933. Riddles of a somewhat similar sort are collected in the headnote to Taylor, *English,* 1100–1108. For a curious parallel to the comparison of the head to a cliff see the crag in the Irish "Four running, four shaking, two on the crag, two cleaving the sky, and the son of Ó Maolshodair (i.e., Gentle Trot) trotting behind" (Ó Cillin, p. 51 = Hull and Taylor, *Irish,* 283c).

936. This is the famous riddle of the Sphinx. For parallels and references to discussions of the riddle see Taylor, *English,* 47 with the headnote and note. See further Korean: F. W. K. Müller, p. 114. Marshallese: Davenport, 6. Cheremis: Sebeok, 1. 2, 1, 1. 2. 2, 1. 2. 3. Finnish: Haavio and Hautala, 1–3. Chuvash: Mészáros, 37. Bulgarian: Stoilov, § 47. Lithuanian: Basanavicius, 204; Mickevicius, p. 590, No. 387. Swedish: Olsson, *Bohuslän,* 1; Wessman, 67. Surinam: Penard and Penard, 34.

937. Mostaert regards the translations of the second and fourth clauses as somewhat uncertain. The import of the riddle is obscure.

938, 939. The corner of the flap is drawn back in the morning, when the weather permits, to form a triangular opening. This act is somewhat differently conceived in No. 796. For a similar use of a variation in shape as the theme of a riddle see the Chuvash "One of its heads is triangular, the other head is quadrangular.—Last" (Mészáros, 111) and the following Mongolian hobble riddle, No. 540. For riddles that refer to a variation in an object between day and night see Nos. 796, 941–944, and 947.

940. Compare the note to No. 940. For the formula "from heaven" see the note to No. 337.

941. For a similar comparison in terms of a grazing sheep see No. 141 above. For riddles contrasting the shapes of an object during the day and at night see the note to Nos. 938, 939.

943. The sleeve covers the arm in the daytime. For riddles contrasting the shapes of an object during the day and at night see the note to Nos. 938, 939.

944. For parallels see the headnote to Taylor, *English,* 1341–1342, § 4. Russian: Sadovnikov, 243. See also a Uraon comparison to a plant: "The flower that shuts by day and opens at night" (Archer, 135) and a Turkish comparison to a house: "It is destroyed in the evening, it is built in the morning" (Yankikoglu, p. 215, No. 1). For riddles contrasting the shapes of an object during the day and at night see the note to Nos. 938, 939.

945. For a survey of riddles for a frog see the note to Nos. 40–42. For the formula "in the steppe" see the note to No. 253.

947. When sheep are driven into the pasture, only manure remains in the sheepfold. At night the sheepfold is white with the sheep crowded into it. For riddles contrasting the shape of an object during the day with its shape at night see the note to Nos. 938, 939.

949. Tatar: Filonenko, 99 (Called *ababit* with rosy wings, it has eyes and a head like a button.—Locust). The

SeSuto "The ox of the father of sticks has a hairy body like a horse or gnu.—Brown locust" (Norton and Velaphe, 43) may be a derivative of the riddle discussed in the note to No. 403.

951. Compare the Hungarian "When he stretches it once, he can't reach out with it. When he stretches it twice, it has the right length.—Man's arm when reaching to his mouth" (*Magyar Nyelvőr* 6: 470, No. 59, [1877]). Swedish: Ström, p. 81, "Näcken" (I see it, but you do not see it, and it is nearer to you than to me). See also the note to No. 808.

952. For another reference to the notion that a rainbow cannot be grasped see No. 854 and the Estonian "In an arch I go over the land, no one gets me in his hand" (Wiedemann, p. 274). There is a similar reference in an Indian riddle for lightning: "It is here, it is there, but even if you give a hundred rupees, you cannot get it" (Saura: Elwin and Archer, p. 379, No. 9). For comparisons to something that cannot be grasped see the headnote to Taylor, *English*, 1643–1654 and especially § 6, where riddles having the answer "shadow" are collected.

953. Yakut: Iastremskii, 183. Mordvin: Ahlqvist, *Moksha Mordvin*, 11 (I have reins, they reach around the earth, but they do not reach around me). Georgian: Glushakov, p. 22, No. 10 (Closed—the size of a coin; open —the size of the earth). For additional parallels see the headnote to Taylor, *English*, 1471.

956. Hungarian: Arany and Gyulai, II, 361, No. 64 (Little, little black thing *ju, ju, ju, ju* [cries of pain]); *Magyar Nyelvőr* 5: 329, 1876; 9: 180, 1880; 13: 285, 1884.

957–959. For other riddles describing buttons see the survey in the note to No. 608. They often have obscene implications; see, for example, Turkish: Kúnos, 1: 144, No. 28.

957. Did the riddler intend to say *angaixu* (to open the mouth) instead of *alcaixu* (to widen)?

959. See Nos. 11, 12 above and the note. Similar conceptions are implied in the Yakut "Something that is goggle-eyed enters somthing that is spread wide" (Piekarski, 284. See also his Nos. 285, 286, 288; Priklonskii, 68) and "When bald old men entered the house, the bald old men remained outside" (Ionova, 125), which means that the button passed through the buttonhole and remained on the farther side.

960. For parallels see Taylor, *English*, 1691 and the headnote to Nos. 1690–1697.

961–964. For discussion of riddles based on a contrast of small and strong see the note to Nos. 32, 33 above.

961. Compare No. 529.

963. Compare the Siberian Turkish parallel, "Smaller than I, but he cheated me" (Katanov, p. 160, No. 1323; Katanov, *Urianchai*, 37). Somewhat different ideas appear in the Turkish "A tiny sharp stone (or: hone), forty men could not hold it.—Dream" (Kúnos, 1: 150, No. 72) and the Icelandic "My substance is of various kinds, but it is always my nature to overtake everyone unawares, particularly as night approaches" (Arnason, 873).

964. See No. 486 and the Khalka Monngolian "Something smaller than you lifts you up" (G. I. Ramstedt, "Ueber die Konjugation des Khalka-Mongolischen," *Mémoires de la Société finno-ougrienne* 19: 15, 1902). Siberian Turkish: Katanov, p. 160, No. 1325 (Smaller than I, but he seated me on a horse); Katanov, *Urianchai*, 38.

965. The meaning of "it threw you away" is not entirely clear and the phrase may not be correctly translated.

966. Turcoman: Samojlovich, 89 (A riddle, a riddle, a jolly riddle, it passes across the tongue and the throat checks it). For similar conceptions see Nos. 8 and 746 above and the note to No. 89.

967. The second clause means "it is transformed by rainwater" and refers to the use of water in making felt.

968. Compare such riddles as the Turcoman "They feed it cunningly, they make it urinate over the side.—Sesame mill" (Samojlovich, 146) and "The old camel nibbles grass and lies down. From its belly it casts forth dung and lies down" (Samojlovich, 147, citing parallels) and the Lappish "It eats and drinks according to measure and urinates according to measure.—Coffee pot or wine barrel" (Qvigstad, 88. See also his No. 69). Turkish: Kowalski, *North Bulgaria*, 6. Bulgarian: Gubov, 415. Polish: Saloni, *Rzeshów*, 146 (watering pot), 160 (cheese in a sack). SeSuto: Norton and Velaphe, 15 (Micturiens per corpus totum.—Beer-strainer woven of grass). Kxatla: Schapera, 106 (beer-strainer).

970. The meaning of *sosalzhin* is obscure.

972. This solution does not occur in discussions of the riddle "How high is heaven?"; see Walter Anderson, *Kaiser und Abt. Die Geschichte eines Schwanks*, FF Communications, 42: 113–129, Helsinki, 1923, and the excellent note in Joseph Gillet, ed., *"Propalladia" and Other Works of Bartolomé Torres de Naharro* 3: 212–213, Bryn Mawr, Pa., 1951.

973. This may involve a reference to the fire god.

974. For parallels see Archer Taylor, "Formelmärchen," *Handwörterbuch des deutschen Märchens* 2: 167, n. 17, Berlin, Walter de Gruyter, 1934–1940.

982. This is perhaps a children's rhyme rather than a riddle. Note a Siberian Turkish parallel: "What pierced you? An auger. What came out of you? Sawdust. What did they shove into you? A strap.—Gratings of the yurt, their preparation, joining them with a strap" (Katanov, p. 113, No. 978). The meaning of *burak* is obscure. It may mean a maroon as in fireworks, a cylindrical birchbark box, or a beet root. Perhaps the birchbark box for an awl is intended.

986. Between the numbers eleven and twelve I have omitted nine questions that do not concern numbers. The first two of these questions are: "What have you done with the black kid of the she-goat? I have killed it and eaten its flesh. What have you done with its hide? The motley dog seized it in his teeth and ran off with it."

990. The first five numbers and the things corresponding to them are lacking. Perhaps the collector intended to imply that they resembled the first five items in Nos. 988 and 989. Zu or Tzu is the name of three famous statues of the Buddha Sakyamuni. Two of them are in Lhasa, one is in Pekin. The temples at Lhasa where the statues are kept, the city of Lhasa, and the country of Tibet are all called Zu. Furthermore, the Kalmucks think that Zu signifies the sacred statue of the god Zunkhara.

991. This series differs from Nos. 986–990 in conception. In Mongolian the numbers and the objects associated with them begin in each instance with the same letter.

995. A mirror is used in Buddhist and lamaist rites.

996. For parallels see Archer Taylor, "Riddles in the 'Emigrant's Penny Magazine'," *Southern Folklore Quarterly* 11: 139, 1947. See a seventeenth-century Latin parallel in Pincier, pp. 75–76. Swedish: Wessman, 681.

997. This is obviously a defective version of Nos. 1006, 1007. For parallels to the ladder with which to ascend see the note to No. 1006. For parallels to the lid with which to cover the ocean see the note to No. 1007. Compare also the Turkish "What is that over which you don't build a bridge? What is that for which you don't find a cure?—Open sea, death" (Hamamizade, 144) and "A bird came and said, 'Hak!' and said 'Hyk!' and said 'There are three things which do not exist in the world: a camel's horseshoe, a stairway to the sky, a lid for the sea'" (Hamamizade, 146).

998. This riddle is, of course, not a triad. I have included it in this section because it involves a reference to the number three. Its import is obscure.

999. The translation of *segdyr* as "shadow, reflection" is uncertain. Compare the last element in the Mongolian riddle with the second element in the Hausa "How many dark things are of use in the world?—Three: dark water (i.e., rain), dark metal (i.e., iron), a dark Koran" (Fletcher, 18). The collector explains that a "dark" Koran means one written or printed. The similarity of these Mongolian and Hausa elements at the eastern and western ends of the Moslem world is worthy of note.

1002. The jabar wind is a cold wind that blows over a valley before and after sunset and sunrise. The lady's cheeks are understood to be red with rouge.

1006. For references to the lack of a ladder reaching to heaven or the sky see the second Turkish riddle quoted in the note to No. 997; the Chuvash and Kabardin riddles quoted in the headnote to Nos. 997–1024; and the Cheremis and Turkish riddles quoted in the note to No. 1007. See also Gen. 28: 12; J. G. Frazer, *Folk-Lore in the Old Testament* **2**: 52–58, London, Macmillan, 1918; Stith Thompson, *Motif-Index of Folk-Literature* **3**: 7–8, F. 52, *Indiana Univ. Studies* **21**, Bloomington, Ind., 1934.

1007. In these triads the elements vary from text to text and a complete parallel to this or any other Mongolian triad is virtually impossible to find. One or more elements of this triad are found in Kashmiri: Knowles, 2 (What is that without a covering? What is that without a pillar? —River and sky), 7 (A golden box with a silver lid; he who can shut it is a brave fellow.—Earth and sky). Cheremis: Wichmann, 173 = Sebeok, 8. 3 (Three sorts of things are not in the world: for climbing to heaven there is no ladder; for going over the sea there is no beam; a white hawk has no milk). Turkish: Hamamizade, 354 (Incapable of begetting offspring, —, unbridgeable, unavoidable. —Mule, heaven, sea, death). The parallels suggest that the untranslated word is "unclimbable."

This triad may be related to the riddles cited in the headnote to Taylor, *English,* 138–140. For additional examples of such riddles see Lithuanian: Volteris, p. 450, No. 19 (The father's girl cannot be tied, the mother's chest cannot be closed, the son's horse cannot be stopped.—Road, ocean, wind); Mickevicius, p. 581, No. 1 (The mother's chest cannot be lifted; the father's belt cannot be tied; the brother's horse cannot be held.—Earth, road, wind). See also a similar riddle with the answers "road, wind, stove" (Mickevicius, p. 589, No. 311). The Lithuanians also use a version of this riddle to describe a stove, smoke, and fire: "It is impossible to lift the father's chest, to hold the brother's horse, to plait the sister's braids" (Sabaliauskas. p. 317, No. 17; Jurgelionis, 339). A description of smoke and a stove may be a fragment of this triad: "The brother's horses are not to be held back, the sister's chest cannot be carried about" (Mickevicius, p. 575, No. 131). See also some riddles having a similar form but entirely different answers in the note to No. 336 above.

1009. For references to a horse's lack of gall see Nos. 461, 462 with the note. Compare also such Yakut riddles as "A lady without a fire-stone [flint] is in labor" (Iastremskii, 59), "A thoroughly, truly honorable man showered with honors. All his life he has occupied high positions, yet he has no dagger" (Iastremskii, 67), and "A worthy man has forgotten his boiler" (Piekarski, 136).

1012. The riddle and the translation are very obscure. According to Golstunskii *asamay* signifies a burro, but the Russian translator interprets it as bull calf and adds a note that the Mongols do not ride on them.

1013. The word here translated "growling" may also mean "bossing." Golstunskii defines Mongolian *kymelky*

as "to pick up from the ground while riding on horseback."

1018. Compare No. 1020.

1020. The Russian translator renders the first statement as "A hedgehog walking on the road is rough."

1022. Tying a knot in silk may refer to the presentation of a ceremonial scarf. The mention of the Nepalese craftsman (*abalbu*) suggests that this riddle has been translated from Tibetan. A knot in iron seems to mean an elaborate pattern wrought in iron. The import of the riddle lies in the various meanings of *zanggilaxu* (to tie a knot).

1024. According to Golstunskii, *zamay*, which is here translated "growing," signifies aquatic plants. This meaning fits the context.

1025. Riddles of this sort are both numerous and widely known. As is obvious, they cannot be easily borrowed from one language to another. Compare the Korean "What kind of rice (*pap*) cannot be eaten?—Sawdust (*toppap*)" and "What kind of a bell (*pang-ool*) cannot be rung? —Pine cone (*sol-pang-ool*)." For these Korean see Bernheisel, p. 82; he cites many more riddles of the same kind. See further Chinese: Serruys, 14 (Vegetables [*ts'ai*] that one cannot reach. Clouds [*yün-ts'ai*]. Vegetables that one cannot cook.—Salad [*sheng-ts'ai*]. Vegetables that are buried in the earth. Coffin [*kuan-ts'ai*]). Japanese: Preston, p. 179, No. 2. 1. Kashmiri: Knowles, 33 (Of four feet, of fourteen feet, of one foot up in a tree.—*Khar*, i.e., an ass, an insect, a muskmelon). See also his No. 88. We see the same theme but a slightly different manner of expression in the Votyak "One is in the field, the other is in the mill, the name is the same.—Mole and millpond" (Wichmann, 56). See also his Nos. 9, 19, 20, 71, 72, 121, 247, 276, 277, 291, 357, 390 and Fuchs, p. 243, Nos. 20, 22 and p. 245, Nos. 45, 46. Hindi: *Panjab Notes and Queries* **2**: 106, § 626, No. 1, 1885 (If it grows in the fields, then all eat it. If it is in the house, then don't go home.—*Phút*, a species of melon and a rent or tear). A Mordvin riddler is content with a partial similarity of the words: "In the house and in the water they have a similar name.—Egg (*alś*) and fish (*kalś*)"; see Paasonen and Ravila, p. 639, No. 3. As examples of the wide distribution of this manner of riddling see Dusun: Evans, 10, 23. Samoan: Heider, 15 (There are two brothers with the same name, one lives in the taro plantation, the other in the ocean.— *Sugale*, the name of a kind of taro and of a fish), 43, 59. Serbian: Novaković, p. 88, No. 7 (I am in both the forest and the water.—*Klen*, wood and a kind of fish). Portuguese: Pires de Lima, 2d ed., 202, 231. Yoruba: Bascom, 3.

1026. The Mongolian *alak dagan* also signifies a piebald stallion.

1027. A Kalmuck's wife must not mention the names of her husband's elders, beginning with his older brothers and sisters. She must avoid naming objects having names similar in sound to the names of these relatives, although such resemblances occur frequently in Kalmuck speech. This riddle, which is represented to be a wife's communication of a domestic accident to her husband, owes its enigmatic quality to the avoidance of such often used nouns as *usun* (water), *modon* (forest), *chono* (wolf), and *khoin* (sheep). Its point lies in the difficulty and confusion caused by the use of periphrastic forms chosen to replace these nouns. In some instances it is possible to see a hunter's tabu in these riddles. See, for example, the Lithuanian "The runner on the road comes running and asks the watchman where the crouching one lies.—Wolf, dog, and pig" (Sabaliauskas, 74). For collections of riddles of this sort, discussions of them, and references to similar tabus see Kenneth Jackson, "The Burning of the Barn," *Folk-Lore*, **47**: 190–203, 1936; Robert Petsch, "Die Scheune Brennt," *Zeitschrift des Vereins für Volkskunde* **26**: 8–18, 1916, with additions by Johannes Bolte, *ibid.* **27**:

135–141, 1917; Martha Long, *Western Folklore* 7: 64, 1948; Kristensen, pp. 164–172 (eleven texts); Olsson, *Bohuslän*, 406–428, 441–449; J. G. Frazer, *The Golden Bough*, Part II, *Taboo and the Perils of the Soul*, 318–418, London, Macmillan, 1922; Wolfgang Krause, *Die Kenning als typische Stilfigur des germanischen und keltischen Dichtersprache*, Schriften der Königsberger gelehrten Gesellschaft, 7, Heft 1: 19–20, 25, and 26, n. 12, Halle, 1930.

Although there are several preliminary investigations of these riddles, we have not yet learned how many independent types exist and what relations, if any, are present among them. Without endeavoring to offer a complete survey I call attention to the following types:

1. The burning of the barn. Swedish: Olsson, *Bohuslän*, 409. See the articles on this riddle that are cited above.

2. A fox (wolf) carries off a chicken (goose, sheep); the farmer calls for his gun. This riddle, which is widely known in western Europe, may perhaps be also found in the Siberian Turkish "The running one found (or: came on), the guarding one guarded.—Wolf" (Katanov, p. 95, No. 815), in which the answer "dog" (the guarding one) seems to have been forgotten. Yakut: Iastremskii, 317 (A hunk of fat and a bit of butter run; a shaman, throwing back his head, pursues; a man striding with difficult —, pursuing it, catches —.—Man takes possession of a fox caught by a dog). The dashes indicates words that cannot be translated. The text is somewhat clarified by comparison with another Yakut version: "A ball of fat and a piece of butter run; a shaman, his head thrown back, chases them; a heavily treading one, having started in pursuit, seizes.—Dog catches a fox; the man seizes it" (Popov, p. 287). Russian: Sadovnikov, 1532 (The blowing one says, "Tiav! Tiav! [barking]. Come to me, mistress of the beehive! Fear is dragging warmth.—Dog, woman, wolf, sheep), 1533 (Thence came Shuru-muru [Soft-stepping], took away Chiki-briki [Dainty, bleating], the chaffy ones have seen it, they informed the grain-ones, the grain-ones overtook Shuru-muru, they grabbed Chiki-briki from him), 1534, 1535. Polish: Saloni, *Rzeshów*, 216 (wolf carries off a hare); Siarkowski, 1. Lithuanian: Schleicher, p. 211; Jurgelionis, 763–768; Basanavicius, 183 (Kudù-budù came running, carried off Kidì-bidì. "Give me Sarapčika or Remenčika, I shall chase Kudù-budù and snatch away Kidì-bidì."—Wolf has carried off a sheep, a man wants to overtake it on a horse), 192 ("Get up, Ass [a proper name], there comes a horror, bring a straight thing, lead the bellowing one."—Hare, hunter, rifle, dog); Daukantas, 6; Volteris, p. 450, No. 25; Mickevicius, p. 588, No. 267. Serbian: Novaković, p. 219, Nos. 7 (Vema calls to Vema: "Give me, Vema, *mil'odrad* so that I may kill Wade-the-puddle. *Dosh'o* came to me last night in the dark."—A neighbor (fem.) asks for a knife from her neighbor to kill a duck; her son-in-law has come to visit her), 8 (the same answer but a different text), and p. 220, No. 3 (calf). These Serbian riddles may belong to the texts discussed in the following section § 3, which deal with a borrowed object. Swedish: Olsson, *Bohuslän*, 406a–406k, 407a–407e. Icelandic: Arnason, 930 (I sat on a roarer [?] and looked at a tumbler [?] and saw a rich bear running with a piece of pleasure in its mouth. Then called my crotch-slammer and guess what she was to do.—He saw a polar bear with a woman's breast in its mouth. Then he called his bitch to set it on the bear). This seems to be confused, for one would expect the "crotch-slammer" to be a gun. See also Arnason, 988 (I saw the deceiver of the forest bear lying down, the whale of the bowstring trudging heavily, the ship of the land rushing on eagerly, and the hart chased by the descendant of Ysjungr.—The forest bear is a mouse, its deceiver is a cat; the whale of the bowstring is an ox; the hart is described by a very obscure kenning [omitted in the translation]; the descendant of Ysjungr is a dog). Perhaps this and similar Icelandic riddles (Arnason, 929, 931–935) belong to a different tradition. German: Wossidlo, 11. English: Emrich and Korson, *The child's book of folklore*, 164, No. 50, New York, Dial Press, 1947. Although the Russian "There flew the savage one, he sat upon a hill, he asked the cackling one, 'Where are my panting ones?' 'My panting ones are in the run-away town.'—Hawk, hen, chickens, nettle" (Sadovnikov, 940) differs greatly from the versions already cited and is furthermore not entirely intelligible, it may be connected with them.

3. A girl borrows a churn (sieve or other domestic object) and promises to return it. Bulgarian: Gubov, 322 (sieve); Iknonomov, 22. Polish: Gustawicz, 223 (One goody called upon another in order to borrow a wriggler. "I'll wriggle it a bit and straightway I'll return it."—Churn), 244–227; Kopernicki, 68 (sieve). Swedish: Sandén, 36; Ström, pp. 311–312. Irish: Ó Dálaigh, 74 = Hull and Taylor, Irish, 693c (My *mam-mam* sent me to get the fetter [churn], the little stick [churnstaff], the bridle bit [table], and the cap [lid]).

A steelyard is the subject of the Modern Greek "My mother's love, and give to me the chink-chink, the jingle-jingle to chink-chink and jingle-jingle, and then she'll send it back to thee" (Abbott, 6). Two riddles with the answer "comb" make reference to borrowing, but their pertinence to this manner of riddling is not entirely clear. The Kashub say, "The gentleman went to the gentleman to borrow a *caban* (a large Wallachian sheep) to drive the cockchafers from the rough (or: green) meadow" (Gulgowski, 17). The collector's comment that the reference to the large Wallachian sheep implies an important object is scarcely correct. For similar riddles in which the sheep or another animal signifies a razor or comb see the headnote to Taylor, *English*, 459–460. The Kashub riddler has adapted an otherwise familiar riddle to this manner of riddling. A Serbian riddle (Novaković, p. 237, No. 5) is, however, similar to the churn or sieve riddles but has the answer "comb." See also a Hungarian spinning wheel riddle in *Magyar Nyelvör* 5: 520, 1876.

4. Cat and rat (mouse). Polish: Siarkowski, 86 (A little taratanuska came along and asked the little bell, "Is the one-who-lies-in-wait at home?"—A mouse came along and asked the rat whether the cat was at home); Kopernicki, p. 129, No. 29 (A *škrápkáryja* [mouse] asked a *piskárya* [rat], "Is *hapko* [cat] at home?" And he answered, "He is, he is, he is lying on the *beretyk* [bed]"). Swedish: Olsson, *Bohuslän*, 408a–408g. A long and difficult Swedish riddle on similar themes may also belong in this class; see Sandén, 138, 139; Ström, pp. 101, 102.

5. dog, wolf, and pig. This is not the riddle cited in § 2 above. Lithuanian: Sabaliauskas, 74 (quoted above); Basanavicius, 185 (The hiding one comes, he asks the holding one [or: the clinging one] where the rooting one is); Mickevicius, p. 588, No. 276; Basanavicius, 181. Russian: Sadovnikov, 1534, 1535. Some of these vary considerably from the texts quoted here.

6. salt, mule, and river. Turkish: Kowalski, *Asia Minor*, 60, citing parallels and explanations of obscure words; Hamamizade, 678 (I took a load from the limitless one, I put a load on the non-multiplying one, I passed over the non-swinging one, I spent it in the one which is not sold.—Earth, mule, stone bridge, mosque), 685 (They loaded what is not sown and not reaped on the one who does not give birth, they passed through the chimney of one who does not lie down and does not sleep.—Salt, mule, river). Armenian: Wingate, 14 (The barren bore the germless/ O'er the crossing of the ceaseless.—Salt, mule, river).

I shall not continue this effort to classify riddles of this type and cite a few examples that do not seem to fall into any of the preceding categories. The texts are not sufficiently numerous and the categories are, at least in the present state of our knowledge, too insecurely established to do more. See Lithuanian: Basanavicius, 56, which is perhaps related to his No. 177. See also Basanavicius, 100, 180, 184; Schleicher, pp, 204, 209. Russian: Sadovnikov, 516 (pancake), 1234 (sheaves, reaper, children, wolf, woman, husband), 1253 (woman, flail, bread, children). Serbian: Novaković, p. 238, Nos. 3-5. White Russian: Wasilewski, 66. Hungarian: *Magyar Nyelvör* **2**: 468, Nos. 78, 79, 1873; **3**: 518, 1874; **5**: 127, 1876; **6**: 372, 1877; **20**: 284, 1891; **40**: 285, 334, 1911; Arany and Gyulai **2**: 363, No. 71. French: Fesquet, p. 177. Spanish: Demófilo, p. 341, No. 7; p. 342, No. 11; p. 377, No. 3; p. 382, No. 4; p. 383,. No. 11; p. 396, No. 65; p. 414, No. 1. Chilean: Laval, 31. Swedish: Hyltén-Cavallius, 73-75; Sandén 68, 130-135; Olsson, *Bohuslän*, 29a-28c; Wessman, 40. German: Wossidlo, 12-14. Note finally the Modern Greek " 'Say, Lady neighbor !' 'What do you want ?' 'Come and smell, will your bottom-ring take my husband's archsoothsayer?'—Washbasin and trousers" (Stathes, p. 352, No. 122).

The familiar use of kennings in Icelandic has been the occasion for the invention of riddles to which no parallels outside of that language can be cited; see, as examples, Arnason, 812, 813, 929, 932. Some curious rhymes or formulas in English and German and no doubt in other languages describe the parts of the human head as "nose-dropper, chin-chopper." These rhymes are now and again cited as riddles; see Swedish: Olsson, *Bohuslän*, 3. Since the speaker does not expect an answer, these rhymes are more properly considered to be children's rhymes and not riddles.

REFERENCES

In addition to the collections of riddles listed in Archer Taylor, *English Riddles from Oral Tradition*, 871–897, Berkeley, Univ. of Calif. Press, 1951, I have consulted the following works. For the reader's convenience I have repeated the titles of the Mongolian collections. Whenever possible, references to riddles are made by number.

BAHAEDDIN, ÖGEL. 1950. Riddles from Erzurum. *Jour. Amer. Folklore* **63**: 413–424.

BALYS, JONAS. 1950. Fifty Lithuanian riddles. *Jour. Amer. Folklore* **63**: 325–327. Cited as Balys, *Fifty riddles*.

——. 1940. Klaipėdiskiu tautosaka. [Folklore in Klaipėda]. *Tautosakos darbai* [*Folklore Studies*] **7**: 154–158. Kaunas. Cited as Balys.

BASANAVICIUS, J. 1887. Oskabalun myslei [Riddles from Oskabaliai]. *Mitteilungen der litauischen litterarischen Gesellschaft* **2**: 189–198.

BASCOM, W. H. 1949. Literary style in Yoruba riddles. *Jour. Amer. Folklore* **62**: 1–16.

BASTIEN, RÉMY. 1946. Anthologie du folklore haïtien. *Acta anthropologica* **1** (4): 93–112, México, D. F.

BAZAROV, S. L. B. 1902. Dvesti zagadok Aginskikh Buriat. *Trudy Troitsko-Savsko-Khiakhtinskogo otdeleniia Priamurskago otdela Imp. Russkago geograficheskago obshchestva*, 5. St. Petersburg.

BORATAV, PERTEV. A manuscript collection of Turkish riddles in my possession.

BROWN, GEORGE. 1910. *Melanesians and Polynesians*, 343–346. London, Macmillan.

BUGA, K. 1923. Seiniu parapijos dzūku males [Riddles of the Dsuk in the Parish of Seinail]. *Tauta ir žodis* **1**: 315–316.

COSTAS ARGUEDAS, J. F. 1950. Folklore de Yamparáez. *Universidad de San Francisco Xavier* **15**: 338–339. Sucré, Bolivia. Also published as a separate work with new pagination: *Folklore de Yamparáez*, Sucré, Bolivia, 1950. See pp. 94–95.

DAUKANTAS, S. 1932. Pasakos massiu, suraszitas 1835 metuose [Riddles of the mass collected in 1835]. *Lietuviu tauta* **4**: 10, 12, 13, 17, 18, 31, 87. Vilnius.

DAVENPORT, W. H. 1952. Fourteen Marshallese riddles. *Jour. Amer. Folklore* **65**: 265–266.

DIAMANTARAS, A. S. 1911. Tourkike laographia. *Laographia* **3**: 227–236, especially pp. 233–234.

ELWIN, VERRIER. [1942]. *The Agaria*. [London], Oxford Univ. Press.

——. [1947]. *The Muria and their Ghotul*. [Bombay], Oxford Univ. Press.

ELWIN, VERRIER, and W. G. ARCHER. 1943. An Indian riddle book. Extracts from a riddle note book. *Man in India* **23**: 265–352. This is whole No. 4, the issue for December, 1943.

See also Hivale, Shamrao, and Verrier Elwin.

EVANS, I. H. N. 1951. Fifty Dusun riddles. *Sarawak Museum Jour.* **5**: 553–561.

FERGUSON, C. A., and W. D. PRESTON. 1946. Seven Bengali riddles. *Jour. Amer. Orient. Soc.* **66**: 299–303.

FOKOS-FUCHS, D. R. 1951. *Volksdichtung der Komi*, 320–321. Budapest, Akadémiai kiadó.

FUCHS, D. R. 1952. *Volksbräuche und Volksdichtung der Wotjaken*, Mémoires de la société finno-ougrienne, **102**: 241–245, 299–301. Notes, pp. 640–643, 644–645.

GETTY, ALICE. 1914. *The Gods of Northern Buddhism*. Oxford, Clarendon Press.

GILL, W. W. 1885. *Jottings from the Pacific*, 217–222. London.

GOLSTUNSKII, K. F. 1893–1895. *Mongol'sko-russkii slovar'*. St. Petersburg.

GOMBOYEV, GALSANG. 1857. Sechzig burjätische Rätsel. *Bulletin de la classe historico-philologique de l'académie impériale des scieinces de Pétersbourg* **14**: 169–174.

GRØNBECH, K. 1936. *Codex Cumanicus*. Monumenta linguarum Asiae Majoris, 1. Copenhagen, Levin & Munksgaard.

HAAVIO, MARTTI, and JOUKO HAUTALA. 1950. Suomen kansan arvoituksia. 3d ed. Helsinki, Werner Söderström Osakeyhtiö.

HARRIES, LYNDON. 1942. Makua song-riddles from the initiation rites. *African Studies* **1**: 27–46. Cited as Harries, *Song-riddles*.

——. 1942. Some riddles of the Makua people. *African Studies* **1**: 275–291. Cited as Harries.

HEIN, WILHELM. 1909. *Mehri- und Hadrami-Texte*. Kaiserliche Akademie der Wissenschaften. Südarabische Expedition, 9. Vienna.

HIVALE, SHAMRAO, and VERRIER ELWIN. [1935.] Songs of the forest, 147–151. London, G. Allen and Unwin.

HUGHES, H. G. A. 1950. Riddles (Kam'aninga) from the Gilbert Islands. *Jour. Polynesian Soc.* **59**: 241–244.

HULL, VERNAM, and ARCHER TAYLOR. Irish riddles. A manuscript compilation of Irish riddles from printed sources. Cited as Hull and Taylor. *Irish*.

IASTREMSKII, S. V. 1929. *Obraztsy narodnoi literatury iakutov*. Akademiia nauk S. S. S. R. Komissiia po izucheniiu Iakutskoi avtonomnoi sovetskoi sotsialisticheskoi respubliki, Trudy, 7: 153–171. Leningrad.

IONOVA, M. N., and M. I. PUGOVKINA. 1936. Iakutskie zagadki. *Sovetskii fol'klor* **4–5**: 243–250. Cited as Ionova.

JARRING, GUNNAR. 1948. Materials to the knowledge of eastern Turki. *Lund Universitets Årsskrift*, N. S., Avd. 1, **45** (7): 134–136.

JOSHI, T. R. 1911. Notes on the ethnography of the Bashahr State, Simla Hills. *Jour. Asiatic Soc. of Bengal*, N. S., 7: 525–613, especially pp. 612–613.

KARAHKA, EINO, and MARTTI RÄSÄNEN. 1949. *Gebräuche und Volksdichtung der Tschuwassen*, Mémoires de la Société finno-ougrienne, **94**: 93–106.

KATANOV, N. 1902. Opyt issledovaniia uriankhaiskago iazyka. *Uchenye zapiski Imp. Kazanskago universiteta* **69** (3): 91–96. Cited as Katanov, *Urianchai*.

KLUKINE, I. A. 1926. *Kliuch k izucheniiu zhivoi mongol'skoi rechi i pis'mennosti*, Trudy Gosudartsvennago dal'nevostochnago universiteta, 6th ser., **4**: 41, 45–46, 54, 68, 71, Vladivostok, 1926.

KOSKIMIES, A. V., and T. ITKONEN. 1910. *Inarinlappalaista kansantietoutta*, Mémoires de la Société finno-ougrienne, **40**: 233–239. Cited as Koskimies.

KOTVICH, V. 1905. *Kalmykskiia zagadki i poslovitsy*. Izdaniia Fakulteta vostochnykh iazykov Imp. St. Petersburgskago universiteta, **16**. Petersburg.

KOUL, ANAND. 1933. Kashmiri riddles. *Indian Antiquary* **62**: 21–28.

KRÜGER, F. 1938. Tlokoa Ueberlieferungen. *Mitteilungen der Ausland-Hochschule an der Universität Berlin* **3**. Abteilung, Afrikanische Studien, 41: 16–35.

——. 1936. Ueberlieferungen der Letsoalo. *Mitteilungen der Ausland-Hochschule an der Universität Berlin*, 3. Abteilung, Afrikanische Studien, **39**: 176–227.

LEHTISALO, T. 1947. Juraksamojedische Volksdichtung. Mémoires de la Société finno-ougrienne, **90**: 592–607.

LESCOT, R. 1937. Proverbes et énigmes kurdes. *Revue des études islamiques* **11**: 307–350.

LIGYROS, G. 1929. In *Pergamos (1300, p. Chr.—1922)*, 300–301. Mytilene, Koinotes Pergamou.

LITTMANN, ENNO. 1937. *Kairener Sprichwörter und Rätsel.* Abhandlungen für Kunde der Morgenlandes, **22** (5). Leipzig.
   The translations are reprinted in *Morgenländische Spruchweisheit. Arabische Sprichwörter und Rätsel.* Morgenland, **29**, Leipzig, 1937.
LOEB, EDWIN M. 1951. Kuanyama Ambo Folklore. *Anthropological Records* **13** (4): 332–335. Berkeley, Univ. of Calif.
LOUBIGNAC, V. 1921–1925. Etude sur le dialecte berbère des Zaïan et Ait Sgougou. *Publications de l'Institut des hautes études marocaines* **14**: 421–423. Paris.
MALECORE, IRENE MARIA. 1940. La poesia poplare nel Salento. *Archivio per la raccolta e lo studio delle tradizioni popolari* **15**: 126–152
MALOV, S. E. 1930. K istorii i kritike Codex Cumanicus. Akademiia nauk U.S.S.R. *Izvestiia,* Serja 7, Otdelenie gumanitarnykh nauk, 347–375. Leningrad.
MELO, VERÍSSIMO DE. 1948. *Adivinhas.* Biblioteca da Sociedade brasileira de folklore, 1. Natal.
MÉSZÁROS, GYULA. 1912. *Csuvas népköltési gyüjtemény.* Budapest.
MICKEVICIUS, V. K. 1928. Misles [Riddles]. *Tauta ir žodis* **5**: 572–591.
MOORE, ELIZABETH I., and W. D. PRESTON. Japanese riddles, I. *Jour. Amer. Orient. Soc.* **71**: 122–134.
MOSTAERT, ANTOINE. 1937. *Textes oraux ordos.* Monumenta Serica, 1. Monograph Series, 1. Peiping, Catholic Univ. 1937. Translated in his *Folklore ordos.* Monumenta Serica, 11. Monograph Series, 11, Peiping; Catholic Univ., 1947.
MÜLLER, F. W. K. 1926. Die Koreaner, in Wilhelm Deegen (ed.), *Unter fremden Völkern,* 114–115. Berlin, O. Stolberg, Verlag für Politik und Wirtschaft.
NAKENE, GODFREY. 1943. Tlokwa riddles. *African Studies* **2**: 125–138.
NÉMETH, JULIUS. 1930. Zu den Rätseln des Codex Cumanicus. *Körösi-Csoma Archivum* **2**: 360–368.
NIC IAIN, ANNA. 1933–1934. Tóimhseachain o Innse Gall. *Béaloideas* **4**: 173–177.
Ó CILLÍN, TOMÁS. 1933–1934. Tomhaiseanna, seanfhocail agus seanphaidreacha ó Umhall uí Mháille. *Béaloideas* **4**: 51.
Ó MAICÍN, TOMÁS. 1929–1930. Tomhaiseanna ó Cho. Thiobrad Árann. *Béaloideas* **2**: 289.
Ó MÁILE, TOMÁS. 1946. Tomhaiseanna Ros Muc. *Béaloideas* **16**: 189–200.
OLSSON, HELMER. 1944. *Folkgåtor från Bohuslän.* Svenska gåtor, 1. Uppsala, Almqvist Wiksells Boktryckeri AB. Cited as Olsson.
——. 1937. Den halländska gåtan. *Vår bygd,* 39–46. Cited as Olsson, *Halland.*
ORHAN, AYDIN. A manuscript collection of Turkish riddles in my possession.
PAASONEN, HEIKKI, and PAAVO RAVILA. 1947. *Mordwinische Volksdichtung* **4**. Mémoires de la Société finno-ougrienne, **91**: 611–693.
PENARD, A. P., and THOMAS E. PENARD. 1925. Negro riddles from Surinam. *West-indische gids* **7**: 411–432.
PESCHUËL-LOESCHE, EDUARD. 1907. Volkskunde von Loango, in Paul Bussfeldt, Julius Falkenstein, and Eduard Peschuël-Loesche, *Die Loango-Expedition,* 3. Abteilung, 2. Hälfte: 100. Stuttgart, Strecher und Schröder.
PIRES DE LIMA, AUGUSTO C. 1943. *O livro das adivinhas.* 2d ed. Porto, Domingo Barreira.
POPPE, N. N. 1936. *Buriat-mongol'skii fol'klornyi i dialektologicheskii sbornik.* Akademiia nauk (Moscow). Trudy instituta vostokovedeniia, **21**: 7–11, 52–53.
——. 1930. *Dagurskoe narechie.* Akademiia nauk S.S.S.R. Materialy Komissii po issledovaniiu Mongol'skoĭ i Tannatuvinskoĭ narodnikh respublik, **6**: 151–156. Leningrad.

PRATT, GEORGE. 1911. *Grammar and dictionary of the Samoan language.* 4th ed. Malua, Samoa, London Missionary Society. See pp. 129–131.
PRESTON, W. D. 1948. Japanese riddle materials. *Jour. Amer. Folklore* **61**: 175–181.
   See also C. A. Ferguson: Elizabeth I. Moore.
RINCHINÉ, A. R. 1947. *Kratkii mongol'sko-russkii solvar'.* Moscow, Gosudarstvennoe izdatel'stvo inostrannykh i natsional'nykh slovareĭ.
RUDNYEV, A. D. 1902. Obraztsy mongol'skago narodnago tvorchestva. *Zapiski Vostochnago otdeleniia Imperatorskago russkago Arkheologicheskago obshchestva* **14**: pp. 092–0106. St. Petersburg.
——. See Zhamtsaranov, Ts. Zh. and A. D. Rudnyev.
SABALIAUSKAS, A. 1923. Pušaloto minos, minutos. *Tauta ir žodis* **1**: 317–322.
SAMOJLOVICH, A. 1924. K istorii i kritike Codex Cumanicus. Akademiia nauk S.S.S.R., *Doklady,* Series B: 86–89.
SANZHEEV, G. D. 1941. *Grammatika buriat-mongol'skogo iazyka.* Moscow, Izdatel'stvo Akademii nauk, S.S.S.R. See pp. 168–169.
SCHWAB, GEORGE. 1947. Tales of the Liberian hinterland. *Papers of the Peabody Museum of Amer. Archaeol.* **31**: 446–447.
SEBEOK, THOMAS A., JR. 1952. *Studies in Cheremis Folklore,* I. Indiana Univ. Publ., Folklore Series, **6**: 170–213. Cited as Sebeok.
SEBEOK, THOMAS A., JR., and others. 1952. Addenda to Studies in Cheremis Folklore, Volume I. *Jour. Amer. Folklore* **65**: 167–177, especially pp. 175–177. Cited as Sebeok-Beke.
SERRUYS, PAUL. 1945. Children's riddles and ditties from the south of Tatung. *Folklore Studies* (Peking) **4**: 213–290. Cited as Serruys, *Riddles.*
——. 1947. Folklore contributions in *"Sino-Mongolica."* *Folklore Studies* **6**: 79–89. Cited as Serruys.
STAMBERG, F. 1942–1944. Rätsel der Dschagga. *Ztschr. für Eingeborenen-Sprachen* **33**: 66–77, 146–156; **34**: 69–76.
TAYLOR, ARCHER. 1951. *English riddles from oral tradition.* Berkeley, Univ. of Calif. Press. Cited as Taylor, *English.*
TURNER, G. 1884. *Samoa a hundred years ago.* London. See pp. 215–216.
VITEVSKII, V. N. 1891. Skazki, zagadki i pesni nagaĭbakov Verkhne-ural'skogo uezda Orenburgskoĭ gubernii. *Trudy chetvertogo Arkheologicheskago s'ezda v Rossii* **2**: 257–280, especially pp. 276–277. Kazan.
VOLTERIS, E. A. 1901–1904. *Lietùvška chrestomatija.* St. Petersburg. See II, 449–451. Cited as Volteris. The Library of Congress catalogues this according to the Russian name and title: Vol'ter, E. A. *Litovskaia khrestomatiia.*
WADDELL, L. A. 1934. *The Buddhism of Tibet.* 2d ed. Cambridge, Eng., W. Heffer & Sons.
WERNER, ALICE. 1896. Sprichwörter und Redensarten der Nyassa-Leute. *Ztschr. für afrikanische und ozeanische Sprachen* **2**: 80–84. Cited as Werner, *Nyassa.*
WESSMAN, V. E. V. 1949. *Gåtor.* Skrifter utgifvna av Svenska Litteratur-sällskapet i Finland, 327; Finlands svenska folkdiktning, 4. Helsingfors.
WHYMANT, A. N. J. 1926. *A Mongolian grammar.* London, K. Paul, Trench, Trübner & Co.
YANIKOGLU, B. A. 1943. *Trabzon ve havalisinde toplanmış folklor malzemesi.* Istanbul, Kenan Matbasi. See pp. 213–242.
ZHAMTSARANOV, TS. ZH. 1907. Materialy k izucheniiu ustnoĭ literatury mongol'skikh plemen. *Zapiski Vostochnago otdeleniia Imp. Arkheologicheskago obshchestva* **17**: 08–0126. St. Petersburg.
ZHAMTSARANOV, TS. ZH., and A. D. RUDNYEV. 1908. *Obraztsy mongol'skoĭ narodnoĭ literatury.* Vypusk I. *Khalkaskoe narechie (teksty v transkriptsii).* St. Petersburg. (Lithographed.)

REFERENCES
COLLECTIONS ARRANGED ACCORDING TO LANGUAGES

The following tabulation includes, except for Mongolian collections, only the titles cited in the preceding bibliography. It supplements a similar tabulation in Taylor, *English Riddles from Oral Tradition*.

African. See Bakongo, Dschagga, Kuanyama Ambo, Letsoalo. Makua, Nyassa, Tlokoa, Yoruba.
Agaria. Elwin.
Arabic. Littmann.
Bakongo. Peschuël-Loesche.
Bengali. Ferguson and Preston.
Berber. Loubignac.
Cheremis. Sebeok; Sebeok-Beke.
Chinese. Serruys; Serruys, *Riddles*.
Chuvash. Karahka and Räsänen; Mészáros.
Cuman. Grönbech, Malov, Samojlovich.
Dusun. Evans.
English. Taylor.
Finnish. Haavio and Hautala.
Gilbertese. Hughes.
Gondi. Hivale and Elwin.
Hadrami. Hein.
Haytian. Bastien.
Indian. Elwin and Archer. See Agaria, Gondi, Kanawari, Muria.
Irish. Hull and Taylor, Nic Iain, Ó Cillín, Ó Maicín, Ó Maille.
Italian. Malecore.
Japanese. Moore and Preston, Preston.
Kanawari. Joshi.
Kashmiri. Koul.
Korean. F. W. K. Müller.
Kuanyama Ambo. Loeb.
Kurd. Lescot.
Lappish. Koskimies and Itkonen.
Letsoalo. Krüger.
Lithuanian. Balys, Basanavicius, Daukantas, Mickevicius, Sabaliauskas, Volteris.
Makua. Harries; Harries, *Song-Riddles*.
Marshallese. Davenport.
Mehri. Hein.
Mongolian. Bazarov, Gomboyev, Klukine, Kotvich, Mostaert, Roppe, Rudnyev, Sanzheev, Whymant, Zhamtsaranov, Zhamtsaranov and Rudnyev.
Mordvin. Paasonen and Ravila.
Muria. Elwin.
Nagaibak. Vitevskii.
Nyassa. Werner.
Portuguese. Pires de Lima.
Samoa. Brown, *Melanesians*.
Samoyede. Lehtisalo.
Surinam. Penard and Penard.
Swedish. Olsson; Olsson, *Halland*; Wessman.
Tlokoa. Krüger, Nakene.
Turkish. Bahaeddin, Boratav, Diamantaras, Jarring, Orhan, Yanikoglu. See also Cuman, Nagaibak.
Votyak. Fuchs.
Yakut. Iastremskii, Ionova.
Yoruba. Bascom.
Zyrian. Fokos-Fuchs.

INDEX OF SOLUTIONS

Numbers refer to riddles

abacus
    rich wise person without tongue, 416
abomasum
    short, potbellied, wooden horns, 45
acorn
    jewel on solitary mountain, 710
adze and ax
    Ōnö and Chonö, 544
agrophyllum
    eighty nests on eighty branches, egg in each nest, 651
akhai, words containing, 1025
alcohol, distilling
    swallow laid eggs, 97
    pig runs around, 108
    gravel-rock is a protuberance, cairn-rock is a boiling spring, 725
    unlucky thing with water and key, 907
    See also brandy, distilling; vessel for making brandy
animal in steppe
    has no owner, 979
anklebone
    small but powerful body, 52
ant
    horse under girl, paces with front legs, 219
    bay pacer carries children, 230
    hero cut in middle does not slip, 536
    young fellow without blood, 543
    many soldiers work in small space, 588a
    universe on a space the size of a saddlecloth, 588b
antelope
    runs by leaps in shagreen boots, 26
——, rump of
    children have white hips, 550
anthill
    black kettle boils, 812
    yellow tea boils, 813
archery
    camel opens mouth, light flashes, 159
    cow lows, stirrup gets loose, 212
    older and younger brothers trot in a game, 564
    See also arrow(s); bow and arrow
arm
    at home in daytime, outside at night, 943
arrow(s)
    arshin-long body, handful of wool, 401
    man carrying wool cannot catch man carrying iron, 576
    See also archery, bow and arrow
——, hunting without
    causes regret, 1004
artery, pulling an
    man throws off cover and moves feet, 481
    weeds pulled out of idol, 655
ashes, heap of ashes
    sheep (ram) grows fat while lying down, 131, 132
    grayish bull under a hollow, 181
    colt gets fat when fed, 261
    See also fire, wood, and ashes

——, fir, smoke, and kettle
    posterior of flour, body of pearls, fiery head, deep well, 404
automobile
    iron carriage fills world, 792
autumn, summer, winter, spring
    four mountain passes, 716
    See also seasons; spring, etc.
awl
    grey she-goat drags rope, 278
ax
    bull with wooden nose-peg, 190
    ferocious dog barks, 297
    See also adze and ax; sound of felling trees
baby
    voice *boo boo*, sleeps in bent tree, has two sacks of food, 510
—— and breast
    guest eats boneless meat, 429
baby, crying
    dog begins to bark, 298
—— in womb
    has no name, 978
——, sex of unborn
    cannot tell whether grandmother is in a heap or a pit, 391
    cannot tell whether anklebone lies with convex or concave side up, 738
    See also boy or girl in womb
bag
    can eat but not eliminate, 17
balalaika
    rabbit with twisted ears screams, 103
    cropeared bay colt with voice of swan and *tsepa*, 257
    cropeared stallion has colt's voice, 258
——, tune of
    ears are turned back, eyes are red, 412
bank
    supports river, 1021
basket
    worthless hobbled goat, 273
beads. See rosary
bee, bumblebee, honey bee
    small body, sonorous voice, 35
    multicolored cow has tasty milk, sharp horns, 187
    multicolored, horned, recites prayers, 760
—— and nectar
    has vessel and holy water and reads scriptures, 343
bell
    voice of rooster on shelf reaches heaven, shadow reaches earth, 76
    posterior the size of a bucket, 439
    Ariābalo speaks from between his thighs, 520
    tree paces around abyss, 654
—— and drum
    ingot of camel dung, lamas let robes fly, 340
——, sound of
    naked lama hits groin, 527

bellows
    stone well, bone trough, flesh boat, 685
——, smoke, tongs, hammer
    horse makes noise, raises dust, 253
belt
    you go this way, I go that way, we meet at Bilȳty River (on Bilȳty Road), 565
    is red, 1001
——, loosening
    nomad horde approaches, loosen the bay's reins, 586
belt for mountains
    is lacking, 1006, 1007
bile
    is green, 1024
birchtree and bark
    white horse with seventy blankets, 226
bird (unidentified)
    runs with a hop, is higher than a camel, lower than a dog, 27
    has a voice *jir jir*, reads sacred book, home is far away, 509
    bronze coin on fence, 899
    has no teats, 1008
    is swift when flying, 1017
——, lama's (a kind of duck)
    tilts beak, is red-colored on leaving water, 950
bird-cherry
    black calf with stone stomach, 185
bit in horse's mouth
    son of heaven chews iron sulfur, 496
boat
    goes without trace, stabs without blood, 15
    walks without feet, carries without neck, 21
bobbin
    sheep conceived while spinning, 130
    See also spindle and thread.
bolt
    solid knot on honey ridge, 879
bones and skull
    twelve pregnant horses, including pregnant stallion, 220
    stallion with young; non-pregnant mares, 221
bones
    are white, 1003
    See anklebone, head, shinbone, vertebra
book, reading a
    black sheep, white pen, shepherd devours it, 128
——, writing a
    parrot drinks, leaves trail on snow mountain, 93
    See also writing
Book, Sacred
    female and male camels, many little camels, reins of silk shreds, 145
    beginning is in Turkish, it cannot be solved in this world, 896
boot, hob of boot
    black horse with green bridle (halter), 225
    Galba licks earth, 497a

rapid tongue licks ground, 729
See also shoe, putting on a
boot, sewing a
  youngest made a hole, 982
boot, sock, leg
  fat boy (yellow girl) in small (red) house in a big house, 390
  hard and black, Tungus white, friendly red, 441
bottle. See flask
bow
  dried-up devil on the road, 395
  strong man with two pillows, 396
  small boy a match for ten men, 397
—— and arrow
  castrated camel yawned; lightning flashed, 158
  See also archery
bowl(s)
  Lama Dondok has seven disciples, 353
  plump red nun in front of statue, 360
  has woolen jacket, leather belt, hat button, water bottle, 367
boy or girl in womb
  grandmother in trunk is in heap or pit, 391
  See also baby in womb
braid (queue)
  thornbush behind a trunk, 656
  cross on cross behind the house, 922
  See also queue
braid, cover and pendant of
  Tunta and Munta are a pair, 545
brain
  ākhä characters in a box, 897
  many-colored characters in a box, 898
  See also mind
——, eating, the
  ate gold and threw away the box, 810
brandy (milk brandy)
  brindled cow produced foolish calf, 210
——, distilling
  Dendžin city from above, Peking city on earth, mule enters, 337a
  mule runs through door, 337b
  Denji River on top, Yuldui River nearby, grass of the well, 657
  Dendein River, Well River, swimming in well, 683
  See also alcohol, distilling
breast, mother's
  family cannot destroy small piece of fat, 820b
  See baby and breast; child, caressing a
breastbone and ribs
  nobleman's wife has suite of twelve and a silver spoon, 374
bride, carrying off the
  red silk hangs; blue silk flutters, 853
broom
  thigh of a dog, 289
brush. See writing brush
buckets
  jangle on going; weep on returning, 593
buckwheat, grinding
  lama makes the sound *khur khur*, cart the sound *jee joo*, 788
Buddha, statue of
  man without tinderbox and tobacco pouch, 462

bullet
  high as a finger, vociferous as a man, 31
  fifteen ducks flew away; fast black duck followed, 77
  hornless devil in well, 394
  little ball, little stone, swifter than a horse, 722
bumblebee. See bee
burrow of mice
  marmot's skin shirt is not tattered, 866
butterfly
  jerboa without bones crosses sea, 100
button, mandarin's (official's)
  particolored magpie on Alkhanai, 90
  like hail fallen from above, like ice trimmed with knife, 915
buttoning clothes
  on spreading legs, a ball appears, 11
  bulb came between sprawled-out legs, 12
  sheep with bad intellects are put together in morning and separated at night, 117
  baby camel strangled on hill, 164
  young camel wrapped up, 165
  goat and ox wrestle on steppe, 318
  Ökhö and Chökhön seize each other, 608
  in widening it, it pops out, 957
  on being pulled asunder, it becomes round, 958
  one sprawls out legs and it goes in, 959
  See also clasps for coat
buttons on pillow
  five flies on shelf, 54

cake
  nestling in fire, 67
—— and griddle
  Gatiga in fire; Mortsokha near fire, 601
calf of leg
  Janggar Jana has belly behind, 435
camel
  trots upstream losing eight buttons, 239
  makes sound *pot pot*, 507
  four tall; five brothers and sisters; two move right and left; one is alone, 571
  five Russians sow; two Russians watch; one Russian chases flies away, 616
  four straight; three protrude; one hangs down, 617
  composed of members of twelve animals, 752
camel in heat, male
  bell in mouth, drum in belly, holy water on back, 346
  carries ice on back, 596
candle
  fat Red over a Buddha, 361
  lanky Russian burns from top, 421
  long man came to his end from top, 422
  protruding pale, 703
  long red nose comes from West, 730
canopy
  tail like lance; ten iron spears, 763
cap
  like cake from East, 916

——, pulling on
  ten men put on something large and shaggy, 556
cart
  voice goes *jing jing*; visits distant places, 508
  See also sleigh, cart, and horse
cash (a coin)
  round, square, four Chinese, two Mongols, 924
cat
  supple bodied, thirty-three vertebrae; bay-bodied; owl's eyes, 751
cattle, brindled, motley, spotted
  cut without measure, sewed without seam, 860a
  connection without seam, 860b
  striped, although seamless, 860c
  See also cow
Cedar
  tree with eighty (eight thousand) branches, nest on each branch, 652, 653
chamberpot
  round body, round mouth, eats flesh, 37
chariot
  patriarch at the start, rampart on leaving road, 937
cheeks of woman
  are red, 1000–1002
chess
  bloodless warriors fight in waterless place, 610
  Torguts and Durbets fight in small space, 611
  soldiers without souls fight without pay, 612
child, caressing a
  everybody ate quail's liver, 820a
——, leaping
  is nice, 1015
churnstaff
  maiden in a well, 393
  wooden thing gurgles among sour things, 817
  See stick for stirring kumiss
cicada
  small body, loud voice, 32
clasps for coat
  take each other by the hand, 570
  See also button
cloud(s)
  walks without legs, flies without wings, 19
  walks without feet, flies without wings, 20
  bluish ox without ribs, 189
  no support below, no hanger above, 829
  carloads of goods from the Tunka country, 839
coals of fire
  bag of red anklebones, 740
  chopped meat in a trough, 800
—— and tongs
  red goats bitten by black goat, 283
cock of rifle
  one-eared soldier, 427
cockroach
  sorrel color, antelope's horns, six feet, 759

companion, nagging
  is annoying, 1014
conch
  cone on crossbeam, 678
coral
  thin red dog (mushroom?) for sale, 302
cord embroidering felt
  firm reed at connecting line, 662
core of reed
  unpeeled silk in closed trunk, 858
core of tree
  thin boy does not see sun, 493
cotton
  white lambs on southern mountains, 124
cow
  has eight cups but does not drink; has a whip but does not drive cart, 499
  lanterns without ropes, cloak without seams, ten thousand white chessmen, embroidered spirals, canine teeth of gazelle, 929
  lasso, straight face, two stakes at cliff, 933
  See also cattle; horns and ears of cow
—— licking nostrils
  two felt tents, one crutch, 770
——, milking a
  four geese come honking, something black caught them, 83, 84
  dark cow makes sound *khud khud,* dark calf makes sound, *up up,* 217
  four brothers, five geese, pretty girl, 321
  four brothers, four geese, smart uncle, 322
  four old women urinate in one hole, 615
  one comes from side and fills one, 618
cow ruminating
  fat lump, hay bunch, 823
crab
  year-old, six-legged sheep, 111
cradle
  wood of Bargusi creaks, 298
craftsman
  ties knot in iron, 1022
cream
  paper (white) caparison (blanket) from white cow, 335
——, milk, sediment
  yellow top, white center, grey bottom, 934, 935
crepitus ventris
  aimed and hit leg; turned and hit nose, 535
crow
  black cow remained when herd went to pasture, 183
crying of baby. See baby, crying
cuckoo
  blue stallion neighs, grayish-white mares become pregnant, 255
cup, drinking
  wooden kettle on stand of flesh, 826
cups on altar
  seven flies on hill, one looks downwards, 53

cup, porcelain
  privileged person with fragile bones, 431
  See also porcelain
cupboard
  Barguzin door faces northwest, 781
cymbals
  small body with voice of Mahākāla, 406
  without flesh but utters piercing sound, 511

daw
  black bottle with red cork, 830
dawn
  elephant yawned, worms began to stir, 286
days
  more numerous than nights, 985
  See also year, months, and days
defecation of cattle
  enters here, protrudes there, 10
  See also stomach, emptying the
dew
  I fall apart if touched, 467
  bowl of broth on point of awl, 802
dipper
  nimble old woman jumps on yurt grate, 471
  hardy knight penetrates among warriors, 569
dirt under fingernails
  dirt under bed, 782
distance between heaven and earth
  as far as thought, 972
distilling. See alcohol, distilling; brandy, distilling; vessel for making brandy
dog
  master passes night with servant, 383
  khan raises dagger, leaves room, 476
  man screams, lifts ax, leaves, 478
  man utters *khong khong,* wears quiver (knife, plume) on hip, 501, 502
  man wears knife on hip (buttocks), 503
  wears plume on rump, 504
  short (low) when standing, high when sitting, 627
dog ignorant of rebirth
  is rough, 1020
dog swallows bones
  bones drift down Yangba River, 746
donkey
  slanting body, Manjushri's hoofs thunderbolts on head, 764
door, door jambs, wings of door or gate
  gray horse swings left and right, 248
  two sisters (brothers) of equal size (same rank), 547
  daughters of Peaceful live in harmony, 563
door and latchet
  small woman has button behind, 436
dream
  fried fat on mountain, nothing fell into my mouth, 821
  delusive letter under pillow, 893
  sweeter than honey, but worthless, 919
  smaller than you but oppresses you, 963
  is empty, 1005

drum
  shoulder blade and bones before a lama, 344
  man with protruding ears, leaden eyes, peacock's tail, 351
——, beating a
  son with felt head seizes and beats father, 603
  See also bell and drum
dune
  is without game, 976
dust in eye
  camel falls in sea but feels no discomfort, 157
  two-year old calf falls in sea, 265

eagle owl. See owl
ear(s)
  yellow foal hitched outside of listener, 232
  cannot stand cold and grows backwards, 674
  slanting trough at the side, 827
  black saucer at the side, 838
  wornout boots at mountainside (by a rock), 872
  slanting summer boots at the side, 873
  See also horns and ears of cow
earrings
  two-year old bay colt is outside of the listener, 233
  two-year old bay colt is tied to stake, 234
  older and younger sister are wholly alike, 546
earth and sky
  shaggy and smooth drums, 843
  cannot step over father's sheepskin, cannot roll up mother's sheepskin, 874
  rugs with and without wool, 875
—— and snow. See snow and earth
eating. See food, eating
echo
  voice without mouth, name without glory, 24
  is empty, 1025
egg
  wooden palace of Mongol's son, 388
  gilded vessel, tea shaped like lamp, 803
  as if descended from heaven, made by master, trimmed by sharp knife, 913
  like hail fallen from above, trimmed with sharp knife, 914
emperor
  ties knot in government affairs, 1022
enclosure of willows
  fallow snake makes a coil, 65
envoy
  is rough (cruel), 1018, 1020
excrements, camel's
  makes sound *pot* here, there, near Engkhe's house, 507
  five peasants want to go out, fat yellow girl opens door, 620a
  knock here, there, on Perlya's door, 954
——, cow's
  sandalwood ornament on road, 850
——, horse's

jumped and jumped and lost silk belt, 482
——, sheep's
  fifty blackies are close, yellow one opened door, 620b
—— of various animals
  round little boy comes unsoiled from land of grease, 468
  See also defecation of cattle; stomach, emptying the
excrement and sun
  sandalwood and silver bowls, 833
eye(s)
  multicolored worm in box, 60
  multicolored ox cannot draw crumb of manure, 198
  particolored two-year old calf behind bristle fence, 200
  motley horse cannot stand dust, 266
  Russian rides piebald horse behind thinly scattered trees, 338
  amber lama in well, 342
  devil in a cup, 392
  Buddha beaten with twigs, 525
  we are both angry; let us not meet, 613
  golden anklebones in cup, 739
  cup (bowl) of motley flesh, 801
  many-colored things in cup, 828
  set free, it fills steppe; taken in one's hand, it doesn't fill the hand, 953
  See dust in eye
eyes of angry person
  are red, 1000, 1002
eyelashes, closing the eyes
  hit Buddha with willow branches, 523
  Buddha's children play with willow branches, 524
  infantry comes from shores of blue sea, 587
  reeds grow along shores of round lake, 660

face, woman's
  Tunka steppe without vegetation, 681
  See also features of the head
fan
  drumlike abdomen, crow's beak, 762
features of head
  stand of a hundred horses is good, seam on counter of show is good, 339
  Russian characters at top of very high tree, 892
  See face, woman's
felt of door to yurt or opening in roof
  yellowish cow with black stripes and shovel-like tail, 186
  half a pretzel on the upper jamb, 794
  crust during day, whole loaf at night, 796
  four wide, two widest, 920
  See also flap
felt, manufacture of
  sneaking up to incautious ones, 631
  pounded many times, 967
fifteenth of the month
  is dark, 999
file
  long thin horse has eighty thousand brands, 218
  is rough, 1018, 1020

finger, fingers and fingernails
  five geese on rack, 80
  ten novices with faces backwards, 548
  ten (five) old women (soldiers) carry ice, 594
  See hand and fingers; mucus; thumb
fingers scratching scurvy head
  five brothers ascend snow-white mountain, 591
fingernail
  thin rock cannot be opened, 724
  See also fingers; hand and fingers
fire
  mist rises, golden gate leans, 376
  walks upwards, 628
  golden stake in yurt, 702
  bag full of anklebones, 741
  bag full of dice, 742
  cannot enter Buddha's temple, cannot eat gruel, 955
——, covering the
  I dig, a small hare lies there, 102
  side of black cow is swollen, 191
  he buried camel's head; I take it and eat it, 728
——, kindling
  iron king (King of Hell) is father, (branchy, tufted) mother, white daughter, black son, 561
  Tolya and Bolya quarreled, 605
  Otso and Totso fight; man's nose between them glows, 607
  See also fire, flint, and spark; steel, flint, and tinder
—— and kettle
  red cow licks black cow, 213
  red cow licks black cow and makes her weep, 214
  black goat runs, cloud moves, white goat runs, 279
——, flint, and spark
  Kerelda and Berelda quarrel, person in squirrel coat separates them, 606
——, wood, and ashes
  many enter, one comes out, 621
fire on steppe (in forest)
  sorrel horse leaves tent and gallops, 247
  red horse causes people to make noise, 259
firebrand
  on coming nearer, it disappears, 13
  See log in fire
fish
  does not walk on ground, fly in air, make nests, but gives birth, 9
  crosseyed girl peeped through sky, 425
  white-eyed youngster flies through soldiers, 568
——, scales of
  blunt-snouted one glitters, 39
flageolet
  has throat, double button, round mouth, eight lotuses, 370
flap
  sheep grazes in back in morning, in front in evening, 141
  square at night, triangular in daytime, 938
  northwards in day, southwards at night, 941

down in evening, up in morning, 942
  See felt of door to yurt or of opening in roof; roof-piece, etc.; smokehole
flask for holy water
  stone, water, plume, 721
flint
  gelded camel takes step, end of lasso glitters, 163
  makes sound *shab shab*, has felt base, hole three fingers wide, 515
  See also fire, flint, and spark
floods, spring
  thirsty dog goes into Lake Elton, 290
flour, bolting of
  drizzling rain (snow in big flakes) falls, 689
fly
  crawling white thing born of flying white thing, 63
  envoy in jacket sings, sits down, strokes beard, 480
—— and mosquito
  Gendel (dog) and Shonkhor (falcon) come singing, 320
foal growing in womb
  is nice, 1015
food. See kettle and food
food, eating or chewing
  going east and west, it is chased away and goes over the Barguzin pass, 8
  magpie chisels and pushes, mouse mixes and throws into well, 89
  white horse kicks and pushes, fallow horse mixes and pushes into well, 262
  white person cuts, mouse stirs, 332
  jarvādai and *jirvēdei* were thrown into hole, 553
  five take and give it to ten; ten give it to naked one; naked one gives it to hole, 619
  chopped in a vessel, mixed with *khuloo*, thrown into well, 806
  ground in a bone mill, it was sent over Chermoyarsky Road, 966
forequarters of sheep
  hawk father, owl or partridge mother, 562
fountain
  twenty shamans shamanized in a ravine, 364
fox
  runs evenly with yellow tail like leaf, 47
  beautiful red-haired maiden with unkempt hair, 423
  yellow-red grandmother at the foot of wormwood, 444
  has noiseless step and lama's yellow fur (coat), 455
  beautiful girl lost comb, 540
  skin of snake, ears of scared camel, 749
  gold wax in ears, 903
  red as flame, six black things, 918
frog
  spotted one with four feet pointing outwards, 40
  spotted one jumps, 41
  spotted one with flat mouth and tongue, 42
  Noyon Denzen with four crooked legs, 440

walks here and there, has cool body, 475
wears silk brocade coat, says *bar bar*, 506
cheese with four crooked legs dropped from sky, 797
hairless brindled ox in steppe, a bow-legged ambler with us, 945

fur, camel's
weed reed grows between two mountains, 663

——, otter's
bay horse suits everybody, 229

gait of cattle
you rise, I sit down, 626

gall bladder. See liver

garment, woman's
black sheep (cow?) without front leg, 114
rams outside, courtyard inside, 119
brindled cow on riverbank, 180

gate
loud sound at emperor's house, creaking sound at wife's house, 634
See also door

girl in womb. See boy or girl in womb

girl without luck
causes regret, 1004

gnat (?)
black bottle with red cork, 830

goat
goes away, growing white; comes along, growing red, 948

—— pursuing female goat
Russian doctor exorcises weeping; Mangut doctor exorcises bleating, 633

goat and sheep, tails of
Circassian keeps door open; Kirghis keeps door closed, 632

gong
shouting black Tibetan, 518

grain not yet harvested
something at mouth of River Tar pricks up ears and goggles eyes, 38
dropped unborn sheep at source of river; it pricked up ears and goggled eyes, 134
unborn child stands guard at a pole with a loop, 532
eighty thousand branches on tree, nest on each branch, nestling in each nest, 647
swaying tree has eighty thousand joints, nest on each joint, egg in each nest, 648
See stalk, ear, and grain

grass
tall white hellion sways morning and night, 445
Tushiyetu khan comes suppressing; Dzasaktu khan goes standing aside, 574

grass called "rolling stone"
flew from here and reaches Lhasa, 658

grasshopper
small body, sonorous voice, 33
seen from behind a camel with a halter, seen from the front a domesticated buck, 765
over there it is camel-colored, closer it is hideous, 949

grasshopper, female
official with tusk behind arrives from the north, 437

grass, mowing
gathered herd of steppe horses with a swift mare, 251

grate of yurt, openings in grate
horns of red cow look in different directions, 192
eagle's hide is worthless, 733
yurt filled with broken tea bricks, 819

growth
is green, 1024

gun
iron snake has wooden feet, 59
leather-covered, spread-legged shooter, 414
Russian official with hole on top, 417
python's body, lion's voice, two feet, 755
dragon's voice, mule's ear, 756

gun, bullet, report, powder
younger brother good at serving, older brother good at commanding herd of horses, two dogs, 384

gunshot, firing a gun
camel throws down rider, dust rises, 168
camel makes noise, dust rises, 169
gray ox is motionless, brindled ox spreads legs, dock-tailed ox runs out, 196
gray horse jumped up, skies thundered, 243
long one emitted sound, three crows scraped ground, 534
ball is quicker than a horse, 723

hair
trees grow beneath summit, 637

hair, cutting
lame crow licked burial mound, 85
sheep beaten with iron lasso, 121
camel prances, grass falls, 156
male camel grinds teeth, grass falls, 170
herd of gray horses collected with bluish-gray steel, 252

hair and louse
tree without branches, sable without bones, 679

hair of the aged
is white, 1003

halter and nosepeg of camel
drags mountain by a cord; lonely elm in front of high mountain, 641

hamlet without sheep
is gloomy, 1010

hammer. See pegs and hammer

hand, back and palm of
tree in north has patterns in bold relief; tree in south has slightly raised patterns, 640

——, hollow of
seems near but is far away, 951

—— and fingers
ten novices with faces backwards, 548

handle of pail, pail, well
high tree, sea, oxhide, 680

handmill. See mill

hare
leaps *bung bung*, jumps awry, 6

at a distance a chamois, alongside a goat, 315
he took camel in his mouth, a horse under his bosom, and led a goat, 316
timid old woman in flimsy house, 463
thimble on birchtree, 847

—— leaving lair
wag of a novice loses his vessel, 362

hat, putting on
ten accompanied the significant master, 352
ten people put on something large and shaggy, 556
ten men put Aksadai on his trail, 584

head
seven holes in a hill, 707
stone *shin* with nine holes, 719
beautiful stone with seven holes, 720
See also bones and skull

——, shaving the
lame crow walks around hillock, 86
black colt paces on a saltmarsh, 242
See also hair, cutting

heart
red (particolored) bird makes sound *gynger*, 69
red house with felt of white thread, 772
white felt in yurt without a grille, 779
without faith is black, 1023
See kidneys and heart

hearth
camel's tracks will not be erased, 172
no grass grows where cow has lain, 207
city without a lord, 973

heaven
has no pillar, 1006
See also sky

heaven and earth, distance between
as far as human thought, 972

hedgehog
is rough, 1018, 1020

hob of boot. See boot

hobble
green-spotted body with three claws, 44
three locks given by us, 777
three locks *dzi dzu*, 778
square is made triangular, 940
strength of brown horse is good, strength of pig skin is good, 1016
See horse, hobbled

hollow in back of thumb
dog's den beyond five hills, 706

—— in nape of neck
well behind the house, 704
hare's lair behind mountain, 705

hoopoe
green mottled one spread a brush, 43
wears Baljing Shaser cap and jacket of tiger fur, 368
wears tiger jacket and reads, 369

horizon
is red when cold wind blows, 1000, 1002

horns of cow
cold when looked at, warm when seized, 946

—— and ears of cow
two men in furs, two men without furs, 557

horse
has no horn or gall and doesn't chew cud, 1009

rages after throwing off saddle, 1013
is swift when galloping, 1017
See sleigh, cart, and horse
——, browsing
little silver tweezers, sable flatiron, 931
——, catching a
son of earth is astonished, tree shakes, 542
——, hobbled
three black devils prevented me from reaching Tugulchin River, 572
three sons are martyrs, one is at large, 636
four pillars and three locks, 777
four pillars *dzing,* three pillars *dzi dzu,* 778
See hobble
horse, mettlesome
is annoying, 1014
—— and rider
sitting Buddha, running tether, 541
—— and tail, horse's tail
walks with proud step, has retinue of ten thousand, 379
rhythmic walk and ten thousand white followers, 380
many enter, one comes out, 622
horse, jaw of
Osoi and Sosoi kneaded until dawn, 614
——, mane and tail of
reed of backlake is beautiful, feathers of front lake are beautiful, 661
——, saddle, stirrups, and tether
mountain of flesh, pass of wood, iron ladder, woolen rope, 714
——, withers of
flesh beneath hollow, 793
house
hollow curved tree, 642
hill of sleeping, hill of fire, hill of the pass, 712
without lamp is black, 1022
——, corners of
deaf oldster has ramifications in four directions, 522
idol
tekelzhin does not walk or eat camel's or goat's meat, 490
bones of a Tungus on mountain, 747
image in a mirage
is empty, 1005
See mirage
incense, incense stick
long yellow worm consumes self, 64
roan horse throws off Bujantui, 327
bald novice from the west, 358
woman with brittle bone, 430
long yellow boy eats self, 446
long red nose from the west, 730
ink and pen
water of deep well is good, snake's tongue is good, 62a
black water, black snout of wattled snake, 62b
intestine
supports belly, 1021
intestines of horse
braided hobbles in a well, 880
bundle of ropes in a house, 881

iron and tongs
bird Kurulda reaches inaccessible place, 72
jamb and threshold
two sisters with equal shoulders, 547a
jaw of horse. See horse, jaw of
jerboa
long tail, face like calf, 48
prince's son-in-law with two hanging ears pursued by dogs, 372
prince with pacing legs, banner-like tail, and calf's snout, 373
official wags rump and walks on two legs, 438
runs with a skip, has face like calf, 472
remains black, 999
has name of domestic animal, color of wild animal, 1026
joodak khorkoi (an insect)
ribbonlike black body, six tufts, smells like resin, 357
jug, mitten for
black sheep lacks lower part of jaw, 113
jujube
one-year old red calf with stone stomach, 184
chamois with bony stomach, 275
juniper
shaggy, curly, northern willow, 639
kaftan, trimming of
curved ram's neck, 110
kettle
black cow at edge of tent, 178
burnt he-goat from Kudara, 270
fire ate protruding black one, 495
fat Russian warms buttocks, 530
remains black when scrubbed, 999
See fire and kettle; tea kettle
kettle, mitten for
sheep lacks lower part of jaw, 113
——, painting of
painted trimmings of saddle, saddle-cloth is tied around, 786
——, plug of
swallow sits on black hillock, 96
hornless black calf with callosity on neck, 188
naughty girl close to fire, 531
knobby nail on smokehole, 780
——, spigot of
watchman's *solovko* is tied up, 784
——, washing of
donkey wags tail in grassless hollow, 249
kettle and fire. See fire and kettle
—— and food
black cow looks upwards; all the living look down, 211
black lama on trunk; all think of him, 341
—— and tripod (tongs)
three officials, three *zassaks,* two corporals, 375
Helun Erendshjen warms liver; three muzhiks warm legs, 600
key
bird Kurulda reaches inaccessible land, 71

long thing enters, 906
See lock and key
kidney(s)
round girl dressed in silver, 457
two red anklebones in courtyard, 745
See liver
—— and heart
two mares tied together; colored colt is tied up, 263
King of Hell
ties knot in sins, 1022
knife, grinding a
black colt paces on saltmarsh mud, 241
knife, knife and sheath
eats goat's meat (mutton), takes shelter in hollow tree, 49
bluish wolf in hollow (cave, hollow tree), 309
after eating meat, it is proper to enter a hole like a polecat, 310
kumiss, preparation of
earless lama performs religious service in well, 363
old woman stoops, old man bows, 630
earth and water are noisy, solitary tree shakes, 688
ladder to heaven
is lacking, 997, 1007
ladle
yellow poppy does not leave alone the poppy that eats, 670
lama
ties knot in silk, 1022
lama reciting spells
is swift, 1017
lama without texts
causes regret, 1004
lamp
black hen with red bill, 73
buxom red nun in front of Buddha, 359
man with coral button and juicy rump, 371
representative of the law in front of an official, 385
lotus flower in small sea, 668
white flower within circular embankment, 669
green garlic plant with small stem, 672
one jujube reddens whole felt tent, 676
large felt tent, in it a small felt tent, in it a lotus flower, 776
copper ladle is good, thin shank is good, 841
lamp, offering, kettle stopper, man
flower on trunk, in front of trunk a flower, at the edge of the fire something rocks, between the floors a poisonous snake, 667
lapwing. See peewit
larch. See pine and larch
larva
white thing born from black thing, 63
larynx and tongue
single reed at the beginning of the ford, 659
latchet. See door and latchet
leaves, falling of
they all went away, the strong ones remained, 624

ten thousand left, the tardy ones remained, 625
darkness has disappeared, stump remains, 697
leg. See boot, sock, and leg
leg, calf of. See calf of leg
legs of horse. See horse, hobbled
legs of table. See table
legs of tripod. See tripod
letter
white corral, black sheep, 129
chip cut here reaches khan, 726
See writing
liars
are more numerous than honest men, 983
lid for ocean
is lacking, 997, 1007
light of lamp
one jujube cannot find room in whole house, 677
lightning
camel opens mouth, rope flashes, 160
makes sound *tes* and camel's tail quivers, 513
See thunder and lightning
lily
fat white horse with seventy pieces of folded saddle cloth, 227
beautiful maiden with winter camp in steppe, father in blue plain, bony, empty mother, 560
pretty, round, made of tallow, 928
See sarana lily
——, stalk of
spread-out tail of calf, 735
lips
touch in saying *aba,* 629
liver and other organs
prince's son in black silk, princess's son in red silk (lungs), 559a, 559d
king's son in black silk, prince's son in green silk (gall bladder), two sons of the people in suet house (kidneys), 559b
king's son in black kaftan, minister's son in green kaftan (gall bladder), 559c
lizard (sheep lizard)
innocent white bird on dune, 68
lock, lock and key, opening a lock
man ousts yavalak bird that is hatching eggs, 99
gray sheep with hole in navel, 115
earless sheep loves lamb, 185
black bull's nose is strong, 194
pricking a grayish bull makes it rise, 202
blue bull rises when pricked, but not when beaten, 203
small boy lifts black cow, 204
bluish ox is lifted by lever, 205
black-bay horse has strong hobble, 228
little black dog lets no one in or out, 303
cat in front of the trunk, 311
old black (parsimonious) woman with hole in cheek, 418
covetous woman with no smell in her nose, 428

boy covered with scratches watches sleeping folk, 466
clever woman watches house, 491
mad boy watches house, 573
See trunk and lock
log in fire
moves and disappears from sight, 14
peaceful when seized from front, ferocious when seized from rear, 50
See firebrand
logs in wall of yurt
tall person has stirrups of thread, 398
women with woolen buttocks, 549
louse
voiceless goose in thick forest, 82
pig in woods, 105
voiceless dog among reeds without joints, 299
See hair and louse
lungs
jumped and jumped and did not reach mother-in-law, 483
See liver and other organs

magpie
leaps in shagreen boots, 25
mottled cow remains when others leave, 183
walks *tek tek* in shagreen boots, wears particolored fur, draws golden rope, 456
early riser, picks up crumbs, 469
bigger than a camel, smaller than a goat, white and black, 909
man
four in the morning, two at noon, three in the evening, 936
without a ship is in the ocean, without a bow is among enemies, without a horse is in the steppe, 1019
—— in saddle
jumped and jumped; did not reach mother-in-law, 483
—— in felt tent
marmot in bottomless burrow, 101
—— plowing
horse cart, wooden body, iron feet, human buttocks, 767
mane of horse. See horse, mane and tail of
marmot
climbed on trunk and called his uncle Adian, 500
yellow butter under the earth, 815
matches
snakchagas (birds) dig earth, 95
mattress
gathered up in daytime, spread out at night, 944
meat in teeth
sheep falling on rock makes rock uncomfortable, 140
fox squeezed between rocks gives pain to rocks, 305
medicine, medicine bag
Precious Thunderbolt has small body, carries blessings, benefits many, 366
Gün Gürwe has a body the size of a stomach, 403

Milk Ocean
has no lid, 1006
milking a cow. See cow, milking a
Milky Way
tall man measures with his arms, 533
mill, handmill
one-horned Chinese goat, 274
round and ambles like a calf, has a horn and ambles like a donkey, 317
millet
tree with seventy-two branches, nest on each branch, egg in each nest, 650
when not sown is black, 1023
——, cooking, grinding, or toasting
many sheep in narrow fold, ram butts, 137
black ram rustles, ten thousand sheep crackle, 138
ten thousand sheep leap, buxom woman jerks, 139
thoughts of all are on big black one, 341b
milt
noble children in green silk, 558
mind
small baby reaches inaccessible places, 489
gold in covered cart, 785
red wineskin cannot be exhausted, 811
See brain
mirage
moving enclosure, ambling horse, 245
running; lingering gazelle cannot be seized, 280
See image in a mirage
moon
bald uncastrated ram, 112
half pancake (loaf) on top of yurt, 795
low bucket on wall, 831
flat pail in the steppe, 832
silver goblet (bowl) on ice, 835
silver clasp on ice, 844
half copeck on cushion, patch of sheepskins, 900
——, reflection of
silver cup on ice, 836
—— and stars. See stars; sun, moon, and stars
month. See fifteenth of the month; year, months, and days
mortar and pestle (tea)
black ram in sheepfold, 125
butting ram in narrow pen, 136, 137
mountains
have no belt, 1007
mouse
grayish hut, grayish food, beautiful child, 386
See burrow of mice
—— entering hole
earthen lock, woolen key, 842
mouth. See head
mucus
gray (bluish) wolf runs through valley, 306
water in a bottomless teapot, 798
real cottage cheese in a pail, 799
——and fingers
Amban Tse is met by five aides, 377
See nose, wiping the

mustache
  black willows under the smaller, 638

name
  strong spike on solid hillock, 708
neck. See hollow in nape of neck
nectar. See bee and nectar
needle, needle and thread
  iron pig with tail of string, 106
  bluish bull drags a halter, 197
  gray she-goat drags rope, 278
  gray wolf drags blanket, 307
  tall man with one eye, 424
  child from market adorns everybody, 452
  person with horseshoe chases person with spear, 577
needle, thread, and thimble
  runs fast, has lash, sits like khan with black cap, 485
needle, threading a
  licking a tasteless thing, 498
nest
  balls of fat and straw container, 822
  ——, eagle's
  impossible to get felt hat thrown on opposite side of the Volga, 869
net for catching horses
  a thousand meshes, ten thousand knots, three pegs, twenty thousand knots, 930
nights. See days
nose
  country without characteristics, building without architecture, 686
  two rooms with one pillar, 771
  ——, wiping (blowing) the
  jumping hare thrown away, 104
  five pages meet great governor, 378
  See mucus and fingers
numbers associated with religious and secular ideas, 986–991
nut
  small kettle, good mush, 807
  took gold, threw away box, 809
nut, cracking of
  butter flows out of little box, 805

omentum
  untorn silk in closed trunk, 857
onion
  red hen with green tail, 74
  white hen with green tail, 75
  sheep with hundred coats, 109
  red novice has seventy pelerines, 450
  Shan Datoi's ball with seventy suits, 863
  See steppe onion
ornaments
  engraved work going to Peking, tawny with white spots in pasture, 840
orobranche
  below an artemisia a yellow arrow, 671
otter, fur of. See fur of otter
owl, eagle owl, horned owl
  disheveled head, sits like Buddha, color of a camel, 408
  brown, eyes like Venus, head like hillock, 409

voice *bar bar*, brocade kaftan, fiery red eyes, 505
ox
  cow that has no calf, 974

pail
  pregnant in coming, non-pregnant in going, 176
  See handle of pail, pail, and well
palm of hand
  cannot take opening of cup in mouth, 808
paper and writing
  white enclosure, black sheep, 126
  black sheep, white enclosure, 127
peewit (lapwing?)
  man in particolored jacket has priest's hat and trumpet, goes thrice daily to church, 347, 348
pegs and hammer
  something with sixty white buttons, two nails, one ambassador, 354
pen
  ring on bow of boat, 845
people who tell the truth
  are rare, 983
periods of a bitch
  three months of a tramp, 998
pestle
  protruding one could not turn his posterior, 474
  See mortar and pestle
pheasant (?)
  small body, loud voice, 32
pig
  four hoofs of cow, ears of gazelle, eyes of wolf, 758
pillow
  gray ram's belly is torn, 116
  beauty this way, bald one that way, 554
  girl's trouser's are torn before marriage, 867
pine
  knotty hand of King Arji Borji, 432
  curly in winter and summer, 921
  —— and larch
  bushy gelded camel, curly camel, 147
pipe
  one sucks its tea and cauterizes its navel, 51
  smoke from courtyard, fire on goblin's head, 419
  See smoking
pit for smoking sheepskins
  grayish hut and grayish food, 387
place where dry dung lies
  grass does not grow where ox has lain, 208
  —— where hare sleeps
  dipper with broken edge on hillside, 824
plane
  Tangut dog vomits brains, 300
  Square boy with hole in middle, 434
Pleiades
  six kinds of flowers grow in winter on mountain, 664–666
  six green ones appear in winter and disappear in summer, 675
plow and man
  horseheaded, iron-footed, man-tailed, 766

cart, wooden body, iron feet, human buttocks, 767
plowing
  goose tracked over earth, 81
  cow arches back, man walks, 323
plug of kettle. See kettle, plug of
pole
  boy makes sing of the fig, 539
  —— in roof of yurt
  king's cows with a halter, 177
porcelain, smashing of
  Chinese goat yelled once and died, 284
  dies on emitting sound, 501
  See cup, porcelain
prince
  without subjects is gloomy, 1011
  supports people, 1021
puppy
  starting to walk is nice, 1015

queue
  whale's bone on mountain, 748
  something dangles behind house, 887
  See braid

rain
  starts from ocean, 981
rain, wind, and thunder
  noise approaches, reins of sorrel horse are down, 256
rafters and flap of tent
  biting black camel among a hundred camels, 167
  See flap; pole in roof of yurt
rainbow
  piece of five-colored silk cannot be grasped, 854
  though near when looking at it, it cannot be grasped, 952
reading
  fast black duck tries to catch ten black ducks, 78
reed
  dog barks at one side, 294
  thirty suits of clothes and cap of fox fur, 449
  lithe body and fox's tail for cap, 451
  tree without color, 543
  ——, core of
  unpeeled silk in closed trunk, 858
  ——, head of
  fox offers sacrifice with tail, 304
  over the vapors the point of a spear, 693
  ——, joints of
  trunk on trunk, 825
  ——, shoot of
  Empress's son with seventy suits, 499
reins of camel
  thread leads (hangs down) mountain, 709
ribbons on hat
  red flag on mountainside, 859
ribs. See breastbone and ribs
rider. See horse and rider
rifle. See gun
ring
  collar on mouse, 288
  golden saddle on knotty tree, 787
  golden ring on many-branched tree, 846

road
  camel without neck goes over ridge, 149
  camel without neck crossed the Kuma, 150
  no one can catch up with camel without neck, 151
  camel without chin reaches Peking, 152
  tall man does not reach colt's mane (sole of boot), 399
  would reach sky, if I could rise; would catch thief, if I could speak, 487
  though blind, I show men's footprints, 492
  white silken ribbon reaches to Peking, 882
  lasso without an end, 883
  multicolored spliced rope cannot be tied together, 884
  lasso cannot be rolled up, 885
  lasso thrown by king cannot be put together, 886
  extremely long, lower than grass, 910
roofpiece, ropes attached to roofpiece, roofpiece and rafters or pole
  eighty thousand marks on black camel, 146
  black camel among many camels, 166
  biting black camel among a hundred camels, 167
  stallion carries seventy poles, 223
  hundred black she-goats, one biting he-goat, 282
  tail attached to tiger's head, 312
  persons are crosswise; the back one looks at the front one, 494
  four women try to outrun one another, 579
  four objects on the boundary, 682
  it is stretched from sky, hitched to tree, 684
  spears in round lake, 700
  supports tent, 1021
rooster
  lama's hat, gold-colored coat, copper and sandalwood trumpet, rites last three seasons, 349
  red flower on his head, gates open at his voice, 453
roots for field mouse
  herd of dark horses, a rich man in goatskin, 330
rope
  big-bellied snake on yurt, 57
  wattled snake in deep well, 61
  four old women run, 579
  thornbush behind the trunk, 656
  four objects at the boundary of Bortin, 682
  offended by the earth, hitched to lonely tree, 684
  tumult behind the mountain, confusion behind the rock, 969
  —— around yurt
  men go apart and meet at Bilȳty River, 565
  men go apart and meet outside the house, 566
  —— for tieing lambs
  thin tree does not raise up leaves, 643

rosary
  eight hundred novices run on same road, 592
  can go over many passes but not the diamond pass, 718
  vertebrae are separated without breaking the marrow, 736
  oxcart comes rolling to the deity, 790
ruins of yurt. See yurt, ruins or traces of
rye
  rams in an iron field, 118
  shamans shamanizing in a hole, 365

sacrifices to statue
  eight yellow goats on slope, 269
saddle, and accessories
  frog Mak with eight (nine) sinews, 56
  crooked mountain pass and eight sinews, 715
  See horse, saddle, stirrup and tether
saddle, arch of
  abdomen of bone, spine of wool, back of flesh, 407
saddle, bridle, whip
  flying bird, sitting Buddha, wise man attacks, 334
  cupboard, plant, tree, 687
saddlebows
  we both curse and do not look at each other's faces, 597
  two sisters (brothers) do not see each other's faces, 598
saddle-girth and loop
  male and female antelopes butt each other, 281
saltwort
  jumps böng böng and has neither kidneys nor heart, 30
  springs from earth, becomes frantic, dies in well, 479
samovar
  iron hook, crooked neck, belly like tureen, Russian cap, 923
sarana lily and flower
  white body with twenty-one joints and red face, 402
  ox's head buried, dog's cap hung up, 753
satchel
  can eat but not eliminate, 17
scales. See steelyard
scissors
  gaping mouth, no throat, 1
  gaping mouth, no food to be swallowed, 2
  frog's body, magpie's bill, 757
scraper
  hungry louse on peg, 55
scythe
  camel without jaws finishes the hay, 171
sea
  has no bottom
  See Milk Ocean, ocean
seasons
  passes of celebration, foliation (?), crackling, desolation, 716
  three mountain passes, three cairns, three icy cavities, three flowery fields, 717a
  See year and seasons

seeds of watermelon. See watermelon
serpent (constellation)
  cannot step over golden spike, 488
sewing
  makes sound *shur shur* and has blue horse, 238
  sowing with harnessed mouse, 287
  make and plug a hole, 982
shadow
  goes without leaving trace, is cut without leaving blood, 16
  cannot kill black sheep, 142
  cannot chap black ox to pieces, 193
  black cow moves around yurt, 195
  catch a black madcap, 443
  foolish old woman cannot overtake husband, 578
  cannot pierce hide of black sheep, 732
  is dark, 999
shakchaga (a bird)
  voice *shak shak*, yellow cap, 516
shamanizing
  two-wheeled cart thunders, Tungus boots gallop, 789
sheep, wolf eats a
  gloves pasture, owl jumps, 331
——, forequarter of
  hawk father, owl or partridge mother, 562
——, tail of. See goat and sheep, tails of
sheep lizard. See lizard
sheepfold
  black in day, white at night, 947
shinbone
  ten men started Arzadai on travels, 585
shelf
  camel without neck carries load, 148
  bow with bony bowstring, 890
shirt, putting on a
shoe. See boot
shoe, putting on a
  naked devil crept into hole, 470
shovel
  flat thing licked earth, 905
sieve
  torn eagle's hide, 734
silver, weighing and handing over
  white bird of Dungkhulä on white dune, 333
skull. See bones and skull
sky, sky and stars
  silk cannot be rolled up, ten thousand pearls cannot be strung, 855
  blue silk cannot be rolled up, 856
  silk without a border, pearls (corals) without holes, 861
  pearl without hole, silk without border, 862
  father's blanket does not end when folded, 877
  has no supports, 1007
  has no rim, 1008
  See earth and sky; heaven
slanderer
  man without friends, 977
sled-runners
  older brothers cannot overtake younger brothers, 581
sleep
  man smaller than you beats you, 529

smaller than you, it bears you down, 961, 962
sleet (?)
   motley one descends, 473
sleigh, cart, and horse
   enjoys self in summer, winter (cart), never (horse), 635
smoke
   cannot catch camel without a neck, 154
   bluish (gray) wolf runs under a hollow (up hollow tree), 308
   iron pole (nail, spike) reaches heaven, 698
   See bellows, smoke, and tongs
smokehole
   black camel among many camels, 166
   ten thousand spears in shore of lake, 700
   feathery like comb, round like moon, 912
   See flap
smoking
   fire lit on Russian's head, 420
   strike him on head, kiss him on mouth, 526
   kindled incense to god, fog spreads over brook, 694
   mist rose on long river, fire started on hill, 695
   nourishment sucked from copper kettle, 804
   See pipe
snake
   bends head without a neck, wriggles without skin, 18
   castrated camel yawned, end of rope flashed, 162
   cannot hold back silver whip (catch braid), 336
   walks without feet, 628
   rosary under the earth, 849
   cannot step over a rope, 888
snow and earth
   white one says, "Let's go!" Black one says, "Let's stay!" 623
sock. See boot, sock, and leg
sole of boot
   Galba licks earth, 497b
   something stinking in yurt (cupboard), 818
   flat thing licked earth, 904
soot and fire
   black goat, white goat, 279
soul of ignorant muznik
   is gloomy, 1010
soul of childless woman
   is gloomy, 1010
sound of felling trees. See trees, felling
spark
   little reddish boy rode in coach, 442
   fire without smoke, 975
   rages, 1013
   See fire, flint, and spark
spider
   climbs on trees, 5
   skew-eyed person climbs up a hair, 426
spigot
   watchman's *solovko* tied up in place of rich man's buggy, 784

spinal cord
   emaciated dog waddled over mountain passes, 292
   fawning dog passed over rivers, 293
spindle and thread
   gray sheep grows too fat to rise, 133
   gray two-year old colt gets fat, 260
   yellow dog grows fat by shaking its tail, 301
   See bobbin
spinning. See wool, spinning
spinning wheel
   thin virgin played, became pregnant, 537
spire
   jewel on mountain, 711
spring, summer, autumn, winter
   three mountain passes, three flowers, three mountain chains, three valleys, 717b
   See autumn, etc.; seasons
stalk, ear, and grain
   eighty-seven limbs on pine, nest on limb, egg in nest, 649
   See grain not yet harvested
stalk of lily. See lily, stalk of
star, morning
   ten thousand sheep go; white ram follows, 123
stars
   Barguzin oxen pasture in the north, 216
   herd of horses in the northwest, 222a
   herd of a hundred thousand; seven count; three rule; two are separated, 222b
   herd of a hundred thousand; seven count; six are crowded, 222c
   seventy thousand buttons on a coat, 865
stars and moon
   massive round ram among a thousand sheep, 120
stars and sky. See sky, sky and stars
stars and sun
   golden ram in stable full of sheep, 122
stars, moon, and sun. See sun, moon, and stars
statue of Buddha. See Buddha, Statue of
steam
   screamed "Oh!" and ran out, 477
steel, flint, and tinder
   two old men fight, a third comes between, 604
   See fire, flint, and spark
steelyard
   span-high body, counts its years when seized, 36
   fallow cow, black calf, 179
   four plaits, forty black eyes, dear to king, 410
   forty black eyes, pigtail of four strands, 411
   twisted feet, clapper with swollen head, 415
   subject to king, trusted by all, 465
   See silver, weighing and handing over
steppe onion
   gray-blue buck with little feet, 277
   See onion
stick for stirring kumiss
   makes sound *khur khur*, 512
   See churnstaff

stinkbug (bedbug?)
   handsome body, six hands, smells of sandalwood, 355
stirrup
   man smaller than you lifts and seats you, 486
   smaller than you, it lifts (carries) you, 964
   smaller than you, it throws you away, 965
   See horse, saddle, stirrups, and tether
stomach, emptying the
   one takes away the hole, throws away the peg, 727
   See defecation of cattle; urinating
stomach of ruminants
   timid old woman in house of fatty skin, 464
   Dalai Lama's purse with seventy compartments, 870
stomach of sheep
   mountainous, impassable roads, 713
   like camel's halter and lama's cloak, 917
Sumeru Mountain
   has no belt, 1006
sun
   falcon penetrates into yurt, 88
   mettlesome horse in courtyard, end of lasso in tent, 224
   all animals overate on a piece of fat, 313
   entire population warm selves at small fire, 602
   chariot rolls from behind mountain, 791
   silver bowl on ice, 833
   silver cup on ice, 834
   See excrement and sun; stars and sun
sun and moon
   among knucklebones two are for throwing, 744
sun, moon, and stars (Milky Way)
   leading camel has star on forehead; wrinkled female camel; many little camels with red silk halters, 144
   anklebones in basket and two brothers, 743
   two hoopnets and thousands of *alchiks*, 868
   silver money and two golden coins, 901
sunset
   is red, 1001
table, legs of table
   four-year old cow has four legs, 174
   four brothers have one hat, 555
tail, camel's
   thick needle hangs from heaven, 699
——, goat's and sheep's
   Circassian keeps door open; Kirghis keeps door closed, 632
——, horse's. See horse and tail
tassel(s) on cap
   red calf tied on mountain, 201
   snow and rain on cone-shaped mountain, 690
   bloody rain went down a pointed peak, 691
tea in mortar; preparation of tea
   gray bull defecates (belches) in morning, 215

deer called every morning, 285
husband and wife fight morning and evening, 609
dried cheese from above, something ample from below, something bluish adds color, white adds flavor, yellow fat adds pleasure, 816

tea, pouring
when lifted, it spits out of itself, 968

tea without milk
is black, 1023

Teachers, the Four
lama in house has bell and drum, 345

teakettle, teapot
miracle with five belts, hole in top, and no chin, 405
Tangut boy with five belts, 459
drum-belled, crow-billed, 761
See kettle, samovar

teats of bitch and mare
eight girls go to banquet; two girls come from banquet, 567

teats of cow
four geese on anvil, 79

teeth
thirty oxen in ditch, 173
twenty goats in hole, 268
thirty poles in ditch, 701
hide of curly sheep fills chest, 731
thirty tents in ditch, 774
are white, 1003

teeth and tongue
dark brown stallion ambles within fences, 246
twenty coupled sheep, red cow (bluish horse) with hollow back, 314
people stand around, stallion ambles, 328
white ship stopped in puddle, 783

teeth, picking the
queen fell ill, five ministers appeared and called Dr. Toothpick, 381
professor fell ill, five ministers galloped off to invite Dr. Incense, 382

telegram
iron tongs filled continent, 848

tendon
sinew plugged a hole, 982b

tent
two feet, empty skin, 750

thimble
ninety-nine eyes in a small thing, 3
many thousand eyes, 4
thin bay horse has eighty thousand brands, 231
small girl full of sores, 400

thong(s) that hold yurt wall together
house full of skin worms, 58
one fist inside, one fist outside, 433
man clenches fist, 528
hammer inside and outside of yurt, 851

thorn
a little *ngī ngū* (cries of pain), 956

thought
a black master, 448

thread. See needle and thread

thread, spinning a
people stand around, stallion ambles, 329

threshold
fallow horse (gray colt) is often straddled, 267

thumb (end of finger)
nape of neck is glossy, abdomen protrudes, 413

thunder and lightning
castrated camel yawned, end of lasso glittered, 161
See lightning

thunder and rain
roan stallion neighed, mares began to foal, 254
See rain, wind, and thunder

tick
a little, boneless bladder that runs, 28
sandalwood cushion, quince wood seat, six hands, feasts on whole sheep, 356

tobacco
unholy thing that seduces all, 971
See smoking

tobacco, snuffing
hornless cow butts, two maidens are like curds, 324

toes
five peasants move in thick fog, 590

toes and nails
women carry ice, 594
soldiers carry ice, 595

tongs
blue ox rolls over on ashes, 182
black dog with white stripe on forehead catches spotted snake on noisy river, 319
long-legged *sosalzhin* does not burn, 970
See bellows, smoke, tongs, hammer; coals and tongs; iron and tongs; kettle and tripod (tongs)

tongue
red calf within bone fence, 199
roan (sorrel) horse within birch fence, 235
sorrel horse behind rocks, 236
green garlic plant with hardly noticeable stem, 673
See larynx and tongue; teeth and tongue

tortoise
Yankhal's son has bone palace, 389

trail of camel
small tobacco pouch on steppe, 871

trees
short dog barks in woods, throws out all he finds, 295
lonely dog barks in woods, 296

trefoil
silver cup on ice, 837

trimming of kaftan. See kaftan, trimming of

tripod, legs of tripod
three year-old cow with three legs, 175
good man has three girdles, 460
three racing women, 589
three old women warm bellies, 599
three hoops, twelve hooks, 927

tripod and fire
three hoops, three hooks, god in middle, 925

three wheels, four hooks, brass statue of Buddha, 926

trousers, putting on
twenty people put Khorkudai on trail, 583

trowel
hungry louse on peg, 55

trumpet
white goat has holes in troin, 276
copper pieces, ox horn, 932
See flageolet

trunk and lock
tie black cow to rock; tie calf to her tail, 206
See lock and key

turquoise
is green, 1024

udder
red bow, white arrows, 889

ulna in cattle
bow with bone string, 891

urinating
pour out tea, carry away container, 814

vapors
driver in cart tries to overtake horseback rider, 575
See mirage

vegetables
are green, 1024

vertebra
feet do not walk, wings do not fly, 22

vessel for making brandy
black sable at end of sleeve, 864

walking
man bows before sheep, sheep bows before cow, cow bows before earth, 325
See gait of cattle

wall of felt tent
seventy shakchaga dug ground, 94
horns point in two directions, 272
monk's carpet fills house, 878

wasp, voice of
small body, masculine voice, 34

watch
bird of Genghis Khan makes sound *shir shir,* has twelve tongues, 70

water, water in well
cannot keep black cow within fence, 209
walks downwards, 628
has no fish, 980

water, drawing
limping magpie makes a turn around a hill, 92

water, pouring
rain without clouds falls in grassless cavity, 692

watermelon
cannot block pig's head, 107
thousands of warriors in doorless house, 551
houseful of people have no door to go in and out, 552
thousands of objects in doorless house, 773

waves
small gray snakes coil, 66

well
  square carpet in middle of village, 876
  See handle of pail, pail, and well
well, digging a
  grows longer by digging, wider by taking away, 960
wheel(s) of cart (carriage)
  older sister (brother) cannot overtake younger sister (brother), 580
  four sons never meet, 582
  has holes like comb, is round like moon, 911
whetstone
  bluish horse with perspiring sides, 237
  cannot grind off cow's anklebone in three years, 737
wind
  opens door without hands or feet, 23
  cannot overtake camel without neck, 153
windhorse
  nicely mottled, ambles like donkey, 240
  flutters in wind until sunset, 696
wings of gate. See door, door jambs, wings of door or gate
wolf
  runs through ravines with bare feet, 7
  has eyes of fire and glass, runs alone, 29
  runs with dun boots and perked-up ears, 46
  has undulations on body, eyes like Venus, 143
  cannot mount gray horse, 336
  man in steppe without flint, 461
  comes from north making sound *khon khon*, ears hang down, tail stands up, 517

wolf devours lamb (sheep)
  gloves pasture, owl jumps, 331
  the howling devours the bleating, 1027
woman, capricious
  is annoying, 1014
woman, fasting
  pacemaker goes thrice monthly to watering place, 244
woman growling at husband
  rages, 1013
woman, unmarried
  three-year old goat with six horns, 271
women
  are more numerous than men, 984
woodpecker
  piebald horse, a carpenter penetrates everywhere, 326
  wears striped kaftan, is subject to Bandida Lama, 350
  tailless, multicolored carpenter, 447
  wears red tassel, 454
wool, spinning
  limping magpie goes around hill, 91
  makes sound *shur shur* and grows fat, 514
writing (script)
  matchmaker (unlucky) man cannot, happy (lucky) man can guess it, 894
  a riddle that one cannot solve, 895
  See book, writing a; letter; paper and writing; reading
writing, act of
  dungping (a bird) bows, drinks from river, makes patterns, 87
  parrot drinks, trail is left on snowy mountain, 93

swan from south quenches thirst in silver channel, grazes on mountain, 98
  camel stamped and arrived at Tibet, fountain flowed, 155
  black dog runs on white snow, 291
  sowed with five oxen and spoke Tibetan, 538
writing brush
  bustard's silk tail, peacock's wise tail, 754

year, months, and days
  twelve branches, 360 leaves, 644
  sandal tree with 12 branches and 365 burs, 645
  tree with 12 branches, each branch has 30 leaves, 646
  cloth measures 12 fathoms and folds in 360 squares, 852
year and seasons
  settlement with four gates, thirty nails on each gate, 775
  See autumn, etc.; seasons; spring, etc.
yurt
  forked wood, sable cap, God's cross, 908
yurt, taking apart a
  drove of horses rounded up by the bay Bultchik, 250
  skin a gray colt while it stands, 264
  he descended at the corner and gathered willow leaves, 484
yurt, ruins or traces of
  camel's footmarks remain three (ten) years, 172
  Byrgyt loses belt, 458
  Solutions lacking: 147a, 902

INDEX OF CONVENTIONAL ELEMENTS AND FORMULAS

Numbers refer to riddles

Animal with legs that pace, 373
Animals in Zodiac, 752
Animals of contrasting colors, 262
At the upper end of the salt marsh (*tsaidam*), 689b
At the mouth (or: source) of the river, 38

Behind the mountain, from behind the mountain, 112

Camel without a neck, 148
Comparison used in two meanings, 476–478
Concave and convex used symbolically, 391
Creature is small but strong, 52
Creature is wounded or lacks a member, 113

Eighty thousand (a very large number), 146

Form in daytime and at night varies, 938, 939
From above, from heaven, from the sky, 337

High and low contrasted, 910

In a grassless hollow, 692
In a hole, ditch, well, 61
In (through) a valley, 306
In the steppe, 253

Man bowing or praying, 363
Man with a defect, 363
Man with a hole in his body, 434

On the top of the Alkhanai (a mountain), 90

On a tree (literal meaning), 846
On a tree (tree = human body), 892

Punning use of words, 661

Riddles enumerating members of various animals, 472
Riddles made on emboxed model, 390

Sky, shaking the fist at or shooting at 539

Tree, hollow, 308b, 308c
Tree, solitary, 542
Thing with a defect, 779

Under the earth, 815

Voice of lama reciting prayers or charms, 343

Yellow cap, cap of fox fur, 449b